Housing Act 1996

CHAPTER 52

ARRANGEMENT OF SECTIONS

Part IV

Housing benefit and related matters

Part V

Conduct of tenants

Chapter I

Introductory tenancies

General provisions

Proceedings for possession

Succession on death of tenant

Assignment

Repairs

Provision of information and consultation

Supplementary

PART VIII

MISCELLANEOUS AND GENERAL PROVISIONS

Miscellaneous

General

Housing Act 1996

1996 CHAPTER 52

An Act to make provision about housing, including provision about the social rented sector, houses in multiple occupation, landlord and tenant matters, the administration of housing benefit, the conduct of tenants, the allocation of housing accommodation by local housing authorities and homelessness; and for connected purposes.   [24th July 1996]

BE IT ENACTED by the Queen's most Excellent Majesty, by and with the advice and consent of the Lords Spiritual and Temporal, and Commons, in this present Parliament assembled, and by the authority of the same, as follows:—

PART I

SOCIAL RENTED SECTOR

CHAPTER I

REGISTERED SOCIAL LANDLORDS

Registration

1.—(1) The Corporation shall maintain a register of social landlords which shall be open to inspection at all reasonable times at the head office of the Corporation. The register of social landlords.

(2) On the commencement of this section every housing association which immediately before commencement was registered in the register kept by the Corporation under Part I of the Housing Associations Act 1985 shall be registered as a social landlord. 1985 c. 69.

2.—(1) A body is eligible for registration as a social landlord if it is— Eligibility for registration.

    (a) a registered charity which is a housing association,

    (b) a society registered under the Industrial and Provident Societies Act 1965 which satisfies the conditions in subsection (2), or 1965 c. 12.

    (c) a company registered under the Companies Act 1985 which satisfies those conditions. 1985 c. 6.

(2) The conditions are that the body is non-profit-making and is established for the purpose of, or has among its objects or powers, the provision, construction, improvement or management of—

    (a) houses to be kept available for letting,

    (b) houses for occupation by members of the body, where the rules of the body restrict membership to persons entitled or prospectively entitled (as tenants or otherwise) to occupy a house provided or managed by the body, or

    (c) hostels,

and that any additional purposes or objects are among those specified in subsection (4).

(3) For the purposes of this section a body is non-profit-making if—

    (a) it does not trade for profit, or

1985 c. 69.

    (b) its constitution or rules prohibit the issue of capital with interest or dividend exceeding the rate prescribed by the Treasury for the purposes of section 1(1)(b) of the Housing Associations Act 1985.

(4) The permissible additional purposes or objects are—

    (a) providing land, amenities or services, or providing, constructing, repairing or improving buildings, for its residents, either exclusively or together with other persons;

    (b) acquiring, or repairing and improving, or creating by the conversion of houses or other property, houses to be disposed of on sale, on lease or on shared ownership terms;

    (c) constructing houses to be disposed of on shared ownership terms;

    (d) managing houses held on leases or other lettings (not being houses within subsection (2)(a) or (b)) or blocks of flats;

    (e) providing services of any description for owners or occupiers of houses in arranging or carrying out works of maintenance, repair or improvement, or encouraging or facilitating the carrying out of such works;

    (f) encouraging and giving advice on the forming of housing associations or providing services for, and giving advice on the running of, such associations and other voluntary organisations concerned with housing, or matters connected with housing.

(5) A body is not ineligible for registration as a social landlord by reason only that its powers include power—

    (a) to acquire commercial premises or businesses as an incidental part of a project or series of projects undertaken for purposes or objects falling within subsection (2) or (4);

    (b) to repair, improve or convert commercial premises acquired as mentioned in paragraph (a) or to carry on for a limited period any business so acquired;

    (c) to repair or improve houses, or buildings in which houses are situated, after a disposal of the houses by the body by way of sale or lease or on shared ownership terms.

(6) In this section—

"block of flats" means a building containing two or more flats which are held on leases or other lettings and which are occupied or intended to be occupied wholly or mainly for residential purposes;

"disposed of on shared ownership terms" means disposed of on a lease—

(a) granted on a payment of a premium calculated by reference to a percentage of the value of the house or of the cost of providing it, or

(b) under which the tenant (or his personal representatives) will or may be entitled to a sum calculated by reference directly or indirectly to the value of the house;

"letting" includes the grant of a licence to occupy;

"residents", in relation to a body, means persons occupying a house or hostel provided or managed by the body; and

"voluntary organisation" means an organisation whose activities are not carried on for profit.

(7) The Secretary of State may by order specify permissible purposes, objects or powers additional to those specified in subsections (4) and (5).

The order may (without prejudice to the inclusion of other incidental or supplementary provisions) contain such provision as the Secretary of State thinks fit with respect to the priority of mortgages entered into in pursuance of any additional purposes, objects or powers.

(8) An order under subsection (7) shall be made by statutory instrument which shall be subject to annulment in pursuance of a resolution of either House of Parliament.

3.—(1) The Corporation may register as a social landlord any body which is eligible for such registration.

Registration.

(2) An application for registration shall be made in such manner, and shall be accompanied by such fee (if any), as the Corporation may determine.

(3) As soon as may be after registering a body as a social landlord the Corporation shall give notice of the registration—

(a) in the case of a registered charity, to the Charity Commissioners,

(b) in the case of an industrial and provident society, to the appropriate registrar, and

(c) in the case of a company registered under the Companies Act 1985 (including such a company which is also a registered charity), to the registrar of companies,

1985 c. 6.

who shall record the registration.

(4) A body which at any time is, or was, registered as a social landlord shall, for all purposes other than rectification of the register, be conclusively presumed to be, or to have been, at that time a body eligible for registration as a social landlord.

4.—(1) A body which has been registered as a social landlord shall not be removed from the register except in accordance with this section.

Removal from the register.

(2) If it appears to the Corporation that a body which is on the register of social landlords—

    (a) is no longer a body eligible for such registration, or

    (b) has ceased to exist or does not operate,

the Corporation shall, after giving the body at least 14 days' notice, remove it from the register.

(3) In the case of a body which appears to the Corporation to have ceased to exist or not to operate, notice under subsection (2) shall be deemed to be given to the body if it is served at the address last known to the Corporation to be the principal place of business of the body.

(4) A body which is registered as a social landlord may request the Corporation to remove it from the register and the Corporation may do so, subject to the following provisions.

(5) Before removing a body from the register of social landlords under subsection (4) the Corporation shall consult the local authorities in whose area the body operates; and the Corporation shall also inform those authorities of its decision.

(6) As soon as may be after removing a body from the register of social landlords the Corporation shall give notice of the removal—

    (a) in the case of a registered charity, to the Charity Commissioners,

    (b) in the case of an industrial and provident society, to the appropriate registrar, and

1985 c. 6.

    (c) in the case of a company registered under the Companies Act 1985 (including such a company which is also a registered charity), to the registrar of companies,

who shall record the removal.

Criteria for registration or removal from register.

5.—(1) The Corporation shall establish (and may from time to time vary) criteria which should be satisfied by a body seeking registration as a social landlord; and in deciding whether to register a body the Corporation shall have regard to whether those criteria are met.

(2) The Corporation shall establish (and may from time to time vary) criteria which should be satisfied where such a body seeks to be removed from the register of social landlords; and in deciding whether to remove a body from the register the Corporation shall have regard to whether those criteria are met.

(3) Before establishing or varying any such criteria the Corporation shall consult such bodies representative of registered social landlords, and such bodies representative of local authorities, as it thinks fit.

(4) The Corporation shall publish the criteria for registration and the criteria for removal from the register in such manner as the Corporation considers appropriate for bringing the criteria to the notice of bodies representative of registered social landlords and bodies representative of local authorities.

Appeal against decision on removal.

6.—(1) A body which is aggrieved by a decision of the Corporation—

    (a) not to register it as a social landlord, or

(b) to remove or not to remove it from the register of social landlords,

may appeal against the decision to the High Court.

(2) If an appeal is brought against a decision relating to the removal of a body from the register, the Corporation shall not remove the body from the register until the appeal has been finally determined or is withdrawn.

(3) As soon as may be after an appeal is brought against a decision relating to the removal of a body from the register, the Corporation shall give notice of the appeal—

(a) in the case of a registered charity, to the Charity Commissioners,

(b) in the case of an industrial and provident society, to the appropriate registrar, and

(c) in the case of a company registered under the Companies Act 1985 (including such a company which is also a registered charity), to the registrar of companies.

1985 c. 6.

Regulation of registered social landlords

7. Schedule 1 has effect for the regulation of registered social landlords.

Part I relates to the control of payments to members and similar matters.

Part II relates to the constitution, change of rules, amalgamation or dissolution of a registered social landlord.

Part III relates to accounts and audit.

Part IV relates to inquiries into the affairs of a registered social landlord.

Regulation of registered social landlords.

CHAPTER II

DISPOSAL OF LAND AND RELATED MATTERS

Power of registered social landlord to dispose of land

8.—(1) A registered social landlord has power by virtue of this section and not otherwise to dispose, in such manner as it thinks fit, of land held by it.

Power of registered social landlord to dispose of land.

(2) Section 39 of the Settled Land Act 1925 (disposal of land by trustees) does not apply to the disposal of land by a registered social landlord; and accordingly the disposal need not be for the best consideration in money that can reasonably be obtained.

1925 c. 18.

Nothing in this subsection shall be taken to authorise any action on the part of a charity which would conflict with the trusts of the charity.

(3) This section has effect subject to section 9 (control by Corporation of land transactions).

Control by Corporation of land transactions

9.—(1) The consent of the Corporation, given by order under the seal of the Corporation, is required for any disposal of land by a registered social landlord under section 8.

Consent required for disposal of land by registered social landlord.

(2) The consent of the Corporation may be so given—

(a) generally to all registered social landlords or to a particular landlord or description of landlords;

(b) in relation to particular land or in relation to a particular description of land,

and may be given subject to conditions.

(3) Before giving any consent other than a consent in relation to a particular landlord or particular land, the Corporation shall consult such bodies representative of registered social landlords as it thinks fit.

(4) A disposal of a house by a registered social landlord made without the consent required by this section is void unless—

(a) the disposal is to an individual (or to two or more individuals),

(b) the disposal does not extend to any other house, and

(c) the landlord reasonably believes that the individual or individuals intend to use the house as their principal dwelling.

(5) Any other disposal by a registered social landlord which requires consent under this section is valid in favour of a person claiming under the landlord notwithstanding that that consent has not been given; and a person dealing with a registered social landlord, or with a person claiming under such a landlord, shall not be concerned to see or inquire whether any such consent has been given.

(6) Where at the time of its removal from the register of social landlords a body owns land, this section continues to apply to that land after the removal as if the body concerned continued to be a registered social landlord.

(7) For the purposes of this section "disposal" means sale, lease, mortgage, charge or any other disposition.

(8) This section has effect subject to section 10 (lettings and other disposals not requiring consent of Corporation).

Lettings and other disposals not requiring consent of Corporation.

10.—(1) A letting by a registered social landlord does not require consent under section 9 if it is—

(a) a letting of land under an assured tenancy or an assured agricultural occupancy, or what would be an assured tenancy or an assured agricultural occupancy but for any of paragraphs 4 to 8, or paragraph 12(1)(h), of Schedule 1 to the Housing Act 1988, or

1988 c. 50.

(b) a letting of land under a secure tenancy or what would be a secure tenancy but for any of paragraphs 2 to 12 of Schedule 1 to the Housing Act 1985.

1985 c. 68.

(2) Consent under section 9 is not required in the case of a disposal to which section 81 or 133 of the Housing Act 1988 applies (certain disposals for which the consent of the Secretary of State is required).

(3) Consent under section 9 is not required for a disposal under Part V of the Housing Act 1985 (the right to buy) or under the right conferred by section 16 below (the right to acquire).

Covenant for repayment of discount on disposal.

11.—(1) Where on a disposal of a house by a registered social landlord, in accordance with a consent given by the Corporation under section 9, a discount has been given to the purchaser, and the consent does not provide otherwise, the conveyance, grant or assignment shall contain a covenant binding on the purchaser and his successors in title to the following effect.

(2) The covenant shall be to pay to the landlord on demand, if within a period of three years there is a relevant disposal which is not an exempted disposal (but if there is more than one such disposal then only on the first of them), an amount equal to the discount reduced by one-third for each complete year which has elapsed after the conveyance, grant or assignment and before the further disposal.

(3) The liability that may arise under the covenant is a charge on the house, taking effect as if it had been created by deed expressed to be by way of legal mortgage.

(4) A charge taking effect by virtue of this section is a land charge for the purposes of section 59 of the Land Registration Act 1925 notwithstanding subsection (5) of that section (exclusion of mortgages), and subsection (2) of that section applies accordingly with respect to its protection and realisation.

1925 c. 21.

(5) Where there is a relevant disposal which is an exempted disposal by virtue of section 15(4)(d) or (e) (compulsory disposal or disposal of yard, garden, &c.)—

    (a) the covenant required by this section is not binding on the person to whom the disposal is made or any successor in title of his, and

    (b) the covenant and the charge taking effect by virtue of this section ceases to apply in relation to the property disposed of.

12.—(1) The charge taking effect by virtue of section 11 (charge for repayment of discount) has priority immediately after any legal charge securing an amount—

Priority of charge for repayment of discount.

    (a) left outstanding by the purchaser, or

    (b) advanced to him by an approved lending institution for the purpose of enabling him to acquire the interest disposed of on the first disposal,

subject to the following provisions.

(2) An advance which is made for a purpose other than that mentioned in subsection (1)(b) and which is secured by a legal charge having priority to the charge taking effect by virtue of section 11, and any further advance which is so secured, shall rank in priority to that charge if, and only if, the registered social landlord by notice served on the institution concerned gives consent.

The landlord shall give consent if the purpose of the advance or further advance is an approved purpose.

(3) The registered social landlord may at any time by notice served on an approved lending institution postpone the charge taking effect by virtue of section 11 to an advance or further advance which—

    (a) is made to the purchaser by that institution, and

    (b) is secured by a legal charge not having priority to that charge;

and the landlord shall serve such a notice if the purpose of the advance or further advance is an approved purpose.

(4) The covenant required by section 11 does not, by virtue of its binding successors in title of the purchaser, bind a person exercising rights under a charge having priority over the charge taking effect by virtue of that section, or a person deriving title under him.

A provision of the conveyance, grant or assignment, or of a collateral agreement, is void in so far as it purports to authorise a forfeiture, or to impose a penalty or disability, in the event of any such person failing to comply with that covenant.

(5) In this section "approved lending institution" means—

(a) a building society, bank, insurance company or friendly society,

(b) the Corporation, or

1985 c. 68.

(c) any body specified, or of a class or description specified, in an order made under section 156 of the Housing Act 1985 (which makes corresponding provision in relation to disposals in pursuance of the right to buy).

(6) The following are "approved purposes" for the purposes of this section—

(a) to enable the purchaser to defray, or to defray on his behalf, any of the following—

(i) the cost of any works to the house,

(ii) any service charge payable in respect of the house for works, whether or not to the house, and

(iii) any service charge or other amount payable in respect of the house for insurance, whether or not of the house, and

(b) to enable the purchaser to discharge, or to discharge on his behalf, any of the following—

(i) so much as is still outstanding of any advance or further advance which ranks in priority to the charge taking effect by virtue of section 11,

(ii) any arrears of interest on such an advance or further advance, and

(iii) any costs and expenses incurred in enforcing payment of any such interest, or repayment (in whole or in part) of any such advance or further advance.

In this subsection "service charge" has the meaning given by section 621A of the Housing Act 1985.

(7) Where different parts of an advance or further advance are made for different purposes, each of those parts shall be regarded as a separate advance or further advance for the purposes of this section.

Restriction on disposal of houses in National Parks, &c.

1949 c. 97.

13.—(1) On the disposal by a registered social landlord, in accordance with a consent given by the Corporation under section 9, of a house situated in—

(a) a National Park,

(b) an area designated under section 87 of the National Parks and Access to the Countryside Act 1949 as an area of outstanding natural beauty, or

(c) an area designated as a rural area by order under section 157 of the Housing Act 1985,

the conveyance, grant or assignment may (unless it contains a condition of a kind mentioned in section 33(2)(b) or (c) of the Housing Act 1985 (right of pre-emption or restriction on assignment)) contain a covenant to the following effect limiting the freedom of the purchaser (including any successor in title of his and any person deriving title under him or such a successor) to dispose of the house.

(2) The limitation is that until such time (if any) as may be notified in writing by the registered social landlord to the purchaser or a successor in title of his, there will be no relevant disposal which is not an exempted disposal without the written consent of the landlord.

(3) That consent shall not be withheld if the person to whom the disposal is made (or, if it is made to more than one person, at least one of them) has, throughout the period of three years immediately preceding the application for consent—

(a) had his place of work in a region designated by order under section 157(3) of the Housing Act 1985 which, or part of which, is comprised in the National Park or area concerned, or

(b) had his only or principal home in such a region,

or if he has had the one in part or parts of that period and the other in the remainder.

The region need not have been the same throughout the period.

(4) A disposal in breach of such a covenant as is mentioned above is void.

(5) The limitation imposed by such a covenant is a local land charge and, if the land is registered under the Land Registration Act 1925, the Chief Land Registrar shall enter the appropriate restriction on the register of title as if an application to that effect had been made under section 58 of that Act.

(6) In this section "purchaser" means the person acquiring the interest disposed of by the first disposal.

(7) Where there is a relevant disposal which is an exempted disposal by virtue of section 15(4)(d) or (e) (compulsory disposal or disposal of yard, garden, &c.), any such covenant as is mentioned in this section ceases to apply in relation to the property disposed of.

14.—(1) For the purposes of sections 9 to 13 the grant of an option enabling a person to call for a relevant disposal which is not an exempted disposal shall be treated as such a disposal made to him.

Treatment of options.

(2) For the purposes of section 13(2) (requirement of consent to disposal of house in National Park, &c.) consent to such a grant shall be treated as consent to a disposal made in pursuance of the option.

15.—(1) In sections 11 to 14 the expression "relevant disposal which is not an exempted disposal" shall be construed as follows.

Relevant and exempted disposals.

(2) A disposal, whether of the whole or part of the house, is a relevant disposal if it is—

(a) a conveyance of the freehold or an assignment of the lease, or

(b) the grant of a lease or sub-lease (other than a mortgage term) for a term of more than 21 years otherwise than at a rack-rent.

(3) For the purposes of subsection (2)(b) it shall be assumed—

(a) that any option to renew or extend a lease or sub-lease, whether or not forming part of a series of options, is exercised, and

(b) that any option to terminate a lease or sub-lease is not exercised.

(4) A disposal is an exempted disposal if—

(a) it is a disposal of the whole of the house and a conveyance of the freehold or an assignment of the lease and the person or each of the persons to whom it is made is a qualifying person (as defined in subsection (5));

(b) it is a vesting of the whole of the house in a person taking under a will or on an intestacy;

(c) it is a disposal of the whole of the house in pursuance of any such order as is mentioned in subsection (6);

(d) it is a compulsory disposal (as defined in subsection (7));

(e) the property disposed of is a yard, garden, outhouses or appurtenances belonging to a house or usually enjoyed with it.

(5) For the purposes of subsection (4)(a) a person is a qualifying person in relation to a disposal if—

(a) he is the person or one of the persons by whom the disposal is made,

(b) he is the spouse or a former spouse of that person or one of those persons, or

(c) he is a member of the family of that person or one of those persons and has resided with him throughout the period of twelve months ending with the disposal.

(6) The orders referred to in subsection (4)(c) are orders under—

1973 c. 18.

(a) section 24 or 24A of the Matrimonial Causes Act 1973 (property adjustment orders or orders for the sale of property in connection with matrimonial proceedings);

1975 c. 63.

(b) section 2 of the Inheritance (Provision for Family and Dependants) Act 1975 (orders as to financial provision to be made from estate);

1984 c. 42.

(c) section 17 of the Matrimonial and Family Proceedings Act 1984 (property adjustment orders or orders for the sale of property after overseas divorce, &c.); or

1989 c. 41.

(d) paragraph 1 of Schedule 1 to the Children Act 1989 (orders for financial relief against parents).

(7) For the purposes of subsection (4)(d) a compulsory disposal is a disposal of property which is acquired compulsorily, or is acquired by a person who has made or would have made, or for whom another person has made or would have made, a compulsory purchase order authorising its compulsory purchase for the purposes for which it is acquired.

Right of tenant to acquire dwelling

16.—(1) A tenant of a registered social landlord has the right to acquire the dwelling of which he is a tenant if—

Right of tenant to acquire dwelling.

   (a) he is a tenant under an assured tenancy, other than an assured shorthold tenancy or a long tenancy, or under a secure tenancy,

   (b) the dwelling was provided with public money and has remained in the social rented sector, and

   (c) he satisfies any further qualifying conditions applicable under Part V of the Housing Act 1985 (the right to buy) as it applies in relation to the right conferred by this section.

1985 c. 68.

(2) For this purpose a dwelling shall be regarded as provided with public money if—

   (a) it was provided or acquired wholly or in part by means of a grant under section 18 (social housing grant),

   (b) it was provided or acquired wholly or in part by applying or appropriating sums standing in the disposal proceeds fund of a registered social landlord (see section 25), or

   (c) it was acquired by a registered social landlord after the commencement of this paragraph on a disposal by a public sector landlord at a time when it was capable of being let as a separate dwelling.

(3) A dwelling shall be regarded for the purposes of this section as having remained within the social rented sector if, since it was so provided or acquired—

   (a) the person holding the freehold interest in the dwelling has been either a registered social landlord or a public sector landlord; and

   (b) any person holding an interest as lessee (otherwise than as mortgagee) in the dwelling has been—

      (i) an individual holding otherwise than under a long tenancy; or

      (ii) a registered social landlord or a public sector landlord.

(4) A dwelling shall be regarded for the purposes of this section as provided by means of a grant under section 18 (social housing grant) if, and only if, the Corporation when making the grant notified the recipient that the dwelling was to be so regarded.

The Corporation shall before making the grant inform the applicant that it proposes to give such a notice and allow him an opportunity to withdraw his application within a specified time.

17.—(1) The Secretary of State may by order—

Right of tenant to acquire dwelling: supplementary provisions.

   (a) specify the amount or rate of discount to be given on the exercise of the right conferred by section 16; and

   (b) designate rural areas in relation to dwellings in which the right conferred by that section does not arise.

(2) The provisions of Part V of the Housing Act 1985 apply in relation to the right to acquire under section 16—

   (a) subject to any order under subsection (1) above, and

(b) subject to such other exceptions, adaptations and other modifications as may be specified by regulations made by the Secretary of State.

(3) The regulations may provide—

(a) that the powers of the Secretary of State under sections 164 to 170 of that Act (powers to intervene, give directions or assist) do not apply,

(b) that paragraphs 1 and 3 (exceptions for charities and certain housing associations), and paragraph 11 (right of appeal to Secretary of State), of Schedule 5 to that Act do not apply,

(c) that the provisions of Part V of that Act relating to the right to acquire on rent to mortgage terms do not apply,

(d) that the provisions of that Part relating to restrictions on disposals in National Parks, &c. do not apply, and

(e) that the provisions of that Part relating to the preserved right to buy do not apply.

Nothing in this subsection affects the generality of the power conferred by subsection (2).

(4) The specified exceptions, adaptations and other modifications shall take the form of textual amendments of the provisions of Part V of that Act as they apply in relation to the right to buy under that Part; and the first regulations, and any subsequent consolidating regulations, shall set out the provisions of Part V as they so apply.

(5) An order or regulations under this section—

(a) may make different provision for different cases or classes of case including different areas, and

(b) may contain such incidental, supplementary and transitional provisions as the Secretary of State considers appropriate.

(6) Before making an order which would have the effect that an area ceased to be designated under subsection (1)(b), the Secretary of State shall consult—

(a) the local housing authority or authorities in whose district the area or any part of it is situated or, if the order is general in its effect, local housing authorities in general, and

(b) such bodies appearing to him to be representative of registered social landlords as he considers appropriate.

(7) An order or regulations under this section shall be made by statutory instrument which shall be subject to annulment in pursuance of a resolution of either House of Parliament.

CHAPTER III

GRANTS AND OTHER FINANCIAL MATTERS

Grants and other financial assistance

18.—(1) The Corporation may make grants to registered social landlords in respect of expenditure incurred or to be incurred by them in connection with their housing activities.

(2) The Corporation, acting in accordance with such principles as it may from time to time determine, shall specify in relation to grants under this section—

   (a) the procedure to be followed in relation to applications for grant,

   (b) the circumstances in which grant is or is not to be payable,

   (c) the method for calculating, and any limitations on, the amount of grant, and

   (d) the manner in which, and time or times at which, grant is to be paid.

(3) In making a grant under this section, the Corporation may provide that the grant is conditional on compliance by the landlord with such conditions as the Corporation may specify.

(4) The Corporation may, with the agreement of a local housing authority, appoint the authority to act as its agent in connection with the assessment and payment of grant under this section.

(5) The appointment shall be on such terms as the Corporation may, with the approval of the Secretary of State given with the consent of the Treasury, specify; and the authority shall act in accordance with those terms.

(6) Where—

   (a) a grant under this section is payable to a registered social landlord, and

   (b) at any time property to which the grant relates becomes vested in, or is leased for a term of years to, or reverts to, another registered social landlord, or trustees for another such landlord,

this section (including this subsection) shall have effect after that time as if the grant, or such proportion of it as is specified or determined under subsection (7), were payable to the other landlord.

(7) The proportion mentioned in subsection (6) is that which, in the circumstances of the particular case—

   (a) the Corporation, acting in accordance with such principles as it may from time to time determine, may specify as being appropriate, or

   (b) the Corporation may determine to be appropriate.

(8) Where one of the landlords mentioned in subsection (6) is registered by the Housing Corporation and another is registered by Housing for Wales, the determination mentioned in subsection (7) shall be such as shall be agreed between the two Corporations.

19. A registered social landlord is not entitled to a grant under section 18 (social housing grant) in respect of land comprised in a management

[margin note: Social housing grants.]

[margin note: Land subject to housing management agreement.]

agreement within the meaning of the Housing Act 1985 (see sections 27(2) and 27B(4) of that Act: delegation of housing management functions by certain authorities).

Purchase grant where right to acquire exercised.

20.—(1) The Corporation shall make grants to registered social landlords in respect of discounts given by them to persons exercising the right to acquire conferred by section 16.

(2) The amount of the grant for any year shall be the aggregate value of the discounts given in that year.

(3) The Corporation, acting in accordance with such principles as it may from time to time determine, shall specify in relation to grants under this section—

    (a) the procedure to be followed in relation to applications for grant,

    (b) the manner in which, and time or times at which, grant is to be paid.

(4) In making a grant the Corporation may provide that the grant is conditional on compliance by the registered social landlord with such conditions as the Corporation may specify.

Purchase grant in respect of other disposals.

21.—(1) The Corporation may make grants to registered social landlords in respect of discounts on disposals by them of dwellings to tenants otherwise than in pursuance of the right conferred by section 16.

(2) The Corporation shall make such a grant if the tenant was entitled to exercise the right conferred by section 16 in relation to another dwelling of the landlord's.

The amount of the grant in such a case shall not exceed the amount of the discount to which the tenant would have been entitled in respect of the other dwelling.

(3) The Corporation, acting in accordance with such principles as it may from time to time determine, shall specify in relation to grants under this section—

    (a) the procedure to be followed in relation to applications for grant;

    (b) the circumstances in which grant is or is not to be payable;

    (c) the method for calculating, and any limitations on, the amount of grant; and

    (d) the manner in which, and time or times at which, grant is to be paid.

(4) In making a grant under this section, the Corporation may provide that the grant is conditional on compliance by the registered social landlord with such conditions as the Corporation may specify.

Assistance from local authorities.

22.—(1) A local authority may promote—

    (a) the formation of bodies to act as registered social landlords, and

    (b) the extension of the objects or activities of registered social landlords.

(2) A local authority may for the assistance of any registered social landlord subscribe for share or loan capital of the landlord.

(3) A local authority may for the assistance of a registered social landlord—

    (a) make grants or loans to the landlord, or

    (b) guarantee or join in guaranteeing the payment of the principal of, and interest on, money borrowed by the landlord (including money borrowed by the issue of loan capital) or of interest on share capital issued by the landlord.

(4) A local housing authority may sell or supply under a hire-purchase agreement furniture to the occupants of houses provided by a registered social landlord, and may buy furniture for that purpose.

In this subsection "hire-purchase agreement" means a hire-purchase agreement or conditional sale agreement within the meaning of the Consumer Credit Act 1974.

1974 c. 39.

23.—(1) The Public Works Loans Commissioners may lend money to a registered social landlord—

Loans by Public Works Loans Commissioners.

    (a) for the purpose of constructing or improving, or facilitating or encouraging the construction or improvement, of dwellings,

    (b) for the purchase of dwellings which the landlord desires to purchase with a view to their improvement, and

    (c) for the purchase and development of land.

(2) A loan for any of those purposes, and interest on the loan, shall be secured by a mortgage of—

    (a) the land in respect of which that purpose is to be carried out, and

    (b) such other lands (if any) as may be offered as security for the loan;

and the money lent shall not exceed three-quarters (or, if the payment of the principal of, and interest on, the loan is guaranteed by a local authority, nine-tenths) of the value, to be ascertained to the satisfaction of the Public Works Commissioners, of the estate or interest in the land proposed to be so mortgaged.

(3) Loans may be made by instalments as the building of dwellings or other work on the land mortgaged under subsection (2) progresses (so, however, that the total amount lent does not at any time exceed the amount specified in that subsection); and a mortgage may accordingly be made to secure such loans to be so made.

(4) If the loan exceeds two-thirds of the value referred to in subsection (2), and is not guaranteed as to principal and interest by a local authority, the Public Works Loans Commissioners shall require, in addition to such a mortgage as is mentioned in that subsection, such further security as they think fit.

(5) Subject to subsection (6), the period for repayment of a loan under this section shall not exceed 40 years, and no money shall be lent on mortgage of any land unless the estate proposed to be mortgaged is either an estate in fee simple absolute in possession or an estate for a term of years absolute of which not less than 50 years are unexpired at the date of the loan.

(6) Where a loan under this section is made for the purpose of carrying out a scheme for the provision of houses approved by the Secretary of State, the maximum period for the repayment of the loan is 50 instead of

40 years, and money may be lent on the mortgage of an estate for a term of years absolute of which a period of not less than ten years in excess of the period fixed for the repayment of the sums advanced remains unexpired at the date of the loan.

Treatment of disposal proceeds

The disposal proceeds fund.

24.—(1) A registered social landlord shall show separately in its accounts for any period ending after the coming into force of this section its net disposal proceeds.

(2) The net disposal proceeds of a registered social landlord are—

(a) the net proceeds of sale received by it in respect of any disposal of land to a tenant—

(i) in pursuance of the right conferred by section 16 (right of tenant to acquire dwelling), or

(ii) in respect of which a grant was made under section 21 (purchase grant in respect of other disposals);

(b) payments of grant received by it under section 20 or 21 (purchase grant);

(c) where any such grant has been paid to it, any repayments of discount in respect of which the grant was given; and

(d) such other proceeds of sale or payments of grant (if any) as the Corporation may from time to time determine.

(3) The net proceeds of sale means the proceeds of sale less an amount calculated in accordance with a determination by the Corporation.

(4) The disposal proceeds shall be shown in a fund to be known as a disposal proceeds fund.

(5) The method of constituting the fund and showing it in the landlord's accounts shall be as required by determination of the Corporation under paragraph 16 of Schedule 1 (general requirements as to accounts).

(6) Interest shall be added to the fund in accordance with a determination made by the Corporation.

(7) Where this section applies in relation to the proceeds of sale arising on a disposal, section 27 below (recovery, &c. of social housing grants) and section 52 of the Housing Act 1988 (recovery, &c. of grants under that Act and earlier enactments) do not apply.

1988 c. 50.

Application or appropriation of disposal proceeds.

25.—(1) The sums standing in the disposal proceeds account of a registered social landlord ("disposal proceeds") may only be applied or appropriated by it for such purposes and in such manner as the Corporation may determine.

(2) If any disposal proceeds are not applied or appropriated as mentioned in subsection (1) within such time as is specified by determination of the Corporation, the Corporation may direct that the whole or part of them shall be paid to it.

Disposal proceeds: power to require information.

26.—(1) The Corporation may give notice—

(a) to all registered social landlords,

(b) to registered social landlords of a particular description, or

(c) to particular registered social landlords,

requiring them to furnish it with such information as it may reasonably require in connection with the exercise of its functions under sections 24 and 25 (treatment of disposal proceeds).

(2) A notice under subsection (1)(a) or (b) may be given by publication in such manner as the Corporation considers appropriate for bringing it to the attention of the landlords concerned.

Recovery, &c. of social housing grants

27.—(1) Where a registered social landlord has received a grant under section 18 (social housing grant), the following powers are exercisable in such events as the Corporation may from time to time determine.

Recovery, &c. of social housing grants.

(2) The Corporation may, acting in accordance with such principles as it has determined—

    (a) reduce any grant payable by it, or suspend or cancel any instalment of any such grant, or

    (b) direct the registered social landlord to apply or appropriate for such purposes as the Corporation may specify, or to pay to the Corporation, such amount as the Corporation may specify.

(3) A direction by the Corporation under subsection (2)(b) may require the application, appropriation or payment of an amount with interest.

(4) Any such direction shall specify—

    (a) the rate or rates of interest (whether fixed or variable) which is or are applicable,

    (b) the date from which interest is payable, and

    (c) any provision for suspended or reduced interest which is applicable.

The date from which interest is payable must not be earlier than the date of the event giving rise to the exercise of the Corporation's powers under this section.

(5) In subsection (4)(c)—

    (a) provision for suspended interest means provision to the effect that if the principal amount is applied, appropriated or paid before a date specified in the direction, no interest will be payable for any period after the date of the direction; and

    (b) provision for reduced interest means provision to the effect that if the principal amount is so applied, appropriated or paid, any interest payable will be payable at a rate or rates lower than the rate or rates which would otherwise be applicable.

(6) Where—

    (a) a registered social landlord has received a payment in respect of a grant under section 18, and

(b) at any time property to which the grant relates becomes vested in, or is leased for a term of years to, or reverts to, some other registered social landlord,

this section (including this subsection) shall have effect in relation to periods after that time as if the grant, or such proportion of it as may be determined by the Corporation to be appropriate, had been made to that other registered social landlord.

(7) The matters specified in a direction under subsection (4)(a) to (c), and the proportion mentioned in subsection (6), shall be—

(a) such as the Corporation, acting in accordance with such principles as it may from time to time determine, may specify as being appropriate, or

(b) such as the Corporation may determine to be appropriate in the particular case.

Grants, &c. under earlier enactments

Grants under
ss.50 to 55 of the
Housing Act 1988.
1988 c. 50.

28.—(1) No application for a grant under section 50 of the Housing Act 1988 (housing association grant) may be made after the commencement of this subsection.

(2) No application for a grant under section 51 of that Act (revenue deficit grant) may be made after the commencement of this subsection except by an association which had such a deficit as is mentioned in that section for any of the years beginning 1st April 1994, 1st April 1995 or 1st April 1996.

(3) Section 52 of that Act (recovery, &c. of grants) is amended as follows—

(a) in subsection (2)(c), for "to pay to it" substitute "to apply or appropriate for such purposes as the Corporation may specify, or to pay to the Corporation,";

(b) in the closing words of subsection (2), for the words from "requiring" to "interest on that amount" substitute "may require the application, appropriation or payment of an amount with interest";

(c) in subsection (7), for the words from "requiring" to "to the Corporation" substitute "requiring the application, appropriation or payment of an amount with interest";

(d) in subsection (8)(a), for the words from "the amount" to "is paid" substitute "the principal amount is applied, appropriated or paid";

(e) in subsection (8)(b), for "that amount is so paid" substitute "the principal amount is so applied, appropriated or paid".

(4) In section 53 of that Act (determinations by Corporation), for subsection (2) (requirement of approval of Secretary of State and, in the case of a general determination, consent of the Treasury) substitute—

"(2) The Corporation shall not make a general determination under the foregoing provisions of this Part except with the approval of the Secretary of State.".

(5) In section 55(1) of that Act (surplus rental income: cases in which section applies), omit paragraph (a).

(6) Any reference in sections 50 to 55 of that Act to registration as a housing association shall be construed after the commencement of section 1 of this Act (the register of social landlords) as a reference to registration as a social landlord.

29.—(1) The Secretary of State may, after consultation with a housing association, determine to commute any payments of special residual subsidy payable to the association under paragraph 2 of Part I of Schedule 5 to the Housing Associations Act 1985 for the financial year 1998-99 and subsequent years.

Commutation of payments of special residual subsidy.
1985 c. 69.

(2) Where the Secretary of State makes such a determination the payments of special residual subsidy payable to a housing association shall be commuted into a single sum calculated in such manner, and payable on such date, as the Secretary of State may consider appropriate.

(3) If after a commuted payment has been made to a housing association it appears to the Secretary of State that the payment was smaller or greater than it should have been, the Secretary of State may make a further payment to the association or require the association to repay to him such sum as he may direct.

(4) The Secretary of State may delegate to the Housing Corporation, to such extent and subject to such conditions as he may specify, any of his functions under this section and, where he does so, references to him in this section shall be construed accordingly.

CHAPTER IV

GENERAL POWERS OF THE CORPORATION

Information

30.—(1) The Corporation may for any purpose connected with the discharge of any of its functions in relation to registered social landlords serve a notice on a person requiring him—

General power to obtain information.

(a) to give to the Corporation, at a time and place and in the form and manner specified in the notice, such information relating to the affairs of a registered social landlord as may be specified or described in the notice, or

(b) to produce to the Corporation or a person authorised by the Corporation, at a time and place specified in the notice, any documents relating to the affairs of the registered social landlord which are specified or described in the notice and are in his custody or under his control.

(2) A notice under this section may be served on—

(a) a registered social landlord,

(b) any person who is, or has been, an officer, member, employee or agent of a registered social landlord,

(c) a subsidiary or associate of a registered social landlord,

(d) any person who is, or has been, an officer, member, employee or agent of a subsidiary or associate of a registered social landlord, or

(e) any other person whom the Corporation has reason to believe is or may be in possession of relevant information.

In this section "agent" includes banker, solicitor and auditor.

(3) No notice shall be served on a person within paragraphs (b) to (e) of subsection (2) unless—

    (a) a notice has been served on the registered social landlord and has not been complied with, or

    (b) the Corporation believes that the information or documents in question are not in the possession of the landlord.

(4) Nothing in this section authorises the Corporation to require—

    (a) the disclosure of anything which a person would be entitled to refuse to disclose on grounds of legal professional privilege in proceedings in the High Court, or

    (b) the disclosure by a banker of anything in breach of any duty of confidentiality owed by him to a person other than a registered social landlord or a subsidiary or associate of a registered social landlord.

(5) A notice under this section shall be given under the seal of the Corporation.

(6) References in this section to a document are to anything in which information of any description is recorded; and in relation to a document in which information is recorded otherwise than in legible form, references to producing it are to producing it in legible form.

(7) Where by virtue of this section documents are produced to any person, he may take copies of or make extracts from them.

Enforcement of notice to provide information, &c.

31.—(1) A person who without reasonable excuse fails to do anything required of him by a notice under section 30 commits an offence and is liable on summary conviction to a fine not exceeding level 5 on the standard scale.

(2) A person who intentionally alters, suppresses or destroys a document which he has been required by a notice under section 30 to produce commits an offence and is liable—

    (a) on summary conviction, to a fine not exceeding the statutory maximum,

    (b) on conviction on indictment, to a fine.

(3) Proceedings for an offence under subsection (1) or (2) may be brought only by or with the consent of the Corporation or the Director of Public Prosecutions.

(4) If a person makes default in complying with a notice under section 30, the High Court may, on the application of the Corporation, make such order as the court thinks fit for requiring the default to be made good.

Any such order may provide that all the costs or expenses of and incidental to the application shall be borne by the person in default or by any officers of a body who are responsible for its default.

Disclosure of information to the Corporation.

32.—(1) A body or person to whom this section applies may, subject to the following provisions, disclose to the Corporation, for the purpose of enabling the Corporation to discharge any of its functions relating to registered social landlords, any information received by that body or person under or for the purposes of any enactment.

(2) This section applies to the following bodies and persons—

(a) any government department (including a Northern Ireland department);

(b) any local authority;

(c) any constable; and

(d) any other body or person discharging functions of a public nature (including a body or person discharging regulatory functions in relation to any description of activities).

(3) This section has effect subject to any express restriction on disclosure imposed by or under any other enactment.

(4) Nothing in this section shall be construed as affecting any power of disclosure exercisable apart from this section.

33.—(1) The Corporation may disclose to a body or person to whom this section applies any information received by it relating to a registered social landlord—

Disclosure of information by the Corporation.

(a) for any purpose connected with the discharge of the functions of the Corporation in relation to such landlords, or

(b) for the purpose of enabling or assisting that body or person to discharge any of its or his functions.

(2) This section applies to the following bodies and persons—

(a) any government department (including a Northern Ireland department);

(b) any local authority;

(c) any constable; and

(d) any other body or person discharging functions of a public nature (including a body or person discharging regulatory functions in relation to any description of activities).

Paragraph (d) extends to any such body or person in a country or territory outside the United Kingdom.

(3) Where any information disclosed to the Corporation under section 32 is so disclosed subject to any express restriction on the further disclosure of the information, the Corporation's power of disclosure under this section is exercisable subject to that restriction.

A person who discloses information in contravention of any such restriction commits an offence and is liable on summary conviction to a fine not exceeding level 3 on the standard scale.

(4) Any information disclosed by the Corporation under this section may be subject by the Corporation to any express restriction on the further disclosure of the information.

(5) A person who discloses information in contravention of any such restriction commits an offence and is liable on summary conviction to a fine not exceeding level 3 on the standard scale.

Proceedings for such an offence may be brought only by or with the consent of the Corporation or the Director of Public Prosecutions.

(6) Nothing in this section shall be construed as affecting any power of disclosure exercisable apart from this section.

Standards of performance

Standards of performance.

34. The Corporation may, after consultation with persons or bodies appearing to it to be representative of registered social landlords, from time to time—

(a) determine such standards of performance in connection with the provision of housing as, in its opinion, ought to be achieved by such landlords, and

(b) arrange for the publication, in such form and in such manner as it considers appropriate, of the standards so determined.

Information as to levels of performance.

35.—(1) The Corporation shall from time to time collect information as to the levels of performance achieved by registered social landlords in connection with the provision of housing.

(2) On or before such date in each year as may be specified in a direction given by the Corporation, each registered social landlord shall provide the Corporation, as respects each standard determined under section 34, with such information as to the level of performance achieved by him as may be so specified.

(3) A registered social landlord who without reasonable excuse fails to do anything required of him by a direction under subsection (2) commits an offence and is liable on summary conviction to a fine not exceeding level 5 on the standard scale.

Proceedings for such an offence may be brought only by or with the consent of the Corporation or the Director of Public Prosecutions.

(4) The Corporation shall at least once in every year arrange for the publication, in such form and in such manner as it considers appropriate, of such of the information collected by or provided to it under this section as appears to it expedient to give to tenants or potential tenants of registered social landlords.

(5) In arranging for the publication of any such information the Corporation shall have regard to the need for excluding, so far as that is practicable—

(a) any matter which relates to the affairs of an individual, where publication of that matter would or might, in the opinion of the Corporation, seriously and prejudicially affect the interests of that individual; and

(b) any matter which relates specifically to the affairs of a particular body of persons, whether corporate or unincorporate, where publication of that matter would or might, in the opinion of the Corporation, seriously and prejudicially affect the interests of that body.

Housing management

36.—(1) The Corporation may issue guidance with respect to the management of housing accommodation by registered social landlords.

Issue of guidance by the Corporation.

(2) Guidance under this section may, in particular, be issued with respect to—

    (a) the housing demands for which provision should be made and the means of meeting those demands;

    (b) the allocation of housing accommodation between individuals;

    (c) the terms of tenancies and the principles upon which levels of rent should be determined;

    (d) standards of maintenance and repair and the means of achieving those standards;

    (e) the services to be provided to tenants;

    (f) the procedures to be adopted to deal with complaints by tenants against a landlord;

    (g) consultation and communication with tenants;

    (h) the devolution to tenants of decisions concerning the management of housing accommodation.

(3) Before issuing any guidance under this section the Corporation shall—

    (a) consult such bodies appearing to it to be representative of registered social landlords as it considers appropriate, and

    (b) submit a draft of the proposed guidance to the Secretary of State for his approval.

(4) If the Secretary of State gives his approval to the draft submitted to him, the Corporation shall issue the guidance in such manner as the Corporation considers appropriate for bringing it to the notice of the landlords concerned.

(5) Guidance issued under this section may be revised or withdrawn; and subsections (3) and (4) apply in relation to the revision of guidance as in relation to its issue.

(6) Guidance under this section may make different provision in relation to different cases and, in particular, in relation to different areas, different descriptions of housing accommodation and different descriptions of registered social landlord.

(7) In considering whether action needs to be taken to secure the proper management of the affairs of a registered social landlord or whether there has been mismanagement, the Corporation may have regard (among other matters) to the extent to which any guidance under this section is being or has been followed.

37.—(1) This section applies where it appears to the Corporation that a registered social landlord may be failing to maintain or repair any premises in accordance with guidance issued under section 36.

Powers of entry.

(2) A person authorised by the Corporation may at any reasonable time, on giving not less than 28 days' notice of his intention to the landlord concerned, enter any such premises for the purpose of survey and examination.

(3) Where such notice is given to the landlord, the landlord shall give the occupier or occupiers of the premises not less than seven days' notice of the proposed survey and examination.

A landlord who fails to do so commits an offence and is liable on summary conviction to a fine not exceeding level 3 on the standard scale.

(4) Proceedings for an offence under subsection (3) may be brought only by or with the consent of the Corporation or the Director of Public Prosecutions.

(5) An authorisation for the purposes of this section shall be in writing stating the particular purpose or purposes for which the entry is authorised and shall, if so required, be produced for inspection by the occupier or anyone acting on his behalf.

(6) The Corporation shall give a copy of any survey carried out in exercise of the powers conferred by this section to the landlord concerned.

(7) The Corporation may require the landlord concerned to pay to it such amount as the Corporation may determine towards the costs of carrying out any survey under this section.

Penalty for obstruction of person exercising power of entry.

38.—(1) It is an offence for a registered social landlord or any of its officers or employees to obstruct a person authorised under section 37 (powers of entry) to enter premises in the performance of anything which he is authorised by that section to do.

(2) A person who commits such an offence is liable on summary conviction to a fine not exceeding level 3 on the standard scale.

(3) Proceedings for such an offence may be brought only by or with the consent of the Corporation or the Director of Public Prosecutions.

Insolvency, &c. of registered social landlord

Insolvency, &c. of registered social landlord: scheme of provisions.

39.—(1) The following sections make provision—

(a) for notice to be given to the Corporation of any proposal to take certain steps in relation to a registered social landlord (section 40), and for further notice to be given when any such step is taken (section 41),

(b) for a moratorium on the disposal of land, and certain other assets, held by the registered social landlord (sections 42 and 43),

(c) for proposals by the Corporation as to the future ownership and management of the land held by the landlord (section 44), which are binding if agreed (section 45),

(d) for the appointment of a manager to implement agreed proposals (section 46) and as to the powers of such a manager (sections 47 and 48),

(e) for the giving of assistance by the Corporation (section 49), and

(f) for application to the court to secure compliance with the agreed proposals (section 50).

(2) In those sections—

"disposal" means sale, lease, mortgage, charge or any other disposition, and includes the grant of an option;

"secured creditor" means a creditor who holds a mortgage or charge (including a floating charge) over land held by the landlord or any existing or future interest of the landlord in rents or other receipts from land; and

"security" means any mortgage, charge or other security.

(3) The Secretary of State may make provision by order defining for the purposes of those sections what is meant by a step to enforce security over land.

Any such order shall be made by statutory instrument which shall be subject to annulment in pursuance of a resolution of either House of Parliament.

40.—(1) Notice must be given to the Corporation before any of the steps mentioned below is taken in relation to a registered social landlord.

The person by whom the notice must be given is indicated in the second column.

(2) Where the registered social landlord is an industrial and provident society, the steps and the person by whom notice must be given are—

Any step to enforce any security over land held by the landlord.	The person proposing to take the step.
Presenting a petition for the winding up of the landlord.	The petitioner.
Passing a resolution for the winding up of the landlord.	The landlord.

(3) Where the registered social landlord is a company registered under the Companies Act 1985 (including a registered charity), the steps and the person by whom notice must be given are—

Any step to enforce any security over land held by the landlord.	The person proposing to take the step.
Applying for an administration order.	The applicant.
Presenting a petition for the winding up of the landlord.	The petitioner.
Passing a resolution for the winding up of the landlord.	The landlord.

(4) Where the registered social landlord is a registered charity (other than a company registered under the Companies Act 1985), the steps and the person by whom notice must be given are—

Any step to enforce any security over land held by the landlord.	The person proposing to take the step.

(5) Notice need not be given under this section in relation to a resolution for voluntary winding up where the consent of the Corporation is required (see paragraphs 12(4) and 13(6) of Schedule 1).

(6) Any step purportedly taken without the requisite notice being given under this section is ineffective.

Further notice to be given to the Corporation.

41.—(1) Notice must be given to the Corporation as soon as may be after any of the steps mentioned below is taken in relation to a registered social landlord.

The person by whom the notice must be given is indicated in the second column.

(2) Where the registered social landlord is an industrial and provident society, the steps and the person by whom notice must be given are—

The taking of a step to enforce any security over land held by the landlord.	The person taking the step.
The making of an order for the winding up of the landlord.	The petitioner.
The passing of a resolution for the winding up of the landlord.	The landlord.

1985 c. 6.

(3) Where the registered social landlord is a company registered under the Companies Act 1985 (including a registered charity), the steps and the person by whom notice must be given are—

The taking of a step to enforce any security over land held by the landlord.	The person taking the step.
The making of an administration order.	The person who applied for the order.
The making of an order for the winding up of the landlord.	The petitioner.
The passing of a resolution for the winding up of the landlord.	The landlord.

(4) Where the registered social landlord is a registered charity (other than a company registered under the Companies Act 1985), the steps and the person by whom notice must be given are—

The taking of a step to enforce any security over land held by the landlord.	The person taking the step.

(5) Failure to give notice under this section does not affect the validity of any step taken; but the period of 28 days mentioned in section 43(1) (period after which moratorium on disposal of land, &c. ends) does not begin to run until any requisite notice has been given under this section.

Moratorium on disposal of land, &c.

42.—(1) Where any of the steps mentioned in section 41 is taken in relation to a registered social landlord, there is a moratorium on the disposal of land held by the landlord.

(2) During the moratorium the consent of the Corporation under this section is required (except as mentioned below) for any disposal of land held by the landlord, whether by the landlord itself or any person having a power of disposal in relation to the land.

Consent under this section may be given in advance and may be given subject to conditions.

(3) Consent is not required under this section for any such disposal as is mentioned in section 10(1), (2) or (3) (lettings and other disposals not requiring consent under section 9).

(4) A disposal made without the consent required by this section is void.

(5) Nothing in this section prevents a liquidator from disclaiming any land held by the landlord as onerous property.

(6) The provisions of this section apply in relation to any existing or future interest of the landlord in rent or other receipts arising from land as they apply to an interest in land.

43.—(1) The moratorium in consequence of the taking of any step as mentioned in section 41—

    (a) begins when the step is taken, and

    (b) ends at the end of the period of 28 days beginning with the day on which notice of its having been taken was given to the Corporation under that section,

subject to the following provisions.

Period of moratorium.

(2) The taking of any further step as mentioned in section 41 at a time when a moratorium is already in force does not start a further moratorium or affect the duration of the existing one.

(3) A moratorium may be extended from time to time with the consent of all the landlord's secured creditors.

Notice of any such extension shall be given by the Corporation to—

    (a) the landlord, and

    (b) any liquidator, administrative receiver, receiver or administrator appointed in respect of the landlord or any land held by it.

(4) If during a moratorium the Corporation considers that the proper management of the landlord's land can be secured without making proposals under section 44 (proposals as to ownership and management of landlord's land), the Corporation may direct that the moratorium shall cease to have effect.

Before making any such direction the Corporation shall consult the person who took the step which brought about the moratorium.

(5) When a moratorium comes to an end, or ceases to have effect under subsection (4), the Corporation shall give notice of that fact to the landlord and the landlord's secured creditors.

(6) When a moratorium comes to an end (but not when it ceases to have effect under subsection (4)), the following provisions of this section apply.

The Corporation's notice shall, in such a case, inform the landlord and the landlord's secured creditors of the effect of those provisions.

(7) If any further step as mentioned in section 41 is taken within the period of three years after the end of the original period of the moratorium, the moratorium may be renewed with the consent of all the landlord's secured creditors (which may be given before or after the step is taken).

Notice of any such renewal shall be given by the Corporation to the persons to whom notice of an extension is required to be given under subsection (3).

(8) If a moratorium ends without any proposals being agreed, then, for a period of three years the taking of any further step as mentioned in section 41 does not start a further moratorium except with the consent of the landlord's secured creditors as mentioned in subsection (7) above.

Proposals as to
ownership and
management of
landlord's land.

44.—(1) During the moratorium (see sections 42 and 43) the Corporation may make proposals as to the future ownership and management of the land held by the registered social landlord, designed to secure the continued proper management of the landlord's land by a registered social landlord.

(2) In drawing up its proposals the Corporation—

    (a) shall consult the landlord and, so far as is practicable, its tenants, and

    (b) shall have regard to the interests of all the landlord's creditors, both secured and unsecured.

(3) The Corporation shall also consult—

    (a) where the landlord is an industrial and provident society, the appropriate registrar, and

    (b) where the landlord is a registered charity, the Charity Commissioners.

(4) No proposals shall be made under which—

    (a) a preferential debt of the landlord is to be paid otherwise than in priority to debts which are not preferential debts, or

    (b) a preferential creditor is to be paid a smaller proportion of his preferential debt than another preferential creditor, except with the concurrence of the creditor concerned.

1986 c. 45.

In this subsection references to preferential debts and preferential creditors have the same meaning as in the Insolvency Act 1986.

(5) So far as practicable no proposals shall be made which have the effect that unsecured creditors of the landlord are in a worse position than they would otherwise be.

(6) Where the landlord is a charity the proposals shall not require the landlord to act outside the terms of its trusts, and any disposal of housing accommodation occupied under a tenancy or licence from the landlord must be to another charity whose objects appear to the Corporation to be, as nearly as practicable, akin to those of the landlord.

(7) The Corporation shall serve a copy of its proposals on—

    (a) the landlord and its officers,

    (b) the secured creditors of the landlord, and

    (c) any liquidator, administrator, administrative receiver or receiver appointed in respect of the landlord or its land;

and it shall make such arrangements as it considers appropriate to see that the members, tenants and unsecured creditors of the landlord are informed of the proposals.

45.—(1) The following provisions apply if proposals made by the Corporation under section 44 are agreed, with or without modifications, by all the secured creditors of the registered social landlord.

Effect of agreed proposals.

    (2) Once agreed the proposals are binding on the Corporation, the landlord, all the landlord's creditors (whether secured or unsecured) and any liquidator, administrator, administrative receiver or receiver appointed in respect of the landlord or its land.

    (3) It is the duty of—

    (a) the members of the committee where the landlord is an industrial and provident society,

    (b) the directors where the landlord is a company registered under the Companies Act 1985 (including a company which is a registered charity), and

1985 c. 6.

    (c) the trustees where the landlord is a charitable trust,

to co-operate in the implementation of the proposals.

This does not mean that they have to do anything contrary to any fiduciary or other duty owed by them.

    (4) The Corporation shall serve a copy of the agreed proposals on—

    (a) the landlord and its officers,

    (b) the secured creditors of the landlord, and

    (c) any liquidator, administrator, administrative receiver or receiver appointed in respect of the landlord or its land, and

    (d) where the landlord is an industrial and provident society or registered charity, the appropriate registrar or the Charity Commissioners, as the case may be;

and it shall make such arrangements as it considers appropriate to see that the members, tenants and unsecured creditors of the landlord are informed of the proposals.

    (5) The proposals may subsequently be amended with the consent of the Corporation and all the landlord's secured creditors.

Section 44(2) to (7) and subsections (2) to (4) above apply in relation to the amended proposals as in relation to the original proposals.

46.—(1) Where proposals agreed as mentioned in section 45 so provide, the Corporation may by order under its seal appoint a manager to implement the proposals or such of them as are specified in the order.

Appointment of manager to implement agreed proposals.

    (2) If the landlord is a registered charity, the Corporation shall give notice to the Charity Commissioners of the appointment.

    (3) Where proposals make provision for the appointment of a manager, they shall also provide for the payment of his reasonable remuneration and expenses.

(4) The Corporation may give the manager directions in relation to the carrying out of his functions.

(5) The manager may apply to the High Court for directions in relation to any particular matter arising in connection with the carrying out of his functions.

A direction of the court supersedes any direction of the Corporation in respect of the same matter.

(6) If a vacancy occurs by death, resignation or otherwise in the office of manager, the Corporation may by further order under its seal fill the vacancy.

Powers of the manager.

47.—(1) An order under section 46(1) shall confer on the manager power generally to do all such things as are necessary for carrying out his functions.

(2) The order may include the following specific powers—

1. Power to take possession of the land held by the landlord and for that purpose to take any legal proceedings which seem to him expedient.

2. Power to sell or otherwise dispose of the land by public auction or private contract.

3. Power to raise or borrow money and for that purpose to grant security over the land.

4. Power to appoint a solicitor or accountant or other professionally qualified person to assist him in the performance of his functions.

5. Power to bring or defend legal proceedings relating to the land in the name and on behalf of the landlord.

6. Power to refer to arbitration any question affecting the land.

7. Power to effect and maintain insurance in respect of the land.

8. Power where the landlord is a body corporate to use the seal of the body corporate for purposes relating to the land.

9. Power to do all acts and to execute in the name and on behalf of the landlord any deed, receipt or other document relating to the land.

10. Power to appoint an agent to do anything which he is unable to do for himself or which can more conveniently be done by an agent, and power to employ and dismiss any employees.

11. Power to do all such things (including the carrying out of works) as may be necessary in connection with the management or transfer of the land.

12. Power to make any payment which is necessary or incidental to the performance of his functions.

13. Power to carry on the business of the landlord so far as relating to the management or transfer of the land.

14. Power to grant or accept a surrender of a lease or tenancy of any of the land, and to take a lease or tenancy of any property required or convenient for the landlord's housing activities.

15. Power to make any arrangement or compromise on behalf of the landlord in relation to the management or transfer of the land.

16. Power to do all other things incidental to the exercise of any of the above powers.

(3) In carrying out his functions the manager acts as the landlord's agent and he is not personally liable on a contract which he enters into as manager.

(4) A person dealing with the manager in good faith and for value is not concerned to inquire whether the manager is acting within his powers.

(5) The manager shall, so far as practicable, consult the landlord's tenants about any exercise of his powers which is likely to affect them and inform them about any such exercise of his powers.

48.—(1) An order under section 46(1) may, where the landlord is an industrial and provident society, give the manager power to make and execute on behalf of the society an instrument transferring the engagements of the society.

Powers of the manager: transfer of engagements.

(2) Any such instrument has the same effect as a transfer of engagements under section 51 or 52 of the Industrial and Provident Societies Act 1965 (transfer of engagements by special resolution to another society or a company).

1965 c. 12.

In particular, its effect is subject to section 54 of that Act (saving for rights of creditors).

(3) A copy of the instrument, signed by the manager, shall be sent to the appropriate registrar and registered by him; and until that copy is so registered the instrument shall not take effect.

(4) It is the duty of the manager to send a copy for registration within 14 days from the day on which the instrument is executed; but this does not invalidate registration after that time.

49.—(1) The Corporation may give such assistance as it thinks fit—

Assistance by the Corporation.

(a) to the landlord, for the purpose of preserving the position pending the making of and agreement to proposals;

(b) to the landlord or a manager appointed under section 46, for the purpose of carrying out any agreed proposals.

(2) The Corporation may, in particular—

(a) lend staff;

(b) pay or secure payment of the manager's reasonable remuneration and expenses;

(c) give such financial assistance as appears to the Corporation to be appropriate.

(3) The following forms of assistance require the consent of the Secretary of State—

(a) making grants or loans;

(b) agreeing to indemnify the manager in respect of liabilities incurred or loss or damage sustained by him in connection with his functions;

(c) paying or guaranteeing the repayment of the principal of, the payment of interest on and the discharge of any other financial obligation in connection with any sum borrowed (before or after the making of the order) and secured on any land disposed of.

Application to court to secure compliance with agreed proposals.

50.—(1) The landlord or any creditor of the landlord may apply to the High Court on the ground that an action of the manager appointed under section 46 is not in accordance with the agreed proposals.

On such an application the court may confirm, reverse or modify any act or decision of the manager, give him directions or make such other order as it thinks fit.

(2) The Corporation or any other person bound by agreed proposals may apply to the High Court on the ground that any action, or proposed action, by another person bound by the proposals is not in accordance with those proposals.

On such an application the court may—

(a) declare any such action to be ineffective, and

(b) grant such relief by way of injunction, damages or otherwise as appears to the court appropriate.

CHAPTER V

MISCELLANEOUS AND GENERAL PROVISIONS

Housing complaints

Schemes for investigation of complaints.

51.—(1) The provisions of Schedule 2 have effect for the purpose of enabling tenants and other individuals to have complaints against social landlords investigated by a housing ombudsman in accordance with a scheme approved by the Secretary of State.

(2) For the purposes of that Schedule a "social landlord" means—

(a) a registered social landlord;

1993 c. 28.

(b) a transferee of housing pursuant to a qualifying disposal under section 135 of the Leasehold Reform, Housing and Urban Development Act 1993;

1988 c. 50.

(c) a body which has acquired dwellings under Part IV of the Housing Act 1988 (change of landlord: secure tenants); or

(d) any other body which was at any time registered with the Corporation and which owns or manages publicly-funded dwellings.

(3) In subsection (2)(d) a "publicly-funded dwelling" means a dwelling which was—

(a) provided by means of a grant under—

section 18 of this Act (social housing grant), or

1985 c. 69.
1974 c. 44.

section 50 of the Housing Act 1988, section 41 of the Housing Associations Act 1985, or section 29 or 29A of the Housing Act 1974 (housing association grant); or

(b) acquired on a disposal by a public sector landlord.

(4) The Secretary of State may by order add to or amend the descriptions of landlords who are to be treated as social landlords for the purposes of Schedule 2.

(5) Before making any such order the Secretary of State shall consult such persons as he considers appropriate.

(6) Any such order shall be made by statutory instrument which shall be subject to annulment in pursuance of a resolution of either House of Parliament.

Orders and determinations

52.—(1) The following provisions apply to any power of the Secretary of State under this Part to make an order.

General provisions as to orders.

(2) An order may make different provision for different cases or descriptions of case.

This includes power to make different provision for different bodies or descriptions of body, different provision for different housing activities and different provision for different areas.

(3) An order may contain such supplementary, incidental, consequential or transitional provisions and savings as the Secretary of State considers appropriate.

53.—(1) The following provisions apply to determinations of the Corporation or the Secretary of State under this Part.

General provisions as to determinations.

(2) A determination may make different provision for different cases or descriptions of case.

This includes power to make—

    (a) different provision for different registered social landlords or descriptions of registered social landlord, and

    (b) different provision for different housing activities and different provision for different areas;

and for the purposes of paragraph (b) descriptions may be framed by reference to any matters whatever, including in particular, in the case of housing activities, the manner in which they are financed.

(3) In this Part a general determination means a determination which does not relate solely to a particular case.

(4) Before making a general determination, the Corporation or the Secretary of State shall consult such bodies appearing to them to be representative of registered social landlords as they consider appropriate.

(5) After making a general determination, the Corporation or the Secretary of State shall publish the determination in such manner as they consider appropriate for bringing the determination to the notice of the landlords concerned.

54. The Corporation shall not make—

    (a) a general determination under paragraph 16 of Schedule 1 (accounting and audit requirements for registered social landlords) or section 18 (social housing grant), or

Determinations of the Corporation requiring approval.

(b) any determination under section 27 (recovery, &c. of social housing grants),

except with the approval of the Secretary of State.

Minor and consequential amendments

55.—(1) The enactments mentioned in Schedule 3 have effect with the minor amendments specified there.

(2) The Secretary of State may by order make such amendments or repeals of any enactment as appear to him necessary or expedient in consequence of the provisions of this Part.

(3) Any such order shall be made by statutory instrument which shall be subject to annulment in pursuance of a resolution of either House of Parliament.

Interpretation

56.—(1) In this Part "the Corporation" means the Housing Corporation or Housing for Wales, as follows.

(2) In relation to a registered social landlord, or a body applying for such registration, which is—

(a) a registered charity which has its address for the purposes of registration by the Charity Commissioners in Wales,

(b) an industrial and provident society which has its registered office for the purposes of the Industrial and Provident Societies Act 1965 in Wales, or

(c) a company registered under the Companies Act 1985 which has its registered office for the purposes of that Act in Wales,

"the Corporation" means Housing for Wales.

(3) In relation to any other registered social landlord or body applying for such registration, "the Corporation" means the Housing Corporation.

(4) Nothing in this Part shall be construed as requiring the Housing Corporation and Housing for Wales to establish the same criteria for registration as a social landlord, or otherwise to act on the same principles in respect of any matter in relation to which they have functions under this Part.

57.—(1) In this Part, in relation to an industrial and provident society—

"appropriate registrar" has the same meaning as in the Industrial and Provident Societies Act 1965 (where it is defined in section 73(1)(c) by reference to the situation of the society's registered office);

"committee" means the committee of management or other directing body of the society; and

"co-opted member", in relation to the committee, includes any person co-opted to serve on the committee, whether he is a member of the society or not.

(2) Any reference in this Part to a member of the committee of an industrial and provident society includes a co-opted member.

58.—(1) In this Part—

(a) "charity" and "trusts", in relation to a charity, have the same meaning as in the Charities Act 1993, and "trustee" means a charitable trustee within the meaning of that Act; and

(b) "registered charity" means a charity which is registered under section 3 of that Act and is not an exempt charity within the meaning of that Act.

(2) References in this Part to a company registered under the Companies Act 1985 do not include a company which is a registered charity, except where otherwise provided.

59.—(1) References in this Part to an officer of a registered social landlord are—

(a) in the case of a registered charity which is not a company registered under the Companies Act 1985, to any trustee, secretary or treasurer of the charity;

(b) in the case of an industrial and provident society, to any officer of the society as defined in section 74 of the Industrial and Provident Societies Act 1965; and

(c) in the case of a company registered under the Companies Act 1985 (including such a company which is also a registered charity), to any director or other officer of the company within the meaning of that Act.

(2) Any such reference includes, in the case of an industrial and provident society, a co-opted member of the committee of the society.

60.—(1) In this Part "subsidiary", in relation to a registered social landlord, means a company with respect to which one of the following conditions is fulfilled—

(a) the landlord is a member of the company and controls the composition of the board of directors;

(b) the landlord holds more than half in nominal value of the company's equity share capital; or

(c) the company is a subsidiary, within the meaning of the Companies Act 1985 or the Friendly and Industrial and Provident Societies Act 1968, of another company which, by virtue of paragraph (a) or paragraph (b), is itself a subsidiary of the landlord.

(2) For the purposes of subsection (1)(a), the composition of a company's board of directors shall be deemed to be controlled by a registered social landlord if, but only if, the landlord, by the exercise of some power exercisable by him without the consent or concurrence of any other person, can appoint or remove the holders of all or a majority of the directorships.

(3) In relation to a company which is an industrial and provident society—

(a) any reference in this section to the board of directors is a reference to the committee of management of the society; and

(b) the reference in subsection (2) to the holders of all or a majority of the directorships is a reference—

(i) to all or a majority of the members of the committee, or

(ii) if the landlord is himself a member of the committee, such number as together with him would constitute a majority.

(4) In the case of a registered social landlord which is a body of trustees, references in this section to the landlord are to the trustees acting as such.

Meaning of
"associate".

61.—(1) In this Part "associate", in relation to a registered social landlord, means—

(a) any body of which the landlord is a subsidiary, and

(b) any other subsidiary of such a body.

1985 c. 6.
1968 c. 55.

(2) In this section "subsidiary" has the same meaning as in the Companies Act 1985 or the Friendly and Industrial and Provident Societies Act 1968 or, in the case of a body which is itself a registered social landlord, has the meaning given by section 60.

Members of a
person's family:
Part I.

62.—(1) A person is a member of another's family within the meaning of this Part if—

(a) he is the spouse of that person, or he and that person live together as husband and wife, or

(b) he is that person's parent, grandparent, child, grandchild, brother, sister, uncle, aunt, nephew or niece.

(2) For the purpose of subsection (1)(b)—

(a) a relationship by marriage shall be treated as a relationship by blood,

(b) a relationship of the half-blood shall be treated as a relationship of the whole blood, and

(c) the stepchild of a person shall be treated as his child.

Minor definitions:
Part I.

63.—(1) In this Part—

"dwelling" means a building or part of a building occupied or intended to be occupied as a separate dwelling, together with any yard, garden, outhouses and appurtenances belonging to it or usually enjoyed with it;

"fully mutual", in relation to a housing association, and "co-operative housing association" have the same meaning as in the Housing Associations Act 1985 (see section 1(2) of that Act);

1985 c. 69.

"hostel" means a building in which is provided for persons generally or for a class or classes of persons—

(a) residential accommodation otherwise than in separate and self-contained premises, and

(b) either board or facilities for the preparation of food adequate to the needs of those persons, or both;

"house" includes—

(a) any part of a building occupied or intended to be occupied as a separate dwelling, and

(b) any yard, garden, outhouses and appurtenances belonging to it or usually enjoyed with it;

"housing accommodation" includes flats, lodging-houses and hostels;

"housing activities" means, in relation to a registered social landlord, all its activities in pursuance of the purposes, objects and powers mentioned in or specified under section 2;

"information" includes accounts, estimates and returns;

"local authority" has the same meaning as in the Housing Associations Act 1985;   1985 c. 69.

"long tenancy" has the same meaning as in Part V of the Housing Act 1985;   1985 c. 68.

"modifications" includes additions, alterations and omissions and cognate expressions shall be construed accordingly;

"notice" means notice in writing;

"public sector landlord" means any of the authorities or bodies within section 80(1) of the Housing Act 1985 (the landlord condition for secure tenancies);

"registrar of companies" has the same meaning as in the Companies Act 1985;   1985 c. 6.

"statutory tenancy" has the same meaning as in the Housing Act 1985.

(2) References in this Part to the provision of a dwelling or house include the provision of a dwelling or house—

(a) by erecting the dwelling or house, or converting a building into dwellings or a house, or

(b) by altering, enlarging, repairing or improving an existing dwelling or house;

and references to a dwelling or house provided by means of a grant or other financial assistance are to its being so provided directly or indirectly.

64. The following Table shows provisions defining or otherwise explaining expressions used in this Part (other than provisions defining or explaining an expression used in the same section)—   Index of defined expressions: Part I.

appointed person (in relation to inquiry into affairs of registered social landlord)	paragraph 20 of Schedule 1
appropriate registrar (in relation to an industrial and provident society)	section 57(1)
associate (in relation to a registered social landlord)	section 61(1)
assured tenancy	section 230
assured agricultural occupancy	section 230
assured shorthold tenancy	section 230
charity	section 58(1)(a)
committee member (in relation to an industrial and provident society)	section 57(2)
company registered under the Companies Act 1985	section 58(2)
co-operative housing association	section 63
co-opted member (of committee of industrial and provident society)	section 57(1)
the Corporation	section 56
disposal proceeds fund	section 24
dwelling	section 63

enactment	section 230
fully mutual housing association	section 63
hostel	section 63
house	section 63
housing accommodation	section 63
housing activities	section 63
housing association	section 230
industrial and provident society	section 2(1)(b)
information	section 63
lease	section 229
local authority	section 63
long tenancy	section 63
member of family	section 62
modifications	section 63
notice	section 63
officer of registered social landlord	section 59
provision (in relation to dwelling or house)	section 63(2)
public sector landlord	section 63
register, registered and registration (in relation to social landlords)	section 1
registered charity	section 58(1)(b)
registrar of companies	section 63
relevant disposal which is not an exempted disposal (in sections 11 to 14)	section 15
secure tenancy	section 230
social housing grant	section 18(1)
statutory tenancy	section 63
subsidiary (in relation to a registered social landlord)	section 60(1)
trustee and trusts (in relation to a charity)	section 58(1)(a)

PART II

HOUSES IN MULTIPLE OCCUPATION

Registration schemes

Making and
approval of
registration
schemes.

1985 c. 68.

"Registration
schemes.

65.—(1) In Part XI of the Housing Act 1985 (houses in multiple occupation), for section 346 (registration schemes) substitute—

346.—(1) A local housing authority may make a registration scheme authorising the authority to compile and maintain a register for their district of houses in multiple occupation.

(2) A registration scheme need not be for the whole of the authority's district and need not apply to every description of house in multiple occupation.

(3) A registration scheme may vary or revoke a previous registration scheme; and the local housing authority may at any time by order revoke a registration scheme.

Contents of
registration
scheme.

346A.—(1) A registration scheme shall make it the duty of such person as may be specified by the scheme to register a house to which the scheme applies and to renew the registration as and when required by the scheme.

(2) A registration scheme shall provide that registration under the scheme—

    (a) shall be for a period of five years from the date of first registration, and

    (b) may on application be renewed, subject to such conditions as are specified in the scheme, for further periods of five years at a time.

(3) A registration scheme may—

    (a) specify the particulars to be inserted in the register,

    (b) make it the duty of such persons as may be specified by the scheme to give the authority as regards a house all or any of the particulars specified in the scheme,

    (c) make it the duty of such persons as may be specified by the scheme to notify the authority of any change which makes it necessary to alter the particulars inserted in the register as regards a house.

(4) A registration scheme shall, subject to subsection (5)—

    (a) require the payment on first registration of a reasonable fee of an amount determined by the local housing authority, and

    (b) require the payment on any renewal of registration of half the fee which would then have been payable on a first registration of the house.

(5) The Secretary of State may by order make provision as to the fee payable on registration—

    (a) specifying the maximum permissible fee (whether by specifying an amount or a method for calculating an amount), and

    (b) specifying cases in which no fee is payable.

(6) An order under subsection (5)—

    (a) may make different provision with respect to different cases or descriptions of case (including different provision for different areas), and

    (b) shall be made by statutory instrument which shall be subject to annulment in pursuance of a resolution of either House of Parliament.

Model schemes
and
confirmation of
schemes.

346B.—(1) The Secretary of State may prepare model registration schemes.

(2) Model registration schemes may be prepared with or without control provisions (see section 347) or special

control provisions (see section 348B); and different model schemes may be prepared for different descriptions of authorities and for different areas.

(3) A registration scheme which conforms to a model scheme—

(a) does not require confirmation by the Secretary of State, and

(b) comes into force on such date (at least one month after the making of the scheme) as may be specified in the scheme.

(4) Any other registration scheme does not come into force unless and until confirmed by the Secretary of State.

(5) The Secretary of State may if he thinks fit confirm such a scheme with or without modifications.

(6) A scheme requiring confirmation shall not come into force before it has been confirmed but, subject to that, comes into force on such date as may be specified in the scheme or, if no date is specified, one month after it is confirmed.".

1985 c. 68.

(2) In section 351(1) of the Housing Act 1985 (proof of matters relating to registration scheme), in paragraph (c) at the beginning insert "that the scheme did not require confirmation by the Secretary of State or".

Registration schemes: control provisions.

66. In Part XI of the Housing Act 1985 (houses in multiple occupation), for sections 347 and 348 (registration schemes: control provisions) substitute—

"Control provisions.

347.—(1) A registration scheme may contain control provisions, that is to say, provisions for preventing multiple occupation of a house unless—

(a) the house is registered, and

(b) the number of households or persons occupying it does not exceed the number registered for it.

(2) Control provisions may prohibit persons from permitting others to take up residence in a house or part of a house but shall not prohibit a person from taking up or remaining in residence in the house.

(3) Control provisions shall not prevent the occupation of a house by a greater number of households or persons than the number registered for it if all of those households or persons have been in occupation of the house without interruption since before the number was first registered.

Control provisions: decisions on applications and appeals.

348.—(1) Control provisions may enable the local housing authority, on an application for first registration of a house or a renewal or variation of registration—

(a) to refuse the application on the ground that the house is unsuitable and incapable of being made suitable for such occupation as would be permitted if the application were granted;

(b) to refuse the application on the ground that the person having control of the house or the person intended to be the person managing the house is not a fit and proper person;

(c) to require as a condition of granting the application that such works as will make the house suitable for such occupation as would be permitted if the application were granted are executed within such time as the authority may determine;

(d) to impose such conditions relating to the management of the house during the period of registration as the authority may determine.

(2) Control provisions shall provide that the local housing authority shall give an applicant a written statement of their reasons where they—

(a) refuse to grant his application for first registration or for a renewal or variation of registration,

(b) require the execution of works as a condition of granting such an application, or

(c) impose conditions relating to the management of the house.

(3) Where the local housing authority—

(a) notify an applicant that they refuse to grant his application for first registration or for the renewal or variation of a registration,

(b) notify an applicant that they require the execution of works as a condition of granting such an application,

(c) notify an applicant that they intend to impose conditions relating to the management of the house, or

(d) do not within five weeks of receiving the application, or such longer period as may be agreed in writing between the authority and the applicant, register the house or vary or renew the registration in accordance with the application,

the applicant may, within 21 days of being so notified or of the end of the period mentioned in paragraph (d), or such longer period as the authority may in writing allow, appeal to the county court.

(4) On appeal the court may confirm, reverse or vary the decision of the authority.

(5) Where the decision of the authority was a refusal—

(a) to grant an application for first registration of a house, or

(b) for the renewal or variation of the registration,

the court may direct the authority to grant the application as made or as varied in such manner as the court may direct.

(6) For the purposes of subsections (4) and (5) an appeal under subsection (3)(d) shall be treated as an appeal against a decision of the authority to refuse the application.

(7) Where the decision of the authority was to impose conditions relating to the management of the house, the court may direct the authority to grant the application without imposing the conditions or to impose the conditions as varied in such manner as the court may direct.

Control provisions: other decisions and appeals.

348A.—(1) Control provisions may enable the local housing authority at any time during a period of registration (whether or not an application has been made)—

(a) to alter the number of households or persons for which a house is registered or revoke the registration on the ground that the house is unsuitable and incapable of being made suitable for such occupation as is permitted by virtue of the registration; or

(b) to alter the number of households or persons for which a house is registered or revoke the registration unless such works are executed within a specified time as will make the house in question suitable for such occupation as is permitted by virtue of the registration.

(2) Control provisions which confer on a local housing authority any such power as is mentioned in subsection (1) shall provide that the authority shall, in deciding whether to exercise the power, apply the same standards in relation to the circumstances existing at the time of the decision as were applied at the beginning of the period of registration.

(3) Control provisions may enable the local housing authority to revoke a registration if they consider that—

(a) the person having control of the house or the person managing it is not a fit and proper person, or

(b) there has been a breach of conditions relating to the management of the house.

(4) Control provisions shall also provide that the local housing authority shall—

(a) notify the person having control of a house and the person managing it of any decision by the authority to exercise a power mentioned in subsection (1) or (3) in relation to the house, and

(b) at the same time give them a written statement of the authority's reasons.

(5) A person who has been so notified may within 21 days of being so notified, or such longer period as the authority may in writing allow, appeal to the county court.

(6) On appeal the court may confirm, reverse or vary the decision of the authority.".

67.—(1) In Part XI of the Housing Act 1985 (houses in multiple occupation), after section 348A (as inserted by section 66 above) insert—

Registration schemes: special control provisions. 1985 c. 68.

"Special control provisions.

348B.—(1) A registration scheme which contains control provisions may also contain special control provisions, that is, provisions for preventing houses in multiple occupation, by reason of their existence or the behaviour of their residents, from adversely affecting the amenity or character of the area in which they are situated.

(2) Special control provisions may provide for the refusal or revocation of registration, for reducing the number of households or persons for which a house is registered and for imposing conditions of registration.

(3) The conditions of registration may include conditions relating to the management of the house or the behaviour of its occupants.

(4) Special control provisions may authorise the revocation of registration in the case of—

(a) occupation of the house by more households or persons than the registration permits, or

(b) a breach of any condition imposed in pursuance of the special control provisions,

which is due to a relevant management failure.

(5) Special control provisions shall not authorise the refusal of—

(a) an application for first registration of a house which has been in operation as a house in multiple occupation since before the introduction by the local housing authority of a registration scheme with special control provisions, or

(b) any application for renewal of registration of a house previously registered under such a scheme,

unless there has been a relevant management failure.

(6) Special control provisions may provide that in any other case where an application is made for first registration of a house the local housing authority may take into account the number of houses in multiple occupation in the vicinity in deciding whether to permit or refuse registration.

Special control
provisions:
general
provisions as to
decisions and
appeals.

348C.—(1) Special control provisions shall provide that the local housing authority shall give a written statement of their reasons to the applicant where they refuse to grant his application for first registration, or for a renewal or variation of a registration, or impose conditions of registration on such an application.

(2) Special control provisions shall provide that the authority shall give written notice to the person having control of the house and the person managing it of any decision by the authority—

    (a) to vary the conditions of registration (otherwise than on an application to which subsection (1) applies), or

    (b) to revoke the registration of the house,

and at the same time give them a written statement of the authority's reasons.

(3) Where in accordance with special control provisions the local housing authority—

    (a) notify an applicant that they refuse to grant his application for first registration or for the renewal or variation of a registration,

    (b) notify such an applicant of the imposition of conditions of registration, or

    (c) give notice to the person having control or the person managing the house of any such decision as is mentioned in subsection (2),

that person may, within 21 days of being so notified, or such longer period as the authority may in writing allow, appeal to the county court.

(4) If on appeal it appears to the court—

    (a) that there has been any informality, defect or error in, or in connection with, the authority's decision, or

    (b) that the authority acted unreasonably,

the court may reverse or vary the decision of the authority.

(5) In so far as an appeal is based on the ground mentioned in subsection (4)(a), the court shall dismiss the appeal if it is satisfied that the informality, defect or error was not a material one.

(6) Where the decision of the authority was a refusal—

    (a) to grant an application for first registration of a house, or

    (b) for the renewal or variation of the registration,

the court may direct the authority to grant the application as made or as varied in such manner as the court may direct.

(7) Where the decision of the authority was to impose conditions of registration, the court may direct the

authority to grant the application without imposing the conditions or to impose the conditions as varied in such manner as the court may direct.

Special control provisions: occupancy directions.

348D.—(1) Special control provisions may provide that where the local housing authority decide that the registration of a house should be revoked the authority may direct that the level of occupation of the house be reduced, within such period of not less than 28 days as they may direct, to a level such that the registration scheme does not apply.

Such a direction is referred to in this Part as an "occupancy direction".

(2) Special control provisions shall provide that the authority shall only make an occupancy direction if it appears to the authority that there has been a relevant management failure resulting in a serious adverse effect on the amenity or character of the area in which the house is situated.

(3) In considering whether to make an occupancy direction the authority shall take into account the interests of the occupants of the house and the person having control of the house as well as the interests of local residents and businesses.

(4) Special control provisions may require the person having control of the house, and the person managing it, to take all reasonably practicable steps to comply with an occupancy direction.

(5) Nothing in Part I of the Housing Act 1988 prevents possession being obtained by any person in order to comply with an occupancy direction.

1988 c. 50.

(6) Nothing in this section affects any liability in respect of any other contravention or failure to comply with control provisions or special control provisions.

Special control provisions: decisions and appeals relating to occupancy directions.

348E.—(1) Special control provisions shall provide that where the local housing authority make an occupancy direction in respect of a house they shall give written notice of the direction to the person having control of the house and the person managing it and at the same time give them a written statement of the authority's reasons.

(2) A person aggrieved by an occupancy direction may, within 21 days after the date of the service of notice as mentioned in subsection (1), appeal to the county court.

(3) If on appeal it appears to the court—

(a) that there has been any informality, defect or error in, or in connection with, the authority's decision, or

(b) that the authority acted unreasonably,

the court may make such order either confirming, quashing or varying the notice as it thinks fit.

(4) In so far as an appeal is based on the ground mentioned in subsection (3)(a), the court shall dismiss the appeal if it is satisfied that the informality, defect or error was not a material one.

(5) If an appeal is brought the direction does not become operative until—

(a) a decision on the appeal confirming the direction (with or without variation) is given and the period within which an appeal to the Court of Appeal may be brought expires without any such appeal having been brought, or

(b) if a further appeal to the Court of Appeal is brought, a decision on that appeal is given confirming the direction (with or without variation).

(6) For this purpose the withdrawal of an appeal has the same effect as a decision confirming the direction or decision appealed against.

Special control provisions: "relevant management failure".

348F. A "relevant management failure" for the purposes of sections 348B to 348E (special control provisions) means a failure on the part of the person having control of, or the person managing, a house in multiple occupation to take such steps as are reasonably practicable to prevent the existence of the house or the behaviour of its residents from adversely affecting the amenity or character of the area in which the house is situated, or to reduce any such adverse effect.".

1985 c. 68.

(2) In section 400 of the Housing Act 1985 (index of defined expressions: Part XI), at the appropriate places insert—

"occupancy direction (in connection with special control provisions)   section 348D

relevant management failure (for purposes of sections 348B to 348E)   section 348F

special control provisions   section 348B".

Offences in connection with registration schemes.

68.—(1) In Part XI of the Housing Act 1985, after section 348F (as inserted by section 67 above) insert—

"Offences in connection with registration schemes.

348G.—(1) A person who contravenes or fails to comply with a provision of a registration scheme commits an offence.

(2) A person who commits an offence under this section consisting of a contravention of so much of control provisions as relates—

(a) to occupation to a greater extent than permitted under those provisions of a house which is not registered, or

(b) to occupation of a house which is registered by more households or persons than the registration permits,

is liable on summary conviction to a fine not exceeding level 5 on the standard scale.

(3) A person who commits an offence under this section consisting of a contravention of so much of special control provisions as requires all reasonably practicable steps to be taken to comply with an occupancy direction is liable on summary conviction to a fine not exceeding level 5 on the standard scale.

(4) A person who commits any other offence under this section is liable on summary conviction to a fine not exceeding level 4 on the standard scale.".

(2) In section 395(2) of the Housing Act 1985 (power of entry to ascertain if offence being committed), for "section 346(6)" substitute "section 348G".

1985 c. 68.

69.—(1) In Part XI of the Housing Act 1985 (houses in multiple occupation), for section 349 (steps required to inform public about registration schemes) substitute—

Information requirements in connection with registration schemes.

"Steps required to inform public about schemes.

349.—(1) Where a local housing authority intend to make a registration scheme which does not require confirmation by the Secretary of State, they shall publish notice of their intention at least one month before the scheme is made.

As soon as the scheme is made, the local housing authority shall publish a notice stating—

(a) that a registration scheme which does not require confirmation has been made, and

(b) the date on which the scheme is to come into force.

(2) Where a local housing authority intend to submit to the Secretary of State a registration scheme which requires his confirmation, they shall publish notice of their intention at least one month before the scheme is submitted.

As soon as the scheme is confirmed, the local housing authority shall publish a notice stating—

(a) that a registration scheme has been confirmed, and

(b) the date on which the scheme is to come into force.

(3) A notice under subsection (1) or (2) of the authority's intention to make a scheme or submit a scheme for confirmation shall—

PART II

> (a) describe any steps which will have to be taken under the scheme by those concerned with registrable houses (other than steps which have only to be taken after a notice from the authority), and
>
> (b) name a place where a copy of the scheme may be seen at all reasonable hours.
>
> (4) After publication of notice under subsection (1) or (2) that a registration scheme has been made or confirmed, and for as long as the scheme is in force, the local housing authority—
>
> (a) shall keep a copy of the scheme, and of the register, available for public inspection at the offices of the authority free of charge at all reasonable hours, and
>
> (b) on request, and on payment of such reasonable fee as the authority may require, shall supply a copy of the scheme or the register, or of any entry in the register, to any person.
>
> (5) If the local housing authority revoke a registration scheme by order they shall publish notice of the order.
>
> (6) In this section "publish" means publish in one or more newspapers circulating in the district of the local housing authority concerned.".

1985 c. 68.

(2) In section 350(1) of the Housing Act 1985 (power to require information for purposes of scheme) for the words "a person" substitute "the person having control of the house or the person managing the house or any person".

Existing registration schemes.

70.—(1) The amendments made by sections 65 to 69 do not apply to registration schemes in force immediately before the coming into force of those sections.

(2) The unamended provisions of Part XI of the Housing Act 1985 continue to apply to such schemes, subject as follows.

(3) Any such scheme may be revoked—

(a) by a new scheme complying with the provisions of that Part as amended, or

(b) by order of the local housing authority.

(4) If not so revoked any such scheme shall cease to have effect at the end of the period of two years beginning with the date on which the amendments come into force.

Other amendments of Part XI of the Housing Act 1985

Restriction on notices requiring execution of works.

71.—(1) In section 352 of the Housing Act 1985 (power to require execution of works to render premises fit for number of occupants), at end insert—

> "(7) Where a local housing authority serve a notice under this section in respect of any of the requirements specified in subsection (1A), and the works specified in the notice are carried out, whether

by the person on whom the notice was served or by the local housing authority under section 375, the authority shall not, within the period of five years from the service of the notice, serve another notice under this section in respect of the same requirement unless they consider that there has been a change of circumstances in relation to the premises.

(8) Such a change may, in particular, relate to the condition of the premises or the availability or use of the facilities mentioned in subsection (1A).".

(2) The above amendment does not apply in relation to a notice served under section 352 of the Housing Act 1985 before this section comes into force.

1985 c. 68.

72.—(1) After section 352 of the Housing Act 1985 insert—

Recovery of expenses of notice requiring execution of works.

"Recovery of expenses of notice under s.352.

352A.—(1) A local housing authority may, as a means of recovering certain administrative and other expenses incurred by them in serving a notice under section 352, make such reasonable charge as they consider appropriate.

(2) The expenses are the expenses incurred in—

  (a) determining whether to serve a notice under that section,

  (b) identifying the works to be specified in the notice, and

  (c) serving the notice.

(3) The amount of the charge shall not exceed such amount as is specified by order of the Secretary of State.

(4) A charge under this section may be recovered by the authority from any person on whom the notice under section 352 is served.

(5) The provisions of Schedule 10 apply to the recovery by the authority of a charge under this section as they apply to the recovery of expenses incurred by the authority under section 375 (expenses of carrying out works required by notice).

(6) An order under this section—

  (a) may make different provision with respect to different cases or descriptions of case (including different provision for different areas), and

  (b) shall be made by statutory instrument which shall be subject to annulment in pursuance of a resolution of either House of Parliament.

(7) This section has effect subject to any order under section 353(6) (power of court on appeal against s.352 notice).".

(2) In section 353 of that Act (appeal against notice under section 352), after subsection (5) insert—

"(6) Where the court allows an appeal under this section or makes an order under subsection (5), it may make such order as it thinks fit reducing, quashing or requiring the repayment of any charge under section 352A made in respect of the notice to which the appeal relates.".

(3) The above amendments do not apply in relation to a notice served under section 352 of the Housing Act 1985 before this section comes into force.

1985 c. 68.

Duty to keep premises fit for number of occupants.

73.—(1) After section 353 of the Housing Act 1985 insert—

"Duty to keep premises fit for number of occupants

353A.—(1) It is the duty of the person having control of a house in multiple occupation, and of the person managing it, to take such steps as are reasonably practicable to prevent the occurrence of a state of affairs calling for the service of a notice or further notice under section 352 (notice requiring execution of works to render house fit for number of occupants).

(2) A breach of that duty is actionable in damages at the suit of any tenant or other occupant of the premises, or any other person who suffers loss, damage or personal injury in consequence of the breach.

(3) A person who fails to comply with the duty imposed on him by subsection (1) commits a summary offence and is liable on conviction to a fine not exceeding level 5 on the standard scale.".

(2) In section 395(2) of the Housing Act 1985 (power of entry to ascertain whether offence being committed), after the entry for section 346(6) insert—

"section 353A (failure to keep premises fit for number of occupants),".

Section 354 direction to be local land charge.

74. In section 354 of the Housing Act 1985 (power to limit number of occupants of house), at the end insert—

"(8) A direction under this section is a local land charge.".

Means of escape from fire.

75.—(1) Section 365 of the Housing Act 1985 (means of escape from fire: general provisions as to exercise of powers) is amended as follows.

(2) In subsection (1)(b) (ground for exercise of additional powers) after "paragraph (d)" insert "or (e)".

(3) For subsection (3) (consultation requirements) substitute—

"(3) The local housing authority shall consult with the fire authority concerned before exercising any of the powers mentioned in subsection (2)—

(a) where they are under a duty to exercise those powers, or

(b) where they are not under such a duty but may exercise those powers and the house is of such description or is occupied in such manner as the Secretary of State may specify by order for the purposes of this subsection.".

(4) In subsection (4) (orders) for "or (2A)" substitute ", (2A) or (3)".

(5) In subsection (5) (other powers unaffected) omit "and (e)".

76. After section 377 of the Housing Act 1985 insert—

Works notices: improvement of enforcement procedures.
1985 c. 68.

"Works notices: improvement of enforcement procedures.

377A.—(1) The Secretary of State may by order provide that a local housing authority shall act as specified in the order before serving a works notice.

In this section a "works notice" means a notice under section 352 or 372 (notices requiring the execution of works).

(2) An order under this section may provide that the authority—

(a) shall as soon as practicable give to the person on whom the works notice is to be served a written notice which satisfies the requirements of subsection (3); and

(b) shall not serve the works notice until after the end of such period beginning with the giving of a notice which satisfies the requirements of subsection (3) as may be determined by or under the order.

(3) A notice satisfies the requirements of this subsection if it—

(a) states the works which in the authority's opinion should be undertaken, and explains why and within what period;

(b) explains the grounds on which it appears to the authority that the works notice might be served;

(c) states the type of works notice which is to be served, the consequences of serving it and whether there is a right to make representations before, or a right of appeal against, the serving of it.

(4) An order under this section may also provide that, before the authority serves the works notice on any person, they—

(a) shall give to that person a written notice stating—

(i) that they are considering serving the works notice and the reasons why they are considering serving the notice; and

(ii) that the person may, within a period specified in the written notice, make written representations to them or, if the person so requests, make oral representations to them in the presence of a person determined by or under the order; and

(b) shall consider any representations which are duly made and not withdrawn.

(5) An order under this section may in particular—

(a) make provision as to the consequences of any failure to comply with a provision made by the order;

(b) contain such consequential, incidental, supplementary or transitional provisions and savings as the Secretary of State considers appropriate (including provisions modifying enactments relating to the periods within which proceedings must be brought).

(6) An order under this section—

(a) may make different provision with respect to different cases or descriptions of case (including different provision for different areas), and

(b) shall be made by statutory instrument which shall be subject to annulment in pursuance of a resolution of either House of Parliament.

(7) Nothing in any order under this section shall—

(a) preclude a local housing authority from serving a works notice on any person, or from requiring any person to take immediate remedial action to avoid a works notice being served on him, in any case where it appears to them to be necessary to serve such a notice or impose such a requirement; or

(b) require such an authority to disclose any information the disclosure of which would be contrary to the public interest.".

Codes of practice.
1985 c. 68.

77. After section 395 of the Housing Act 1985 insert—

"Codes of practice.

395A.—(1) The Secretary of State may by order—

(a) approve any code of practice (whether prepared by him or another person) which, in his opinion, gives suitable guidance to any person in relation to any matter arising under this Part;

(b) approve any modification of such a code; or

(c) withdraw such a code or modification.

(2) The Secretary of State shall only approve a code of practice or a modification of a code if he is satisfied that—

(a) the code or modification has been published (whether by him or by another person) in such manner as he considers appropriate for the purpose of bringing the code or modification to the notice of those likely to be affected by it; or

(b) arrangements have been made for the code or modification to be so published.

(3) The Secretary of State may approve—

(a) more than one code of practice in relation to the same matter;

(b) a code of practice which makes different provision with respect to different cases or descriptions of case (including different provision for different areas).

(4) A failure to comply with a code of practice for the time being approved under this section shall not of itself render a person liable to any civil or criminal proceedings; but in any civil or criminal proceedings—

(a) any code of practice approved under this section shall be admissible in evidence, and

(b) any provision of any such code which appears to the court to be relevant to any question arising in the proceedings shall be taken into account in determining that question.

(5) An order under this section shall be made by statutory instrument which shall be subject to annulment in pursuance of a resolution of either House of Parliament.

(6) In this section references to a code of practice include references to a part of a code of practice.".

78.—(1) In section 350(2) of the Housing Act 1985 (information in relation to registration schemes)—

Increase of fines, &c.
1985 c. 68.

(a) in paragraph (a) (failure to give information) for "level 2" substitute "level 3", and

(b) in paragraph (b) (mis-statement) for "level 3" substitute "level 5".

(2) In section 355(2) of that Act (failure to comply with occupancy restrictions) for "level 4" substitute "level 5".

(3) In section 356(2) of that Act (information in relation to occupation of house) for "level 2" substitute "level 3".

(4) In section 364(2) of that Act (information in relation to overcrowding) for "level 2 on the standard scale" substitute ", in the case of such failure, level 3 on the standard scale and, in the case of furnishing such a statement, level 5 on the standard scale".

(5) In section 368(3) of that Act (use of house in contravention of undertaking) omit from "and if" to the end.

(6) In section 369(5) of that Act (failure to comply with management code) for "level 3" substitute "level 5".

(7) In section 376(1) and (2) of that Act (penalties for failures to execute works) for "level 4" substitute in each case "level 5".

(8) In section 377(3) of that Act (failure to permit execution of works) for the words from "level 3" to the end substitute "level 5 on the standard scale".

(9) In section 387(5) of that Act (failure to permit carrying out of works) for the words from "level 3" to the end substitute "level 5 on the standard scale".

(10) In section 396(2) of that Act (penalty for obstruction) for the words "level 3" substitute "level 4".

Minor
amendments.
1985 c. 68.

79.—(1) In section 355(1) of the Housing Act 1985 (effect of direction limiting number of occupants) for the words from "the number" to the end substitute "any individual to take up residence in that house or part unless the number of individuals or households then occupying the house or part would not exceed the limit specified in the direction.".

(2) In section 398 of the Housing Act 1985 for subsection (6) (meaning of "person managing") substitute—

"(6) "Person managing"—

(a) means the person who, being an owner or lessee of the premises—

(i) receives, directly or through an agent or trustee, rents or other payments from persons who are tenants of parts of the premises, or who are lodgers, or

(ii) would so receive those rents or other payments but for having entered into an arrangement (whether in pursuance of a court order or otherwise) with another person who is not an owner or lessee of the premises by virtue of which that other person receives the rents or other payments, and

(b) includes, where those rents or other payments are received through another person as agent or trustee, that other person.".

(3) In Part IV of Schedule 13 to the Housing Act 1985 (control order followed by compulsory purchase order), in paragraph 22 (application of provisions where compulsory purchase order is made within 28 days of a control order), for "28 days" substitute "eight weeks".

Common lodging houses

Repeal of Part XII
of the Housing
Act 1985.

80.—(1) Part XII of the Housing Act 1985 (common lodging houses) is hereby repealed.

(2) In consequence of the above repeal—

(a) in section 619(2) of the Housing Act 1985, for "The other provisions of this Act" substitute "The provisions of Parts I to XI and XIII to XVIII of this Act"; and

1988 c. 50.

(b) in section 65(2)(a) of the Housing Act 1988, for "XII" substitute "XI".

(3) The Secretary of State may by order make such consequential amendments or repeals in any local Act as he considers necessary or expedient.

Any such order shall be made by statutory instrument which shall be subject to annulment in pursuance of a resolution of either House of Parliament.

Part III

Landlord and tenant

Chapter I

Tenants' rights

Forfeiture

81.—(1) A landlord may not, in relation to premises let as a dwelling, exercise a right of re-entry or forfeiture for failure to pay a service charge unless the amount of the service charge—

    (a) is agreed or admitted by the tenant, or

    (b) has been the subject of determination by a court or by an arbitral tribunal in proceedings pursuant to an arbitration agreement (within the meaning of Part I of the Arbitration Act 1996).

(2) Where the amount is the subject of determination, the landlord may not exercise any such right of re-entry or forfeiture until after the end of the period of 14 days beginning with the day after that on which the decision of the court or arbitral tribunal is given.

(3) For the purposes of this section the amount of a service charge shall be taken to be determined when the decision of the court or arbitral tribunal is given, notwithstanding the possibility of an appeal or other legal challenge to the decision.

(4) The reference in subsection (1) to premises let as a dwelling does not include premises let on—

    (a) a tenancy to which Part II of the Landlord and Tenant Act 1954 applies (business tenancies),

    (b) a tenancy of an agricultural holding within the meaning of the Agricultural Holdings Act 1986 in relation to which that Act applies, or

    (c) a farm business tenancy within the meaning of the Agricultural Tenancies Act 1995.

(5) In this section "service charge" means a service charge within the meaning of section 18(1) of the Landlord and Tenant Act 1985, other than one excluded from that section by section 27 of that Act (rent of dwelling registered and not entered as variable).

(6) Nothing in this section affects the exercise of a right of re-entry or forfeiture on other grounds.

82.—(1) Nothing in section 81 (restriction on termination of tenancy for failure to pay service charge) affects the power of a landlord to serve a notice under section 146(1) of the Law of Property Act 1925 (restrictions on and relief against forfeiture: notice of breach of covenant or condition).

(2) But such a notice in respect of premises let as a dwelling and failure to pay a service charge is ineffective unless it complies with the following requirements.

(3) It must state that section 81 applies and set out the effect of subsection (1) of that section.

The Secretary of State may by regulations prescribe a form of words to be used for that purpose.

Marginal notes:

Restriction on termination of tenancy for failure to pay service charge.

1996 c. 23.

1954 c. 56.

1986 c. 5.

1995 c. 8.

1985 c. 70.

Notice under s.146 of the Law of Property Act 1925.

1925 c. 20.

(4) The information or words required must be in characters not less conspicuous than those used in the notice—

(a) to indicate that the tenancy may be forfeited, or

(b) to specify the breach complained of,

whichever is the more conspicuous.

(5) In this section "premises let as a dwelling" and "service charge" have the same meaning as in section 81.

(6) Regulations under this section—

(a) shall be made by statutory instrument, and

(b) may make different provision for different cases or classes of case including different areas.

Service charges

Determination of
reasonableness of
service charges.
1985 c. 70.

83.—(1) In section 19 of the Landlord and Tenant Act 1985 (limitation of service charges: reasonableness), after subsection (2) insert—

"(2A) A tenant by whom, or a landlord to whom, a service charge is alleged to be payable may apply to a leasehold valuation tribunal for a determination—

(a) whether costs incurred for services, repairs, maintenance, insurance or management were reasonably incurred,

(b) whether services or works for which costs were incurred are of a reasonable standard, or

(c) whether an amount payable before costs are incurred is reasonable.

(2B) An application may also be made to a leasehold valuation tribunal by a tenant by whom, or landlord to whom, a service charge may be payable for a determination—

(a) whether if costs were incurred for services, repairs, maintenance, insurance or management of any specified description they would be reasonable,

(b) whether services provided or works carried out to a particular specification would be of a reasonable standard, or

(c) what amount payable before costs are incurred would be reasonable.

(2C) No application under subsection (2A) or (2B) may be made in respect of a matter which—

(a) has been agreed or admitted by the tenant,

(b) under an arbitration agreement to which the tenant is a party is to be referred to arbitration, or

(c) has been the subject of determination by a court or arbitral tribunal.".

(2) In the Schedule to the Landlord and Tenant Act 1985, for paragraph 8 (right to challenge landlord's choice of insurers) substitute—

"8.—(1) This paragraph applies where a tenancy of a dwelling requires the tenant to insure the dwelling with an insurer nominated by the landlord.

(2) The tenant or landlord may apply to a county court or leasehold valuation tribunal for a determination whether—

    (a) the insurance which is available from the nominated insurer for insuring the tenant's dwelling is unsatisfactory in any respect, or

    (b) the premiums payable in respect of any such insurance are excessive.

(3) No such application may be made in respect of a matter which—

    (a) has been agreed or admitted by the tenant,

    (b) under an arbitration agreement to which the tenant is a party is to be referred to arbitration, or

    (c) has been the subject of determination by a court or arbitral tribunal.

(4) On an application under this paragraph the court or tribunal may make—

    (a) an order requiring the landlord to nominate such other insurer as is specified in the order, or

    (b) an order requiring him to nominate another insurer who satisfies such requirements in relation to the insurance of the dwelling as are specified in the order.

(5) Any such order of a leasehold valuation tribunal may, with the leave of the court, be enforced in the same way as an order of a county court to the same effect.

(6) An agreement by the tenant of a dwelling (other than an arbitration agreement) is void in so far as it purports to provide for a determination in a particular manner, or on particular evidence, of any question which may be the subject of an application under this paragraph.".

(3) In the Landlord and Tenant Act 1985 before section 32 under the heading "*Supplementary provisions*" insert—   1985 c. 70.

"Jurisdiction of leasehold valuation tribunal.   31A.—(1) The jurisdiction conferred by this Act on a leasehold valuation tribunal is exercisable by a rent assessment committee constituted in accordance with Schedule 10 to the Rent Act 1977 which when so   1977 c. 42. constituted for the purposes of exercising any such jurisdiction shall be known as a leasehold valuation tribunal.

    (2) The power to make regulations under section 74(1)(b) of the Rent Act 1977 (procedure of rent assessment committees) extends to prescribing the procedure to be followed in connection with any proceedings before a leasehold valuation tribunal under this Act.

    (3) Such regulations may, in particular, make provision—

(a) for securing consistency where numerous applications under this Act are or may be brought in respect of the same or substantially the same matters; and

(b) empowering a leasehold valuation tribunal to dismiss an application, in whole or in part, on the ground that it is frivolous or vexatious or otherwise an abuse of the process of the tribunal."

(4) No costs incurred by a party in connection with proceedings under this Act before a leasehold valuation tribunal shall be recoverable by order of any court.

1980 c. 51.

(5) Paragraphs 2, 3 and 7 of Schedule 22 to the Housing Act 1980 (supplementary provisions relating to leasehold valuation tribunals: appeals and provision of information) apply to a leasehold valuation tribunal constituted for the purposes of this section.

(6) No appeal shall lie to the Lands Tribunal from a decision of a leasehold valuation tribunal under this Act without the leave of the leasehold valuation tribunal concerned or the Lands Tribunal.

(7) On any such appeal—

(a) the Lands Tribunal may exercise any power available to the leasehold valuation tribunal in relation to the original matter, and

(b) an order of the Lands Tribunal may be enforced in the same way as an order of the leasehold valuation tribunal.

Leasehold valuation tribunal: applications and fees.

31B.—(1) The Secretary of State may make provision by order as to the form of, or the particulars to be contained in, an application made to a leasehold valuation tribunal under this Act.

(2) The Secretary of State may make provision by order—

(a) requiring the payment of fees in respect of any such application, or in respect of any proceedings before, a leasehold valuation tribunal under this Act; and

(b) empowering a leasehold valuation tribunal to require a party to proceedings before it to reimburse any other party the whole or part of any fees paid by him.

(3) The fees payable shall be such as may be specified in or determined in accordance with the order subject to this limit, that the fees payable in respect of any one application or reference by the court together with any proceedings before the tribunal arising out of that application or reference shall not exceed £500 or such other amount as may be specified by order of the Secretary of State.

(4) An order under this section may make different provision for different cases or classes of case or for different areas.

(5) An order may in particular—

   (a) make different provision in relation to proceedings transferred to the tribunal from that applicable where an application was made to the tribunal, and

   (b) provide for the reduction or waiver of fees by reference to the financial resources of the party by whom they are to be paid or met.

(6) In the latter case the order may apply, subject to such modifications as may be specified in the order, any other statutory means-testing regime as it has effect from time to time.

(7) An order under this section shall be made by statutory instrument.

(8) No order altering the limit under subsection (3) shall be made unless a draft of the order has been laid before and approved by a resolution of each House of Parliament.

(9) Any other order under this section, unless it contains only such provision as is mentioned in subsection (1), shall be subject to annulment in pursuance of a resolution of either House of Parliament.

Transfer of cases from county court.

31C.—(1) Where in any proceedings before a court there falls for determination a question falling within the jurisdiction of a leasehold valuation tribunal under this Act, the court—

   (a) may by order transfer to such a tribunal so much of the proceedings as relate to the determination of that question, and

   (b) may then dispose of all or any remaining proceedings, or adjourn the disposal of all or any of such proceedings, pending the determination of that question by the tribunal, as it thinks fit.

(2) When the tribunal has determined the question, the court may give effect to the determination in an order of the court.

(3) Any such order shall be treated as a determination by the court for the purposes of section 81 of the Housing Act 1996 (restriction on termination of tenancy for failure to pay service charge).

(4) Rules of court may prescribe the procedure to be followed in the court in connection with or in consequence of a transfer under this section.".

(4) For section 20C of the Landlord and Tenant Act 1985 (limitation of service charges: costs of court proceedings) substitute—

1985 c. 70.

"Limitation of service charges: costs of proceedings.

20C.—(1) A tenant may make an application for an order that all or any of the costs incurred, or to be incurred, by the landlord in connection with proceedings before a court or leasehold valuation tribunal, or the Lands Tribunal, or in connection with arbitration proceedings, are not to be regarded as relevant costs to be taken into account in determining the amount of any service charge payable by the tenant or any other person or persons specified in the application.

(2) The application shall be made—

(a) in the case of court proceedings, to the court before which the proceedings are taking place or, if the application is made after the proceedings are concluded, to a county court;

(b) in the case of proceedings before a leasehold valuation tribunal, to the tribunal before which the proceedings are taking place or, if the application is made after the proceedings are concluded, to any leasehold valuation tribunal;

(c) in the case of proceedings before the Lands Tribunal, to the tribunal;

(d) in the case of arbitration proceedings, to the arbitral tribunal or, if the application is made after the proceedings are concluded, to a county court.

(3) The court or tribunal to which the application is made may make such order on the application as it considers just and equitable in the circumstances.".

1985 c. 70.

(5) In section 38 of the Landlord and Tenant Act 1985 (minor definitions), at the appropriate place insert—

""arbitration agreement", "arbitration proceedings" and "arbitral tribunal" have the same meaning as in Part I of the Arbitration Act 1996;".

1996 c. 23.

(6) In section 39 of that Act (index of defined expressions), at the appropriate place insert—

"arbitration agreement,   section 38"
  arbitration proceedings
  and arbitral tribunal

Right to appoint surveyor to advise on matters relating to service charges.

84.—(1) A recognised tenants' association may appoint a surveyor for the purposes of this section to advise on any matters relating to, or which may give rise to, service charges payable to a landlord by one or more members of the association.

The provisions of Schedule 4 have effect for conferring on a surveyor so appointed rights of access to documents and premises.

(2) A person shall not be so appointed unless he is a qualified surveyor.

1993 c. 28.

For this purpose "qualified surveyor" has the same meaning as in section 78(4)(a) of the Leasehold Reform, Housing and Urban Development Act 1993 (persons qualified for appointment to carry out management audit).

(3) The appointment shall take effect for the purposes of this section upon notice in writing being given to the landlord by the association stating the name and address of the surveyor, the duration of his appointment and the matters in respect of which he is appointed.

(4) An appointment shall cease to have effect for the purposes of this section if the association gives notice in writing to the landlord to that effect or if the association ceases to exist.

(5) A notice is duly given under this section to a landlord of any tenants if it is given to a person who receives on behalf of the landlord the rent payable by those tenants; and a person to whom such a notice is so given shall forward it as soon as may be to the landlord.

(6) In this section—

"recognised tenants' association" has the same meaning as in the provisions of the Landlord and Tenant Act 1985 relating to service charges (see section 29 of that Act); and

"service charge" means a service charge within the meaning of section 18(1) of that Act, other than one excluded from that section by section 27 of that Act (rent of dwelling registered and not entered as variable).

1985 c. 70.

Appointment of manager

85.—(1) Section 24 of the Landlord and Tenant Act 1987 (appointment of manager by the court) is amended as follows.

Appointment of manager by the court.
1987 c. 31.

(2) In subsection (2) (circumstances in which order may be made), in paragraph (a) (breach of obligation by landlord), omit sub-paragraph (ii) (requirement that circumstances likely to continue).

(3) In that subsection, after paragraph (a), and before the word "or" following that paragraph, insert—

"(ab) where the court is satisfied—

(i) that unreasonable service charges have been made, or are proposed or likely to be made, and

(ii) that it is just and convenient to make the order in all the circumstances of the case;

(ac) where the court is satisfied—

(i) that the landlord has failed to comply with any relevant provision of a code of practice approved by the Secretary of State under section 87 of the Leasehold Reform, Housing and Urban Development Act 1993 (codes of management practice), and

(ii) that it is just and convenient to make the order in all the circumstances of the case;".

1993 c. 28.

(4) After that subsection insert—

"(2A) For the purposes of subsection (2)(ab) a service charge shall be taken to be unreasonable—

(a) if the amount is unreasonable having regard to the items for which it is payable,

(b) if the items for which it is payable are of an unnecessarily high standard, or

(c) if the items for which it is payable are of an insufficient standard with the result that additional service charges are or may be incurred.

1985 c. 70.

In that provision and this subsection "service charge" means a service charge within the meaning of section 18(1) of the Landlord and Tenant Act 1985, other than one excluded from that section by section 27 of that Act (rent of dwelling registered and not entered as variable).".

1987 c. 31.

(5) The above amendments apply to applications for an order under section 24 of the Landlord and Tenant Act 1987 which are made after this section comes into force.

In relation to any such application the reference in the inserted subsection (2)(ab) to service charges which have been made includes services charges made before that date.

(6) After subsection (9) insert—

"(9A) The court shall not vary or discharge an order under subsection (9) on a landlord's application unless it is satisfied—

(a) that the variation or discharge of the order will not result in a recurrence of the circumstances which led to the order being made, and

(b) that it is just and convenient in all the circumstances of the case to vary or discharge the order.".

Appointment of manager: transfer of jurisdiction to leasehold valuation tribunal.

86.—(1) Part II of the Landlord and Tenant Act 1987 (appointment of managers by the court) is amended as follows for the purpose of transferring to a leasehold valuation tribunal the jurisdiction of the court under that Part.

(2) In the following contexts for "the court", in the first (or only) place where it occurs, substitute "a leasehold valuation tribunal": section 21(1), section 22(2)(b), section 22(3), section 23(1), section 24(1), (2), (9) and (10); and in every other context in those sections, except section 21(6), for "the court" substitute "the tribunal".

(3) In section 21(6) (exclusion of application under inherent jurisdiction of court) for "any jurisdiction existing apart from this Act" substitute "any jurisdiction".

(4) In section 23(2)—

(a) for "Rules of court" substitute "Procedure regulations", and

(b) in paragraph (a), for "rules" substitute "regulations".

(5) After section 24 insert—

"Jurisdiction of leasehold valuation tribunal.

1977 c. 42.

24A.—(1) The jurisdiction conferred by this Part on a leasehold valuation tribunal is exercisable by a rent assessment committee constituted in accordance with Schedule 10 to the Rent Act 1977 which when so constituted for the purposes of exercising any such jurisdiction shall be known as a leasehold valuation tribunal.

(2) The power to make regulations under section 74(1)(b) of the Rent Act 1977 (procedure of rent assessment committees) extends to prescribing the

procedure to be followed in connection with any proceedings before a leasehold valuation tribunal under this Part.

Such regulations are referred to in this Part as "procedure regulations".

(3) Procedure regulations may, in particular, make provision—

(a) for securing consistency where numerous applications under this Part are or may be brought in respect of the same or substantially the same matters; and

(b) empowering a leasehold valuation tribunal to dismiss an application, in whole or in part, on the ground that it is frivolous or vexatious or otherwise an abuse of the process of the tribunal.

(4) Any order made by a leasehold valuation tribunal under this Part may, with the leave of the court, be enforced in the same way as an order of the county court.

(5) No costs incurred by a party in connection with proceedings under this Part before a leasehold valuation tribunal shall be recoverable by order of any court.

(6) Paragraphs 2, 3 and 7 of Schedule 22 to the Housing Act 1980 (supplementary provisions relating to leasehold valuation tribunals: appeals and provision of information) apply to a leasehold valuation tribunal constituted for the purposes of this section.

1980 c. 51.

(7) No appeal shall lie to the Lands Tribunal from a decision of a leasehold valuation tribunal under this Part without the leave of the leasehold valuation tribunal concerned or the Lands Tribunal.

(8) On an appeal to the Lands Tribunal from a decision of a leasehold valuation tribunal under this Part—

(a) the Lands Tribunal may exercise any power available to the leasehold valuation tribunal in relation to the original matter, and

(b) an order of the Lands Tribunal may be enforced in the same way as an order of the leasehold valuation tribunal.

Leasehold valuation tribunal: applications and fees.

24B.—(1) The Secretary of State may make provision by order as to the form of, or the particulars to be contained in, an application made to a leasehold valuation tribunal under this Part.

(2) The Secretary of State may make provision by order—

(a) requiring the payment of fees in respect of any such application, or in respect of any proceedings before, a leasehold valuation tribunal under this Part; and

(b) empowering a leasehold valuation tribunal to require a party to proceedings before it to reimburse any other party the whole or part of any fees paid by him.

(3) The fees payable shall be such as may be specified in or determined in accordance with the order subject to this limit, that the fees payable in respect of any one application or reference by the court together with any proceedings before the tribunal arising out of that application or reference shall not exceed £500 or such other amount as may be specified by order of the Secretary of State.

(4) An order under this section may make different provision for different cases or classes of case or for different areas.

(5) An order may, in particular, provide for the reduction or waiver of fees by reference to the financial resources of the party by whom they are to be paid or met.

Any such order may apply, subject to such modifications as may be specified in the order, any other statutory means-testing regime as it has effect from time to time.

(6) An order under this section shall be made by statutory instrument.

(7) No order altering the limit under subsection (3) shall be made unless a draft of the order has been laid before and approved by a resolution of each House of Parliament.

(8) Any other order under this section, unless it contains only such provision as is mentioned in subsection (1), shall be subject to annulment in pursuance of a resolution of either House of Parliament.".

1987 c. 31.

(6) In section 52 of the Landlord and Tenant Act 1987 (jurisdiction of county courts), in subsection (2)(a) for "Parts I to IV" substitute "Parts I, III and IV".

Text of Part II of the Landlord and Tenant Act 1987, as amended.

87. The text of Part II of the Landlord and Tenant Act 1987 as amended by this Act is set out in Schedule 5.

Period after which acquisition order may be made.

88. In Part III of the Landlord and Tenant Act 1987 (compulsory acquisition by tenants of their landlord's interest), in section 29(3) (conditions for making acquisition orders: period since appointment of manager under Part II) for "three years" substitute "two years".

Right of first refusal

89.—(1) After section 4 of the Landlord and Tenant Act 1987 (relevant disposals) insert—

Application of
right of first
refusal in relation
to contracts.
1987 c. 31.

"Application of
provisions to
contracts.

4A.—(1) The provisions of this Part apply to a contract to create or transfer an estate or interest in land, whether conditional or unconditional and whether or not enforceable by specific performance, as they apply in relation to a disposal consisting of the creation or transfer of such an estate or interest.

As they so apply—

(a) references to a disposal of any description shall be construed as references to a contract to make such a disposal;

(b) references to making a disposal of any description shall be construed as references to entering into a contract to make such a disposal; and

(c) references to the transferee under the disposal shall be construed as references to the other party to the contract and include a reference to any other person to whom an estate or interest is to be granted or transferred in pursuance of the contract.

(2) The provisions of this Part apply to an assignment of rights under such a contract as is mentioned in subsection (1) as they apply in relation to a disposal consisting of the transfer of an estate or interest in land.

As they so apply—

(a) references to a disposal of any description shall be construed as references to an assignment of rights under a contract to make such a disposal;

(b) references to making a disposal of any description shall be construed as references to making an assignment of rights under a contract to make such a disposal;

(c) references to the landlord shall be construed as references to the assignor; and

(d) references to the transferee under the disposal shall be construed as references to the assignee of such rights.

(3) The provisions of this Part apply to a contract to make such an assignment as is mentioned in subsection (2) as they apply (in accordance with subsection (1)) to a contract to create or transfer an estate or interest in land.

(4) Nothing in this section affects the operation of the provisions of this Part relating to options or rights of pre-emption.".

(2) In section 4(2) of the Landlord and Tenant Act 1987 (relevant disposals: excluded disposals), for paragraph (i) (certain disposals in pursuance of existing obligations) substitute—

"(i) a disposal in pursuance of a contract, option or right of pre-emption binding on the landlord (except as provided by section 8D (application of sections 11 to 17 to disposal in pursuance of option or right of pre-emption));".

(3) In section 20(1) (interpretation), in the definition of "disposal" for "has the meaning given by section 4(3)" substitute "shall be construed in accordance with section 4(3) and section 4A (application of provisions to contracts)".

Notice required to be given by landlord making disposal.

1987 c. 31.

90.—(1) In section 4(2) of the Landlord and Tenant Act 1987 (disposals which are not relevant disposals for the purposes of Part I of that Act), for paragraph (l) substitute—

"(l) a disposal by a body corporate to a company which has been an associated company of that body for at least two years.".

(2) The above amendment does not apply to a disposal made in pursuance of an obligation entered into before the commencement of this section.

Offence of failure to comply with requirements of Part I.

91.—(1) After section 10 of the Landlord and Tenant Act 1987 insert—

"Offence of failure to comply with requirements of Part I.

10A.—(1) A landlord commits an offence if, without reasonable excuse, he makes a relevant disposal affecting premises to which this Part applies—

(a) without having first complied with the requirements of section 5 as regards the service of notices on the qualifying tenants of flats contained in the premises, or

(b) in contravention of any prohibition or restriction imposed by sections 6 to 10.

(2) A person guilty of an offence under this section is liable on summary conviction to a fine not exceeding level 5 on the standard scale.

(3) Where an offence under this section committed by a body corporate is proved—

(a) to have been committed with the consent or connivance of a director, manager, secretary or other similar officer of the body corporate, or a person purporting to act in such a capacity, or

(b) to be due to any neglect on the part of such an officer or person,

he, as well as the body corporate, is guilty of the offence and liable to be proceeded against and punished accordingly.

Where the affairs of a body corporate are managed by its members, the above provision applies in relation to the acts and defaults of a member in connection with his functions of management as if he were a director of the body corporate.

(4) Proceedings for an offence under this section may be brought by a local housing authority (within the meaning of section 1 of the Housing Act 1985).

1985 c. 68.

(5) Nothing in this section affects the validity of the disposal.".

(2) The above amendment does not apply to a disposal made in pursuance of an obligation entered into before the commencement of this section.

92.—(1) Part I of the Landlord and Tenant Act 1987 (tenants' rights of first refusal) is amended in accordance with Schedule 6.

Procedure for exercise of rights of first refusal.
1987 c. 31.

(2) The amendments restate the principal provisions of that Part so as to—

(a) simplify the procedures for the exercise of the rights conferred on tenants, and

(b) apply those procedures in relation to contracts and certain special cases.

(3) In Schedule 6—

Part I sets out provisions replacing sections 5 to 10 of the Act (rights of first refusal),

Part II sets out provisions replacing sections 11 to 15 of the Act (enforcement by tenants of rights against purchaser),

Part III sets out provisions replacing sections 16 and 17 of the Act (enforcement of rights against subsequent purchasers and termination of rights), and

Part IV contains consequential amendments.

93.—(1) In the Landlord and Tenant Act 1985, after section 3 (duty to inform tenant of assignment of landlord's interest) insert—

Duty of new landlord to inform tenant of rights.
1985 c. 70.

"Duty to inform tenant of possible right to acquire landlord's interest.

3A.—(1) Where a new landlord is required by section 3(1) to give notice to a tenant of an assignment to him, then if—

(a) the tenant is a qualifying tenant within the meaning of Part I of the Landlord and Tenant Act 1987 (tenants' rights of first refusal), and

(b) the assignment was a relevant disposal within the meaning of that Part affecting premises to which at the time of the disposal that Part applied,

the landlord shall give also notice in writing to the tenant to the following effect.

(2) The notice shall state—

(a) that the disposal to the landlord was one to which Part I of the Landlord and Tenant Act 1987 applied;

(b) that the tenant (together with other qualifying tenants) may have the right under that Part—

(i) to obtain information about the disposal, and

> > (ii) to acquire the landlord's interest in the whole or part of the premises in which the tenant's flat is situated; and

> (c) the time within which any such right must be exercised, and the fact that the time would run from the date of receipt of notice under this section by the requisite majority of qualifying tenants (within the meaning of that Part).

> (3) A person who is required to give notice under this section and who fails, without reasonable excuse, to do so within the time allowed for giving notice under section 3(1) commits a summary offence and is liable on conviction to a fine not exceeding level 4 on the standard scale.".

1985 c. 70.
1954 c. 56.

(2) In section 32(1) of the Landlord and Tenant Act 1985 (provisions not applying to tenancies within Part II of the Landlord and Tenant Act 1954), for "sections 1 to 3" substitute "sections 1 to 3A".

General legal advice

Provision of general legal advice about residential tenancies.

94.—(1) The Secretary of State may give financial assistance to any person in relation to the provision by that person of general advice about—

(a) any aspect of the law of landlord and tenant, so far as relating to residential tenancies, or

1993 c. 28.

(b) Chapter IV of Part I of the Leasehold Reform, Housing and Urban Development Act 1993 (estate management schemes in connection with enfranchisement).

(2) Financial assistance under this section may be given in such form and on such terms as the Secretary of State considers appropriate.

(3) The terms on which financial assistance under this section may be given may, in particular, include provision as to the circumstances in which the assistance must be repaid or otherwise made good to the Secretary of State and the manner in which that is to be done.

Supplementary

Jurisdiction of county courts.

95.—(1) Any jurisdiction expressed by a provision to which this section applies to be conferred on the court shall be exercised by a county court.

(2) There shall also be brought in a county court any proceedings for determining any question arising under or by virtue of any provision to which this section applies.

(3) Where, however, other proceedings are properly brought in the High Court, that court has jurisdiction to hear and determine proceedings to which subsection (1) or (2) applies which are joined with those proceedings.

(4) Where proceedings are brought in a county court by virtue of subsection (1) or (2), that court has jurisdiction to hear and determine other proceedings joined with those proceedings despite the fact that they would otherwise be outside its jurisdiction.

(5) The provisions to which this section applies are—

(a) section 81 (restriction on termination of tenancy for failure to pay service charge), and

(b) section 84 (right to appoint surveyor to advise on matters relating to service charges) and Schedule 4 (rights exercisable by surveyor appointed by tenants' association).

CHAPTER II

ASSURED TENANCIES

Assured shorthold tenancies

96.—(1) In Chapter II of Part I of the Housing Act 1988 (assured shorthold tenancies) there shall be inserted at the beginning—

"Assured shorthold tenancies: post-Housing Act 1996 tenancies.

Tenancies which are assured shorthold tenancies.

1988 c. 50.

19A. An assured tenancy which—

(a) is entered into on or after the day on which section 96 of the Housing Act 1996 comes into force (otherwise than pursuant to a contract made before that day), or

(b) comes into being by virtue of section 5 above on the coming to an end of an assured tenancy within paragraph (a) above,

is an assured shorthold tenancy unless it falls within any paragraph in Schedule 2A to this Act.".

(2) After Schedule 2 to that Act there shall be inserted the Schedule set out in Schedule 7 to this Act.

97. After section 20 of the Housing Act 1988 there shall be inserted—

"Post-Housing Act 1996 tenancies: duty of landlord to provide statement as to terms of tenancy.

Duty of landlord to provide statement of terms of assured shorthold tenancy.

20A.—(1) Subject to subsection (3) below, a tenant under an assured shorthold tenancy to which section 19A above applies may, by notice in writing, require the landlord under that tenancy to provide him with a written statement of any term of the tenancy which—

(a) falls within subsection (2) below, and

(b) is not evidenced in writing.

(2) The following terms of a tenancy fall within this subsection, namely—

(a) the date on which the tenancy began or, if it is a statutory periodic tenancy or a tenancy to which section 39(7) below applies, the date on which the tenancy came into being,

(b) the rent payable under the tenancy and the dates on which that rent is payable,

(c) any term providing for a review of the rent payable under the tenancy, and

(d) in the case of a fixed term tenancy, the length of the fixed term.

(3) No notice may be given under subsection (1) above in relation to a term of the tenancy if—

    (a) the landlord under the tenancy has provided a statement of that term in response to an earlier notice under that subsection given by the tenant under the tenancy, and

    (b) the term has not been varied since the provision of the statement referred to in paragraph (a) above.

(4) A landlord who fails, without reasonable excuse, to comply with a notice under subsection (1) above within the period of 28 days beginning with the date on which he received the notice is liable on summary conviction to a fine not exceeding level 4 on the standard scale.

(5) A statement provided for the purposes of subsection (1) above shall not be regarded as conclusive evidence of what was agreed by the parties to the tenancy in question.

(6) Where—

    (a) a term of a statutory periodic tenancy is one which has effect by virtue of section 5(3)(e) above, or

    (b) a term of a tenancy to which subsection (7) of section 39 below applies is one which has effect by virtue of subsection (6)(e) of that section,

subsection (1) above shall have effect in relation to it as if paragraph (b) related to the term of the tenancy from which it derives.

(7) In subsections (1) and (3) above—

    (a) references to the tenant under the tenancy shall, in the case of joint tenants, be taken to be references to any of the tenants, and

    (b) references to the landlord under the tenancy shall, in the case of joint landlords, be taken to be references to any of the landlords."

Form of notices under s. 21 of the Housing Act 1988.
1988 c. 50.

98.—(1) Section 21 of the Housing Act 1988 (recovery of possession on expiry or termination of assured shorthold tenancy) shall be amended as follows.

(2) In subsection (1)(b) (which requires the landlord under a fixed term tenancy to give two months' notice to recover possession), after "notice" there shall be inserted "in writing".

(3) In subsection (4)(a) (corresponding provision for periodic tenancies), after "notice", where it first occurs, there shall be inserted "in writing".

Restriction on recovery of possession on expiry or termination.

99. In section 21 of the Housing Act 1988 there shall be inserted at the end—

"(5) Where an order for possession under subsection (1) or (4) above is made in relation to a dwelling-house let on a tenancy to which section 19A above applies, the order may not be made so as to take effect earlier than—

(a) in the case of a tenancy which is not a replacement tenancy, six months after the beginning of the tenancy, and

(b) in the case of a replacement tenancy, six months after the beginning of the original tenancy.

(6) In subsection (5)(b) above, the reference to the original tenancy is—

(a) where the replacement tenancy came into being on the coming to an end of a tenancy which was not a replacement tenancy, to the immediately preceding tenancy, and

(b) where there have been successive replacement tenancies, to the tenancy immediately preceding the first in the succession of replacement tenancies.

(7) For the purposes of this section, a replacement tenancy is a tenancy—

(a) which comes into being on the coming to an end of an assured shorthold tenancy, and

(b) under which, on its coming into being—

(i) the landlord and tenant are the same as under the earlier tenancy as at its coming to an end, and

(ii) the premises let are the same or substantially the same as those let under the earlier tenancy as at that time.".

100.—(1) Section 22 of the Housing Act 1988 (reference of excessive rents to rent assessment committee) shall be amended as follows.

Applications for determination of rent: time limit.
1988 c. 50.

(2) In subsection (2) (circumstances in which no application under the section may be made) after paragraph (a) there shall be inserted—

"(aa) the tenancy is one to which section 19A above applies and more than six months have elapsed since the beginning of the tenancy or, in the case of a replacement tenancy, since the beginning of the original tenancy; or".

(3) At the end there shall be inserted—

"(6) In subsection (2)(aa) above, the references to the original tenancy and to a replacement tenancy shall be construed in accordance with subsections (6) and (7) respectively of section 21 above.".

Grounds for possession

101. In Part I of Schedule 2 to the Housing Act 1988 (grounds on which court must order possession) in Ground 8 (rent unpaid for certain periods)—

Mandatory possession for non-payment of rent: reduction in arrears required.

(a) in paragraph (a) (rent payable weekly or fortnightly) for "thirteen weeks'" there shall be substituted "eight weeks'", and

(b) in paragraph (b) (rent payable monthly) for "three months'" there shall be substituted "two months'".

102. In Part II of Schedule 2 to the Housing Act 1988 (grounds on which court may order possession) there shall be inserted at the end—

Recovery of possession where grant induced by false statement.

"Ground 17

The tenant is the person, or one of the persons, to whom the tenancy was granted and the landlord was induced to grant the tenancy by a false statement made knowingly or recklessly by—

(a) the tenant, or

(b) a person acting at the tenant's instigation.".

Assured agricultural occupancies

Assured agricultural occupancies: exclusion of tenancies of agricultural holdings and farm business tenancies.

1988 c. 50.

103.—(1) Section 24 of the Housing Act 1988 (assured agricultural occupancies) shall be amended as follows.

(2) In subsection (2)(b) (under which a tenancy is an assured agricultural occupancy if it would be an assured tenancy, but for paragraph 7 of Schedule 1 to that Act) there shall be inserted at the end "and is not an excepted tenancy".

(3) After subsection (2) there shall be inserted—

"(2A) For the purposes of subsection (2)(b) above, a tenancy is an excepted tenancy if it is—

1986 c. 5.

(a) a tenancy of an agricultural holding within the meaning of the Agricultural Holdings Act 1986 in relation to which that Act applies, or

1995 c. 8.

(b) a farm business tenancy within the meaning of the Agricultural Tenancies Act 1995.".

Consequential amendments

Consequential amendments: assured tenancies.

104. The enactments mentioned in Schedule 8 have effect with the amendments specified there which are consequential on the provisions of this Chapter.

CHAPTER III

LEASEHOLD REFORM

Scope of rights

Low rent test: nil rateable values.

1967 c. 88.

105.—(1) In section 4(1) of the Leasehold Reform Act 1967 (meaning of "low rent") —

(a) in paragraph (i) (cases where rent limit of two-thirds of rateable value on later of appropriate day and first day of term applies), for the words from "or (where" to "that date" there shall be substituted ", or on or after 1st April 1990 in pursuance of a contract made before that date, and the property had a rateable value other than nil at the date of the commencement of the tenancy or else at any time before 1st April 1990,",

(b) in paragraph (ii) (other cases), for the words from "is entered" to "1990)," there shall be substituted "does not fall within paragraph (i) above,", and

1977 c. 42.

(c) in paragraph (a) (definition of "appropriate day" by reference to section 25(3) of the Rent Act 1977), there shall be inserted at the end "if the reference in paragraph (a) of that provision to a rateable value were to a rateable value other than nil".

(2) In section 4A of the Leasehold Reform Act 1967 (alternative rent limits for the purposes of section 1A(2) of that Act)— 1967 c. 88.

(a) in subsection (1)(b) (cases where rent limit of two-thirds of rateable value on the relevant date applies), for sub-paragraph (ii) there shall be substituted—

> "(ii) the property had a rateable value other than nil at the date of commencement of the tenancy or else at any time before 1st April 1990,", and

(b) in subsection (2), for paragraph (b) there shall be substituted—

> "(b) "the relevant date" means the date of the commencement of the tenancy or, if the property did not have a rateable value, or had a rateable value of nil, on that date, the date on which it first had a rateable value other than nil;".

(3) In section 8 of the Leasehold Reform, Housing and Urban Development Act 1993 (leases at a low rent)— 1993 c. 28.

(a) in subsection (1)(b) (cases where rent limit of two-thirds of rateable value on the appropriate date applies), for sub-paragraph (ii) there shall be substituted—

> "(ii) the flat had a rateable value other than nil at the date of the commencement of the lease or else at any time before 1st April 1990,", and

(b) in subsection (2), for paragraph (b) there shall be substituted—

> "(b) "the appropriate date" means the date of commencement of the lease or, if the flat in question did not have a rateable value, or had a rateable value of nil, on that date, the date on which the flat first had a rateable value other than nil;".

106. Schedule 9 (which makes provision for conferring an additional right to enfranchisement in relation to tenancies which fail the low rent test and for introducing an alternative to the low rent test in the case of the right to collective enfranchisement and the right to a new lease) shall have effect. Low rent test: extension of rights.

107.—(1) In section 3 of the Leasehold Reform, Housing and Urban Development Act 1993 (premises in respect of which the right to collective enfranchisement is exercisable), in subsection (1)(a), the words "and the freehold of the whole of the building or of that part of the building is owned by the same person" shall be omitted. Collective enfranchisement: multiple freeholders.

(2) In section 4 of that Act (premises excluded from the right to collective enfranchisement), after subsection (3) there shall be inserted—

> "(3A) Where different persons own the freehold of different parts of premises within subsection (1) of section 3, this Chapter does not apply to the premises if any of those parts is a self-contained part of a building for the purposes of that section.".

(3) In section 1(3) of that Act (additional property which may be acquired by tenants exercising the right to collective enfranchisement), the words "the freehold of it is owned by the person who owns the freehold of the relevant premises and" shall be omitted.

(4) Schedule 10 (amendments consequential on this section) shall have effect.

Valuation

Collective
enfranchisement:
removal of need
for professional
valuation of
interests to be
acquired.
1993 c. 28.

108. In section 13 of the Leasehold Reform, Housing and Urban Development Act 1993 (notice by qualifying tenants of claim to exercise right to collective enfranchisement) subsection (6) (tenants to obtain professional valuation of interests proposed to be acquired before giving notice) shall cease to have effect.

Collective
enfranchisement:
valuation
principles.

109.—(1) Schedule 6 to the Leasehold Reform, Housing and Urban Development Act 1993 (purchase price payable by nominee purchaser) shall be amended as follows.

(2) In paragraph 3(1) (freeholder's interest to be valued on the basis that neither the nominee purchaser nor any participating tenant is in the market) for "neither the nominee purchaser nor any participating tenant" there shall be substituted "no person who falls within sub-paragraph (1A)".

(3) After paragraph 3(1) there shall be inserted—

"(1A) A person falls within this sub-paragraph if he is—

(a) the nominee purchaser, or

(b) a tenant of premises contained in the specified premises, or

(c) an owner of an interest which the nominee purchaser is to acquire in pursuance of section 2(1)(b).".

(4) In paragraph 7 (value of intermediate leasehold interests) after sub-paragraph (1) there shall be inserted—

"(1A) In its application in accordance with sub-paragraph (1), paragraph 3(1A) shall have effect with the addition after paragraph (a) of—

"(aa) an owner of a freehold interest in the specified premises, or"".

(5) In paragraph 11 (value of other interests) after sub-paragraph (3) there shall be inserted—

"(4) In its application in accordance with sub-paragraph (2) above, paragraph 3(1A) shall have effect with the addition after paragraph (a) of—

"(aa) an owner of a freehold interest in the specified premises, or"".

New leases:
valuation
principles.

110.—(1) Schedule 13 to the Leasehold Reform, Housing and Urban Development Act 1993 (premium and other amounts payable by tenant on grant of new lease) shall be amended as mentioned in subsections (2) to (4) below.

(2) In paragraph 3(2) (landlord's interest to be valued on the basis that the tenant is not buying or seeking to buy) for "the tenant not" there shall be substituted "neither the tenant nor any owner of an intermediate leasehold interest".

(3) In paragraph 4(3) (calculation of marriage value) for paragraph (a) (value of tenant's interest) there shall be substituted—

"(a) the value of the interest of the tenant under his existing
    lease shall be determined in accordance with paragraph
    4A;

(aa) the value of the interest to be held by the tenant under the
     new lease shall be determined in accordance with
     paragraph 4B;",

and, in paragraph (b), for "that sub-paragraph" there shall be substituted
"sub-paragraph (2)".

(4) After paragraph 4 there shall be inserted—

"4A.—(1) Subject to the provisions of this paragraph, the value
of the interest of the tenant under the existing lease is the amount
which at the valuation date that interest might be expected to realise
if sold on the open market by a willing seller (with neither the
landlord nor any owner of an intermediate leasehold interest buying
or seeking to buy) on the following assumptions—

(a) on the assumption that the vendor is selling such interest as
    is held by the tenant subject to any interest inferior to the
    interest of the tenant;

(b) on the assumption that Chapter I and this Chapter confer
    no right to acquire any interest in any premises containing
    the tenant's flat or to acquire any new lease;

(c) on the assumption that any increase in the value of the flat
    which is attributable to an improvement carried out at his
    own expense by the tenant or by any predecessor in title is
    to be disregarded; and

(d) on the assumption that (subject to paragraph (b)) the
    vendor is selling with and subject to the rights and burdens
    with and subject to which any interest inferior to the
    existing lease of the tenant has effect.

(2) It is hereby declared that the fact that sub-paragraph (1)
requires assumptions to be made in relation to particular matters
does not preclude the making of assumptions as to other matters
where those assumptions are appropriate for determining the
amount which at the valuation date the interest of the tenant under
his existing lease might be expected to realise if sold as mentioned in
that sub-paragraph.

(3) In determining any such amount there shall be made such
deduction (if any) in respect of any defect in title as on a sale of that
interest on the open market might be expected to be allowed between
a willing seller and a willing buyer.

(4) Subject to sub-paragraph (5), the value of the interest of the
tenant under his existing lease shall not be increased by reason of—

(a) any transaction which—

    (i) is entered into after 19th January 1996, and

    (ii) involves the creation or transfer of an interest
    inferior to the tenant's existing lease; or

(b) any alteration after that date of the terms on which any
    such inferior interest is held.

(5) Sub-paragraph (4) shall not apply to any transaction which
falls within paragraph (a) of that sub-paragraph if—

(a) the transaction is entered into in pursuance of a contract entered into on or before the date mentioned in that paragraph; and

(b) the amount of the premium payable by the tenant in respect of the grant of the new lease was determined on or before that date either by agreement or by a leasehold valuation tribunal under this Chapter.

4B.—(1) Subject to the provisions of this paragraph, the value of the interest to be held by the tenant under the new lease is the amount which at the valuation date that interest (assuming it to have been granted to him at that date) might be expected to realise if sold on the open market by a willing seller (with the owner of any interest superior to the interest of the tenant not buying or seeking to buy) on the following assumptions—

(a) on the assumption that the vendor is selling such interest as is to be held by the tenant under the new lease subject to the inferior interests to which the tenant's existing lease is subject at the valuation date;

(b) on the assumption that Chapter I and this Chapter confer no right to acquire any interest in any premises containing the tenant's flat or to acquire any new lease;

(c) on the assumption that there is to be disregarded any increase in the value of the flat which would fall to be disregarded under paragraph (c) of sub-paragraph (1) of paragraph 4A in valuing in accordance with that sub-paragraph the interest of the tenant under his existing lease; and

(d) on the assumption that (subject to paragraph (b)) the vendor is selling with and subject to the rights and burdens with and subject to which any interest inferior to the tenant's existing lease at the valuation date then has effect.

(2) It is hereby declared that the fact that sub-paragraph (1) requires assumptions to be made in relation to particular matters does not preclude the making of assumptions as to other matters where those assumptions are appropriate for determining the amount which at the valuation date the interest to be held by the tenant under the new lease might be expected to realise if sold as mentioned in that sub-paragraph.

(3) In determining any such amount there shall be made such deduction (if any) in respect of any defect in title as on a sale of that interest on the open market might be expected to be allowed between a willing seller and a willing buyer.

(4) Subject to sub-paragraph (5), the value of the interest to be held by the tenant under the new lease shall not be decreased by reason of—

(a) any transaction which—

(i) is entered into after 19th January 1996, and

(ii) involves the creation or transfer of an interest inferior to the tenant's existing lease; or

(b) any alteration after that date of the terms on which any such inferior interest is held.

(5) Sub-paragraph (4) shall not apply to any transaction which falls within paragraph (a) of that sub-paragraph if—

    (a) the transaction is entered into in pursuance of a contract entered into on or before the date mentioned in that paragraph; and

    (b) the amount of the premium payable by the tenant in respect of the grant of the new lease was determined on or before that date either by agreement or by a leasehold valuation tribunal under this Chapter.".

(5) This section applies in relation to any claim made after 19th January 1996 by the giving of notice under section 42 of the Act of 1993 unless the amount of the premium payable in pursuance of the claim has been determined, either by agreement or by a leasehold valuation tribunal under Chapter II of the Act of 1993, before the day on which this Act is passed.

Trusts

111.—(1) In section 6 of the Leasehold Reform, Housing and Urban Development Act 1993 (which provides when a qualifying tenant of a flat satisfies the residence condition) for subsection (4) there shall be substituted—

> Satisfaction of residence condition: collective enfranchisement.
>
> 1993 c. 28.
> 1925 c. 18.

    "(4) Subsection (1) shall not apply where a lease is vested in trustees (other than a sole tenant for life within the meaning of the Settled Land Act 1925), and, in that case, a qualifying tenant of a flat shall, for the purposes of this Chapter, be treated as satisfying the residence condition at any time when the condition in subsection (5) is satisfied with respect to an individual having an interest under the trust (whether or not also a trustee).

    (5) That condition is that the individual has occupied the flat as his only or principal home—

        (a) for the last twelve months, or

        (b) for periods amounting to three years in the last ten years,

whether or not he has used the flat also for other purposes.

    (6) For the purposes of subsection (5)—

        (a) any reference to the flat includes a reference to part of it; and

        (b) it is immaterial whether at any particular time the individual's occupation was in right of the lease by virtue of which the trustees are a qualifying tenant or in right of some other lease or otherwise.".

(2) In section 13(3)(e)(iii) of that Act (particulars of satisfaction of residence condition to be included in the notice by which qualifying tenants exercise right to collective enfranchisement)—

    (a) after "which he" there shall be inserted ", or, where the tenant's lease is vested as mentioned in section 6(4), the individual concerned,", and

    (b) for "his", in the first place where it occurs, there shall be substituted "the".

Satisfaction of
residence
condition: new
leases.

1993 c. 28.

1925 c. 18.

112.—(1) Section 39 of the Leasehold Reform, Housing and Urban Development Act 1993 (right of qualifying tenant of flat to acquire new lease) shall be amended as mentioned in subsections (2) to (4) below.

(2) In subsection (2) (circumstances in which the right conferred) for paragraph (b) (residence condition) there shall be substituted—

> "(b) the condition specified in subsection (2A) or, as the case may be, (2B) is satisfied.

(2A) Where the lease by virtue of which the tenant is a qualifying tenant is vested in trustees (other than a sole tenant for life within the meaning of the Settled Land Act 1925), the condition is that an individual having an interest under the trust (whether or not also a trustee) has occupied the flat as his only or principal home—

> (a) for the last three years, or

> (b) for periods amounting to three years in the last ten years,

whether or not he has used it also for other purposes.

(2B) Where the lease by virtue of which the tenant is a qualifying tenant is not vested as mentioned in subsection (2A), the condition is that the tenant has occupied the flat as his only or principal home—

> (a) for the last three years, or

> (b) for periods amounting to three years in the last ten years,

whether or not he has used it also for other purposes.".

(3) After subsection (4) there shall be inserted—

> "(4A) For the purposes of subsection (2A)—

> (a) any reference to the flat includes a reference to part of it; and

> (b) it is immaterial whether at any particular time the individual's occupation was in right of the lease by virtue of which the trustees are a qualifying tenant or in right of some other lease or otherwise.".

(4) In subsection (5), for "(2)(b)" there shall be substituted "(2B)".

(5) In section 42 of that Act (notice by qualifying tenant of claim to exercise right) for subsection (4) there shall be substituted—

> "(4) If the tenant's lease is vested as mentioned in section 39(2A), the reference to the tenant in subsection (3)(b)(iv) shall be read as a reference to any individual with respect to whom it is claimed the condition in section 39(2A) is satisfied.".

Powers of trustees.

113. After section 93 of the Leasehold Reform, Housing and Urban Development Act 1993 there shall be inserted—

"Powers of
trustees in
relation to rights
under Chapters I
and II.

93A.—(1) Where trustees are a qualifying tenant of a flat for the purposes of Chapter I or II, their powers under the instrument regulating the trusts shall include power to participate in the exercise of the right to collective enfranchisement under Chapter I or, as the case may be, to exercise the right to a new lease under Chapter II.

(2) Subsection (1) shall not apply where the instrument regulating the trusts—

    (a) is made on or after the day on which section 113 of the Housing Act 1996 comes into force, and

    (b) contains an explicit direction to the contrary.

(3) The powers conferred by subsection (1) shall be exercisable with the like consent or on the like direction (if any) as may be required for the exercise of the trustees' powers (or ordinary powers) of investment.

(4) The following purposes, namely—

    (a) those authorised for the application of capital money by section 73 of the Settled Land Act 1925, or by that section as applied by section 28 of the Law of Property Act 1925 in relation to trusts for sale, and

    (b) those authorised by section 71 of the Settled Land Act 1925, or by that section as so applied, as purposes for which moneys may be raised by mortgage,

shall include the payment of any expenses incurred by a tenant for life or statutory owners or by trustees for sale, as the case may be, in or in connection with participation in the exercise of the right to collective enfranchisement under Chapter I or in or in connection with the exercise of the right to a new lease under Chapter II.".

1925 c. 18.

1925 c. 20.

Miscellaneous

114. In section 1 of the Leasehold Reform Act 1967 (tenants entitled to enfranchisement or extension), in subsection (1)(a)—

    (a) in sub-paragraph (i), for the words from "or (where" to "that date," there shall be substituted ", or on or after 1st April 1990 in pursuance of a contract made before that date, and the house and premises had a rateable value at the date of commencement of the tenancy or else at any time before 1st April 1990,", and

    (b) in sub-paragraph (ii), for the words from "is entered" to "1990)," there shall be substituted "does not fall within sub-paragraph (i) above,".

Minor amendment of section 1(1)(a) of Leasehold Reform Act 1967.

1967 c. 88.

115. In section 21(1) of the Leasehold Reform Act 1967 (matters to be determined by leasehold valuation tribunal), after paragraph (b) there shall be inserted—

"(ba) the amount of any costs payable under section 9(4) or 14(2);".

Power for leasehold valuation tribunal to determine amount of costs payable under Leasehold Reform Act 1967.

116. Schedule 11 (which makes, in relation to claims to enfranchisement or an extended lease under Part I of the Leasehold Reform Act 1967 and claims to collective enfranchisement or a new lease under Chapter I or II of Part I of the Leasehold Reform, Housing and Urban Development Act 1993, provision for compensation of the landlord where the claim has prolonged an existing tenancy, but is ineffective) shall have effect.

Compensation for postponement of termination in connection with ineffective claims.

1993 c. 28.

Priority of
interests on grant
of new lease.

1993 c. 28.

117. After section 58 of the Leasehold Reform, Housing and Urban Development Act 1993 there shall be inserted—

"Priority of
interests on
grant of new
lease.

58A.—(1) Where a lease granted under section 56 takes effect subject to two or more interests to which the existing lease was subject immediately before its surrender, the interests shall have the same priority in relation to one another on the grant of the new lease as they had immediately before the surrender of the existing lease.

(2) Subsection (1) is subject to agreement to the contrary.

(3) Where a person who is entitled on the grant of a lease under section 56 to rights of occupation in relation to the flat comprised in that lease was entitled immediately before the surrender of the existing lease to rights of occupation in relation to the flat comprised in that lease, the rights to which he is entitled on the grant of the new lease shall be treated as a continuation of the rights to which he was entitled immediately before the surrender of the existing lease.

(4) In this section—

"the existing lease", in relation to a lease granted under section 56, means the lease surrendered on the grant of the new lease, and

1983 c. 19.

"rights of occupation" has the same meaning as in the Matrimonial Homes Act 1983.".

Estate
management
schemes in
connection with
enfranchisement
by virtue of s. 106.

118.—(1) Chapter IV of Part I of the 1993 Act, except section 75(1), (estate management schemes in connection with enfranchisement by virtue of that Act) shall also have effect subject to the modifications mentioned in subsections (2) to (4) below.

(2) In section 69(1) (definition of estate management schemes), for paragraphs (a) and (b) there shall be substituted—

1967 c. 88.

"(a) acquiring the landlord's interest in their house and premises ("the house") under Part I of the Leasehold Reform Act 1967 by virtue of the provisions of section 1AA of that Act (as inserted by paragraph 1 of Schedule 9 to the Housing Act 1996), or

(b) acquiring the landlord's interest in any premises ("the premises") in accordance with Chapter I of this Part of this Act by virtue of the amendments of that Chapter made by paragraph 3 of Schedule 9 to the Housing Act 1996,".

(3) In section 70 (time limit for applications for approval), for "two years beginning with the date of the coming into force of this section" there shall be substituted "two years beginning with the coming into force of section 118 of the Housing Act 1996".

(4) In section 74 (effect of application for approval on claim to acquire freehold), in subsection (1)—

(a) in paragraph (b), in sub-paragraph (i), the words from "being" to the end shall be omitted, and

(b) after that paragraph there shall be inserted "and

(c) in the case of an application for the approval of a scheme as an estate management scheme, the scheme would extend to the house or premises if acquired in pursuance of the notice.".

(5) Section 94(6) to (8) of the 1993 Act (estate management schemes relating to Crown land) shall also have effect with the substitution for any reference to a provision of Chapter IV of Part I of that Act of a reference to that provision as it has effect by virtue of subsection (1) above.

(6) In section 33 of the National Heritage Act 1983 (general functions of the Historic Buildings and Monuments Commission for England), after subsection (2B) there shall be inserted—

1983 c. 47.

"(2C) In subsection (2B), references to provisions of the Leasehold Reform, Housing and Urban Development Act 1993 include references to those provisions as they have effect by virtue of section 118(1) of the Housing Act 1996.".

1993 c. 28.

(7) In section 72 of the Planning (Listed Buildings and Conservation Areas) Act 1990 (general duty as respects conservation area in exercise of planning functions), at the end there shall be inserted—

1990 c. 9.

"(3) In subsection (2), references to provisions of the Leasehold Reform, Housing and Urban Development Act 1993 include references to those provisions as they have effect by virtue of section 118(1) of the Housing Act 1996.".

(8) In this section, "the 1993 Act" means the Leasehold Reform, Housing and Urban Development Act 1993.

119.—(1) Procedure regulations may make provision in relation to proceedings before a leasehold valuation tribunal—

Leasehold valuation tribunals: pre-trial review.

(a) for the holding of a pre-trial review, on the application of a party to the proceedings or of the tribunal's own motion; and

(b) for the exercise of the functions of the tribunal in relation to, or at, a pre-trial review by a single member who is qualified to exercise them.

(2) In subsection (1) "procedure regulations" means regulations under section 74(1)(b) of the Rent Act 1977, as that section applies in relation to leasehold valuation tribunals.

1977 c. 42.

(3) For the purposes of subsection (1)(b)—

(a) a "member" means a member of the panel provided for in Schedule 10 to that Act, and

(b) a member is qualified to exercise the functions referred to if he was appointed to that panel by the Lord Chancellor.

PART IV

HOUSING BENEFIT AND RELATED MATTERS

Payment of
housing benefit to
third parties.
1992 c. 5.

120.—(1) In section 5 of the Social Security Administration Act 1992 (regulations about claims for and payments of benefit), after subsection (5) insert—

> "(6) As it has effect in relation to housing benefit subsection (1)(p) above authorises provision requiring the making of payments of benefit to another person, on behalf of the beneficiary, in such circumstances as may be prescribed.".

(2) The above amendment shall be deemed always to have had effect; and provision corresponding to that made by the amendment shall be deemed to have had effect at all material times in relation to corresponding earlier enactments.

Administration of
housing benefit,
&c.

121. Part VIII of the Social Security Administration Act 1992 (arrangements for housing benefit and council tax benefit and related subsidies) is amended in accordance with Schedule 12.

Functions of rent
officers in
connection with
housing benefit
and rent
allowance subsidy.

122.—(1) The Secretary of State may by order require rent officers to carry out such functions as may be specified in the order in connection with housing benefit and rent allowance subsidy.

(2) Without prejudice to the generality of subsection (1), an order under this section may contain provision—

(a) enabling a prospective landlord to apply for a determination for the purposes of any application for housing benefit which may be made by a tenant of a dwelling which he proposes to let;

(b) as to the payment of a fee by the landlord for that determination;

(c) requiring the landlord to give a copy of the determination to the appropriate local authority; and

(d) enabling the appropriate local authority to seek a redetermination when a claim for housing benefit or rent allowance subsidy is made.

1992 c. 4.

(3) Regulations under section 130(4) of the Social Security Contributions and Benefits Act 1992 (housing benefit: manner of determining appropriate maximum benefit) may provide for benefit to be limited by reference to determinations made by rent officers in exercise of functions conferred under this section.

(4) In relation to rent allowance subsidy, the Secretary of State may by order under section 140B of the Social Security Administration Act 1992—

(a) provide for any calculation under subsection (2) of that section to be made,

(b) specify any additions and deductions as are referred to in that subsection, and

(c) exercise his discretion as to what is unreasonable for the purposes of subsection (4) of that section,

by reference to determinations made by rent officers in exercise of functions conferred on them under this section.

(5) The Secretary of State may by any such regulations or order as are mentioned in subsection (3) or (4) require a local authority in any prescribed case—

    (a) to apply to a rent officer for a determination to be made in pursuance of the functions conferred on them under this section, and

    (b) to do so within such time as may be specified in the order or regulations.

(6) An order under this section—

    (a) shall be made by statutory instrument which shall be subject to annulment in pursuance of a resolution of either House of Parliament;

    (b) may make different provision for different cases or classes of case and for different areas; and

    (c) may contain such transitional, incidental and supplementary provisions as appear to the Secretary of State to be desirable.

(7) In this section "housing benefit" and "rent allowance subsidy" have the same meaning as in Part VIII of the Social Security Administration Act 1992.

1992 c. 5.

123. The enactments mentioned in Schedule 13 have effect with the amendments specified there which are consequential on the provisions of this Part.

Consequential amendments: Part IV.

PART V

CONDUCT OF TENANTS

CHAPTER I

INTRODUCTORY TENANCIES

General provisions

124.—(1) A local housing authority or a housing action trust may elect to operate an introductory tenancy regime.

Introductory tenancies.

(2) When such an election is in force, every periodic tenancy of a dwelling-house entered into or adopted by the authority or trust shall, if it would otherwise be a secure tenancy, be an introductory tenancy, unless immediately before the tenancy was entered into or adopted the tenant or, in the case of joint tenants, one or more of them was—

    (a) a secure tenant of the same or another dwelling-house, or

    (b) an assured tenant of a registered social landlord (otherwise than under an assured shorthold tenancy) in respect of the same or another dwelling-house.

(3) Subsection (2) does not apply to a tenancy entered into or adopted in pursuance of a contract made before the election was made.

(4) For the purposes of this Chapter a periodic tenancy is adopted by a person if that person becomes the landlord under the tenancy, whether on a disposal or surrender of the interest of the former landlord.

(5) An election under this section may be revoked at any time, without prejudice to the making of a further election.

Duration of
introductory
tenancy.

125.—(1) A tenancy remains an introductory tenancy until the end of the trial period, unless one of the events mentioned in subsection (5) occurs before the end of that period.

(2) The "trial period" is the period of one year beginning with—

    (a) in the case of a tenancy which was entered into by a local housing authority or housing action trust—

        (i) the date on which the tenancy was entered into, or

        (ii) if later, the date on which a tenant was first entitled to possession under the tenancy; or

    (b) in the case of a tenancy which was adopted by a local housing authority or housing action trust, the date of adoption;

subject as follows.

(3) Where the tenant under an introductory tenancy was formerly a tenant under another introductory tenancy, or held an assured shorthold tenancy from a registered social landlord, any period or periods during which he was such a tenant shall count towards the trial period, provided—

    (a) if there was one such period, it ended immediately before the date specified in subsection (2), and

    (b) if there was more than one such period, the most recent period ended immediately before that date and each period succeeded the other without interruption.

(4) Where there are joint tenants under an introductory tenancy, the reference in subsection (3) to the tenant shall be construed as referring to the joint tenant in whose case the application of that subsection produces the earliest starting date for the trial period.

(5) A tenancy ceases to be an introductory tenancy if, before the end of the trial period—

    (a) the circumstances are such that the tenancy would not otherwise be a secure tenancy,

    (b) a person or body other than a local housing authority or housing action trust becomes the landlord under the tenancy,

    (c) the election in force when the tenancy was entered into or adopted is revoked, or

    (d) the tenancy ceases to be an introductory tenancy by virtue of section 133(3) (succession).

(6) A tenancy does not come to an end merely because it ceases to be an introductory tenancy, but a tenancy which has once ceased to be an introductory tenancy cannot subsequently become an introductory tenancy.

(7) This section has effect subject to section 130 (effect of beginning proceedings for possession).

Licences.

126.—(1) The provisions of this Chapter apply in relation to a licence to occupy a dwelling-house (whether or not granted for a consideration) as they apply in relation to a tenancy.

(2) Subsection (1) does not apply to a licence granted as a temporary expedient to a person who entered the dwelling-house or any other land as a trespasser (whether or not, before the grant of that licence, another licence to occupy that or another dwelling-house had been granted to him).

Proceedings for possession

127.—(1) The landlord may only bring an introductory tenancy to an end by obtaining an order of the court for the possession of the dwelling-house.

(2) The court shall make such an order unless the provisions of section 128 apply.

(3) Where the court makes such an order, the tenancy comes to an end on the date on which the tenant is to give up possession in pursuance of the order.

Proceedings for possession.

128.—(1) The court shall not entertain proceedings for the possession of a dwelling-house let under an introductory tenancy unless the landlord has served on the tenant a notice of proceedings complying with this section.

(2) The notice shall state that the court will be asked to make an order for the possession of the dwelling-house.

(3) The notice shall set out the reasons for the landlord's decision to apply for such an order.

(4) The notice shall specify a date after which proceedings for the possession of the dwelling-house may be begun.

The date so specified must not be earlier than the date on which the tenancy could, apart from this Chapter, be brought to an end by notice to quit given by the landlord on the same date as the notice of proceedings.

(5) The court shall not entertain any proceedings for possession of the dwelling-house unless they are begun after the date specified in the notice of proceedings.

(6) The notice shall inform the tenant of his right to request a review of the landlord's decision to seek an order for possession and of the time within which such a request must be made.

(7) The notice shall also inform the tenant that if he needs help or advice about the notice, and what to do about it, he should take it immediately to a Citizens' Advice Bureau, a housing aid centre, a law centre or a solicitor.

Notice of proceedings for possession.

129.—(1) A request for review of the landlord's decision to seek an order for possession of a dwelling-house let under an introductory tenancy must be made before the end of the period of 14 days beginning with the day on which the notice of proceedings is served.

(2) On a request being duly made to it, the landlord shall review its decision.

(3) The Secretary of State may make provision by regulations as to the procedure to be followed in connection with a review under this section.

Nothing in the following provisions affects the generality of this power.

Review of decision to seek possession.

(4) Provision may be made by regulations—

    (a) requiring the decision on review to be made by a person of appropriate seniority who was not involved in the original decision, and

    (b) as to the circumstances in which the person concerned is entitled to an oral hearing, and whether and by whom he may be represented at such a hearing.

(5) The landlord shall notify the person concerned of the decision on the review.

If the decision is to confirm the original decision, the landlord shall also notify him of the reasons for the decision.

(6) The review shall be carried out and the tenant notified before the date specified in the notice of proceedings as the date after which proceedings for the possession of the dwelling-house may be begun.

Effect of beginning proceedings for possession.

130.—(1) This section applies where the landlord has begun proceedings for the possession of a dwelling-house let under an introductory tenancy and—

    (a) the trial period ends, or

    (b) any of the events specified in section 125(5) occurs (events on which a tenancy ceases to be an introductory tenancy).

(2) Subject to the following provisions, the tenancy remains an introductory tenancy until—

    (a) the tenancy comes to an end in pursuance of section 127(3) (that is, on the date on which the tenant is to give up possession in pursuance of an order of the court), or

    (b) the proceedings are otherwise finally determined.

(3) If any of the events specified in section 125(5)(b) to (d) occurs, the tenancy shall thereupon cease to be an introductory tenancy but—

    (a) the landlord (or, as the case may be, the new landlord) may continue the proceedings, and

    (b) if he does so, section 127(2) and (3) (termination by landlord) apply as if the tenancy had remained an introductory tenancy.

1985 c. 68.

(4) Where in accordance with subsection (3) a tenancy ceases to be an introductory tenancy and becomes a secure tenancy, the tenant is not entitled to exercise the right to buy under Part V of the Housing Act 1985 unless and until the proceedings are finally determined on terms such that he is not required to give up possession of the dwelling-house.

(5) For the purposes of this section proceedings shall be treated as finally determined if they are withdrawn or any appeal is abandoned or the time for appealing expires without an appeal being brought.

Succession on death of tenant

Persons qualified to succeed tenant.

131. A person is qualified to succeed the tenant under an introductory tenancy if he occupies the dwelling-house as his only or principal home at the time of the tenant's death and either—

    (a) he is the tenant's spouse, or

(b) he is another member of the tenant's family and has resided with the tenant throughout the period of twelve months ending with the tenant's death;

unless, in either case, the tenant was himself a successor, as defined in section 132.

132.—(1) The tenant is himself a successor if— Cases where the tenant is a successor.

(a) the tenancy vested in him by virtue of section 133 (succession to introductory tenancy),

(b) he was a joint tenant and has become the sole tenant,

(c) he became the tenant on the tenancy being assigned to him (but subject to subsections (2) and (3)), or

(d) he became the tenant on the tenancy being vested in him on the death of the previous tenant.

(2) A tenant to whom the tenancy was assigned in pursuance of an order under section 24 of the Matrimonial Causes Act 1973 (property adjustment orders in connection with matrimonial proceedings) or section 17(1) of the Matrimonial and Family Proceedings Act 1984 (property adjustment orders after overseas divorce, &c.) is a successor only if the other party to the marriage was a successor. 1973 c. 18.
1984 c. 42.

(3) Where within six months of the coming to an end of an introductory tenancy ("the former tenancy") the tenant becomes a tenant under another introductory tenancy, and—

(a) the tenant was a successor in relation to the former tenancy, and

(b) under the other tenancy either the dwelling-house or the landlord, or both, are the same as under the former tenancy,

the tenant is also a successor in relation to the other tenancy unless the agreement creating that tenancy otherwise provides.

133.—(1) This section applies where a tenant under an introductory tenancy dies. Succession to introductory tenancy.

(2) Where there is a person qualified to succeed the tenant, the tenancy vests by virtue of this section in that person, or if there is more than one such person in the one to be preferred in accordance with the following rules—

(a) the tenant's spouse is to be preferred to another member of the tenant's family;

(b) of two or more other members of the tenant's family such of them is to be preferred as may be agreed between them or as may, where there is no such agreement, be selected by the landlord.

(3) Where there is no person qualified to succeed the tenant, the tenancy ceases to be an introductory tenancy—

(a) when it is vested or otherwise disposed of in the course of the administration of the tenant's estate, unless the vesting or other disposal is in pursuance of an order made under—

(i) section 24 of the Matrimonial Causes Act 1973 (property adjustment orders made in connection with matrimonial proceedings),

1984 c. 42.

> (ii) section 17(1) of the Matrimonial and Family Proceedings Act 1984 (property adjustment orders after overseas divorce, &c.), or

1989 c. 41.

> (iii) paragraph 1 of Schedule 1 to the Children Act 1989 (orders for financial relief against parents); or

(b) when it is known that when the tenancy is so vested or disposed of it will not be in pursuance of such an order.

Assignment

Assignment in general prohibited.

134.—(1) An introductory tenancy is not capable of being assigned except in the cases mentioned in subsection (2).

(2) The exceptions are—

(a) an assignment in pursuance of an order made under—

1973 c. 18.

> (i) section 24 of the Matrimonial Causes Act 1973 (property adjustment orders in connection with matrimonial proceedings),

> (ii) section 17(1) of the Matrimonial and Family Proceedings Act 1984 (property adjustment orders after overseas divorce, &c.), or

> (iii) paragraph 1 of Schedule 1 to the Children Act 1989 (orders for financial relief against parents);

(b) an assignment to a person who would be qualified to succeed the tenant if the tenant died immediately before the assignment.

(3) Subsection (1) also applies to a tenancy which is not an introductory tenancy but would be if the tenant, or where the tenancy is a joint tenancy, at least one of the tenants, were occupying or continuing to occupy the dwelling-house as his only or principal home.

Repairs

Right to carry out repairs.
1985 c. 68.

135. The Secretary of State may by regulations under section 96 of the Housing Act 1985 (secure tenants: right to carry out repairs) apply to introductory tenants any provision made under that section in relation to secure tenants.

Provision of information and consultation

Provision of information about tenancies.

136.—(1) Every local housing authority or housing action trust which lets dwelling-houses under introductory tenancies shall from time to time publish information about its introductory tenancies, in such form as it considers best suited to explain in simple terms, and, so far as it considers it appropriate, the effect of—

(a) the express terms of its introductory tenancies,

(b) the provisions of this Chapter, and

1985 c. 70.

(c) the provisions of sections 11 to 16 of the Landlord and Tenant Act 1985 (landlord's repairing obligations),

and shall ensure that so far as is reasonably practicable the information so published is kept up to date.

(2) The landlord under an introductory tenancy shall supply the tenant with—

(a) a copy of the information for introductory tenants published by it under subsection (1), and

(b) a written statement of the terms of the tenancy, so far as they are neither expressed in the lease or written tenancy agreement (if any) nor implied by law;

and the statement required by paragraph (b) shall be supplied on the grant of the tenancy or as soon as practicable afterwards.

137.—(1) This section applies in relation to every local housing authority and housing action trust which lets dwelling-houses under introductory tenancies and which is a landlord authority for the purposes of Part IV of the Housing Act 1985 (secure tenancies).

Consultation on matters of housing management.
1985 c. 68.

(2) The authority or trust shall maintain such arrangements as it considers appropriate to enable those of its introductory tenants who are likely to be substantially affected by a relevant matter of housing management—

(a) to be informed of the proposals of the authority or trust in respect of the matter, and

(b) to make their views known to the authority or trust within a specified period;

and the authority or trust shall, before making a decision on the matter, consider any representations made to it in accordance with those arrangements.

(3) A matter is one of housing management if, in the opinion of the authority or trust concerned, it relates to—

(a) the management, improvement, maintenance or demolition of dwelling-houses let by the authority or trust under introductory or secure tenancies, or

(b) the provision of services or amenities in connection with such dwelling-houses;

but not so far as it relates to the rent payable under an introductory or secure tenancy or to charges for services or facilities provided by the authority or trust.

(4) A matter is relevant if, in the opinion of the authority or trust concerned, it represents—

(a) a new programme of maintenance, improvement or demolition, or

(b) a change in the practice or policy of the authority or trust,

and is likely substantially to affect either its introductory tenants as a whole or a group of them who form a distinct social group or occupy dwelling-houses which constitute a distinct class (whether by reference to the kind of dwelling-house, or the housing estate or other larger area in which they are situated).

(5) In the case of a local housing authority, the reference in subsection (3) to the provision of services or amenities is a reference only to the provision of services or amenities by the authority acting in its capacity as landlord of the dwelling-houses concerned.

(6) The authority or trust shall publish details of the arrangements which it makes under this section, and a copy of the documents published under this subsection shall—

(a) be made available at its principal office for inspection at all reasonable hours, without charge, by members of the public, and

(b) be given, on payment of a reasonable fee, to any member of the public who asks for one.

Supplementary

Jurisdiction of county court.

138.—(1) A county court has jurisdiction to determine questions arising under this Chapter and to entertain proceedings brought under this Chapter and claims, for whatever amount, in connection with an introductory tenancy.

(2) That jurisdiction includes jurisdiction to entertain proceedings as to whether a statement supplied in pursuance of section 136(2)(b) (written statement of certain terms of tenancy) is accurate notwithstanding that no other relief is sought than a declaration.

(3) If a person takes proceedings in the High Court which, by virtue of this section, he could have taken in the county court, he is not entitled to recover any costs.

(4) The Lord Chancellor may make such rules and give such directions as he thinks fit for the purpose of giving effect to this section.

(5) The rules and directions may provide—

(a) for the exercise by a district judge of a county court of any jurisdiction exercisable under this section, and

(b) for the conduct of proceedings in private.

(6) The power to make rules is exercisable by statutory instrument which shall be subject to annulment in pursuance of a resolution of either House of Parliament.

Meaning of "dwelling-house".

139.—(1) For the purposes of this Chapter a dwelling-house may be a house or a part of a house.

(2) Land let together with a dwelling-house shall be treated for the purposes of this Chapter as part of the dwelling-house unless the land is agricultural land which would not be treated as part of a dwelling-house for the purposes of Part IV of the Housing Act 1985 (see section 112(2) of that Act).

1985 c. 68.

Members of a person's family: Chapter I.

140.—(1) A person is a member of another's family within the meaning of this Chapter if—

(a) he is the spouse of that person, or he and that person live together as husband and wife, or

(b) he is that person's parent, grandparent, child, grandchild, brother, sister, uncle, aunt, nephew or niece.

(2) For the purpose of subsection (1)(b)—

(a) a relationship by marriage shall be treated as a relationship by blood,

(b) a relationship of the half-blood shall be treated as a relationship of the whole blood, and

(c) the stepchild of a person shall be treated as his child.

141.—(1) The enactments mentioned in Schedule 14 have effect with the amendments specified there which are consequential on the provisions of this Chapter.

(2) The Secretary of State may by order make such other amendments or repeals of any enactment as appear to him necessary or expedient in consequence of the provisions of this Chapter.

(3) Without prejudice to the generality of subsection (2), an order under that subsection may make such provision in relation to an enactment as the Secretary of State considers appropriate as regards its application (with or without modifications) or non-application in relation to introductory tenants or introductory tenancies.

Consequential amendments: introductory tenancies.

142. Any regulations or order under this Part—

(a) may contain such incidental, supplementary or transitional provisions, or savings, as the Secretary of State thinks fit, and

(b) shall be made by statutory instrument which shall be subject to annulment in pursuance of a resolution of either House of Parliament.

Regulations and orders.

143. The following Table shows provisions defining or otherwise explaining provisions used in this Chapter (other than provisions defining or explaining an expression in the same section)—

Index of defined expressions: introductory tenancies.

adopt (in relation to periodic tenancy)	section 124(4)
assured tenancy and assured shorthold tenancy	section 230
dwelling-house	section 139
housing action trust	section 230
introductory tenancy and introductory tenant	section 124
local housing authority	section 230
member of family	section 140
registered social landlord	section 2
secure tenancy and secure tenant	section 230

CHAPTER II

REPOSSESSION, &C.: SECURE AND ASSURED TENANCIES

Secure tenancies

144. For Ground 2 in Schedule 2 to the Housing Act 1985 (nuisance or annoyance to neighbours, &c.) substitute—

Extension of ground of nuisance or annoyance to neighbours, &c. 1985 c. 68.

"Ground 2

The tenant or a person residing in or visiting the dwelling-house—

(a) has been guilty of conduct causing or likely to cause a nuisance or annoyance to a person residing, visiting or otherwise engaging in a lawful activity in the locality, or

(b) has been convicted of—

(i) using the dwelling-house or allowing it to be used for immoral or illegal purposes, or

(ii) an arrestable offence committed in, or in the locality of, the dwelling-house.".

New ground of domestic violence: secure tenancies.

1985 c. 68.

145. After Ground 2 in Schedule 2 to the Housing Act 1985 (as substituted by section 144) insert—

"Ground 2A

The dwelling-house was occupied (whether alone or with others) by a married couple or a couple living together as husband and wife and—

(a) one or both of the partners is a tenant of the dwelling-house,

(b) one partner has left because of violence or threats of violence by the other towards—

(i) that partner, or

(ii) a member of the family of that partner who was residing with that partner immediately before the partner left, and

(c) the court is satisfied that the partner who has left is unlikely to return.".

Extension of ground that grant of tenancy induced by false statement.

146. In Ground 5 in Schedule 2 to the Housing Act 1985 (grant of tenancy induced by false statement) for "by the tenant" substitute "by—

(a) the tenant, or

(b) a person acting at the tenant's instigation".

Proceedings for possession or termination.

147.—(1) For section 83 of the Housing Act 1985 (notice of proceedings for possession or termination) substitute—

"Proceedings for possession or termination: notice requirements.

83.—(1) The court shall not entertain proceedings for the possession of a dwelling-house let under a secure tenancy or proceedings for the termination of a secure tenancy unless—

(a) the landlord has served a notice on the tenant complying with the provisions of this section, or

(b) the court considers it just and equitable to dispense with the requirement of such a notice.

(2) A notice under this section shall—

(a) be in a form prescribed by regulations made by the Secretary of State,

(b) specify the ground on which the court will be asked to make an order for the possession of the dwelling-house or for the termination of the tenancy, and

(c) give particulars of that ground.

(3) Where the tenancy is a periodic tenancy and the ground or one of the grounds specified in the notice is Ground 2 in Schedule 2 (nuisance or other anti-social behaviour), the notice—

(a) shall also—

      (i) state that proceedings for the possession of the dwelling-house may be begun immediately, and

      (ii) specify the date sought by the landlord as the date on which the tenant is to give up possession of the dwelling-house, and

    (b) ceases to be in force twelve months after the date so specified.

(4) Where the tenancy is a periodic tenancy and Ground 2 in Schedule 2 is not specified in the notice, the notice—

    (a) shall also specify the date after which proceedings for the possession of the dwelling-house may be begun, and

    (b) ceases to be in force twelve months after the date so specified.

(5) The date specified in accordance with subsection (3) or (4) must not be earlier than the date on which the tenancy could, apart from this Part, be brought to an end by notice to quit given by the landlord on the same date as the notice under this section.

(6) Where a notice under this section is served with respect to a secure tenancy for a term certain, it has effect also with respect to any periodic tenancy arising on the termination of that tenancy by virtue of section 86; and subsections (3) to (5) of this section do not apply to the notice.

(7) Regulations under this section shall be made by statutory instrument and may make different provision with respect to different cases or descriptions of case, including different provision for different areas.

Additional requirements in relation to certain proceedings for possession.

83A.—(1) Where a notice under section 83 has been served on a tenant containing the information mentioned in subsection (3)(a) of that section, the court shall not entertain proceedings for the possession of the dwelling-house unless they are begun at a time when the notice is still in force.

(2) Where—

    (a) a notice under section 83 has been served on a tenant, and

    (b) a date after which proceedings may be begun has been specified in the notice in accordance with subsection (4)(a) of that section,

the court shall not entertain proceedings for the possession of the dwelling-house unless they are begun after the date so specified and at a time when the notice is still in force.

(3) Where—

> > (a) the ground or one of the grounds specified in a
> >   notice under section 83 is Ground 2A in
> >   Schedule 2 (domestic violence), and
> >
> > (b) the partner who has left the dwelling-house as
> >   mentioned in that ground is not a tenant of the
> >   dwelling-house,
>
> the court shall not entertain proceedings for the
> possession of the dwelling-house unless it is satisfied that
> the landlord has served a copy of the notice on the partner
> who has left or has taken all reasonable steps to serve a
> copy of the notice on that partner.
>
> This subsection has effect subject to subsection (5).
>
> (4) Where—
>
> > (a) Ground 2A in Schedule 2 is added to a notice
> >   under section 83 with the leave of the court after
> >   proceedings for possession are begun, and
> >
> > (b) the partner who has left the dwelling-house as
> >   mentioned in that ground is not a party to the
> >   proceedings,
>
> the court shall not continue to entertain the proceedings
> unless it is satisfied that the landlord has served a notice
> under subsection (6) on the partner who has left or has
> taken all reasonable steps to serve such a notice on that
> partner.
>
> This subsection has effect subject to subsection (5).
>
> (5) Where subsection (3) or (4) applies and Ground 2
> in Schedule 2 (nuisance or other anti-social behaviour) is
> also specified in the notice under section 83, the court may
> dispense with the requirements as to service in relation to
> the partner who has left the dwelling-house if it considers
> it just and equitable to do so.
>
> (6) A notice under this subsection shall—
>
> > (a) state that proceedings for the possession of the
> >   dwelling-house have begun,
> >
> > (b) specify the ground or grounds on which
> >   possession is being sought, and
> >
> > (c) give particulars of the ground or grounds.".

(2) In section 84 of that Act (grounds and orders for possession), for
subsection (3) substitute—

> "(3) Where a notice under section 83 has been served on the
> tenant, the court shall not make such an order on any of those
> grounds above unless the ground is specified in the notice; but the
> grounds so specified may be altered or added to with the leave of
> the court.
>
> (4) Where a date is specified in a notice under section 83 in
> accordance with subsection (3) of that section, the court shall not
> make an order which requires the tenant to give up possession of the
> dwelling-house in question before the date so specified.".

(3) In Schedule 2 to that Act, in Ground 16, after "notice of the proceedings for possession was served under section 83" insert "(or, where no such notice was served, the proceedings for possession were begun)".

Assured tenancies

148. For Ground 14 in Schedule 2 to the Housing Act 1988 (nuisance or annoyance to adjoining occupiers etc.) substitute—

"Ground 14

The tenant or a person residing in or visiting the dwelling-house—

    (a) has been guilty of conduct causing or likely to cause a nuisance or annoyance to a person residing, visiting or otherwise engaging in a lawful activity in the locality, or

    (b) has been convicted of—

        (i) using the dwelling-house or allowing it to be used for immoral or illegal purposes, or

        (ii) an arrestable offence committed in, or in the locality of, the dwelling-house.".

> Extension of ground of nuisance or annoyance to adjoining occupiers &c.
> 1988 c. 50.

149. After Ground 14 in Schedule 2 to the Housing Act 1988 (as substituted by section 148) insert—

"Ground 14A

The dwelling-house was occupied (whether alone or with others) by a married couple or a couple living together as husband and wife and—

    (a) one or both of the partners is a tenant of the dwelling-house,

    (b) the landlord who is seeking possession is a registered social landlord or a charitable housing trust,

    (c) one partner has left the dwelling-house because of violence or threats of violence by the other towards—

        (i) that partner, or

        (ii) a member of the family of that partner who was residing with that partner immediately before the partner left, and

    (d) the court is satisfied that the partner who has left is unlikely to return.

For the purposes of this ground "registered social landlord" and "member of the family" have the same meaning as in Part I of the Housing Act 1996 and "charitable housing trust" means a housing trust, within the meaning of the Housing Associations Act 1985, which is a charity within the meaning of the Charities Act 1993.".

> New ground of domestic violence: assured tenancies.

> 1985 c. 69.
> 1993 c. 10.

Additional notice
requirements:
domestic violence.

150. After section 8 of the Housing Act 1988 insert—

"Additional
notice
requirements:
ground of
domestic
violence.

8A.—(1) Where the ground specified in a notice under section 8 (whether with or without other grounds) is Ground 14A in Schedule 2 to this Act and the partner who has left the dwelling-house as mentioned in that ground is not a tenant of the dwelling-house, the court shall not entertain proceedings for possession of the dwelling-house unless—

> (a) the landlord or, in the case of joint landlords, at least one of them has served on the partner who has left a copy of the notice or has taken all reasonable steps to serve a copy of the notice on that partner, or
>
> (b) the court considers it just and equitable to dispense with such requirements as to service.

(2) Where Ground 14A in Schedule 2 to this Act is added to a notice under section 8 with the leave of the court after proceedings for possession are begun and the partner who has left the dwelling-house as mentioned in that ground is not a party to the proceedings, the court shall not continue to entertain the proceedings unless—

> (a) the landlord or, in the case of joint landlords, at least one of them has served a notice under subsection (3) below on the partner who has left or has taken all reasonable steps to serve such a notice on that partner, or
>
> (b) the court considers it just and equitable to dispense with the requirement of such a notice.

(3) A notice under this subsection shall—

> (a) state that proceedings for the possession of the dwelling-house have begun,
>
> (b) specify the ground or grounds on which possession is being sought, and
>
> (c) give particulars of the ground or grounds.".

Early
commencement of
certain
proceedings for
possession.
1988 c. 50.

151.—(1) Section 8 of the Housing Act 1988 (notice of proceedings for possession) is amended as follows.

(2) In subsection (1)(a) for the words "subsections (3) and (4)" substitute "subsections (3) to (4B)".

(3) In subsection (3)(b) for the words from "which," to "of the notice" substitute "in accordance with subsections (4) to (4B) below".

(4) For subsection (4) substitute—

> "(4) If a notice under this section specifies in accordance with subsection (3)(a) above Ground 14 in Schedule 2 to this Act (whether with or without other grounds), the date specified in the notice as mentioned in subsection (3)(b) above shall not be earlier than the date of the service of the notice.
>
> (4A) If a notice under this section specifies in accordance with subsection (3)(a) above, any of Grounds 1, 2, 5 to 7, 9 and 16 in

Schedule 2 to this Act (whether without other grounds or with any ground other than Ground 14), the date specified in the notice as mentioned in subsection (3)(b) above shall not be earlier than—

(a) two months from the date of service of the notice; and

(b) if the tenancy is a periodic tenancy, the earliest date on which, apart from section 5(1) above, the tenancy could be brought to an end by a notice to quit given by the landlord on the same date as the date of service of the notice under this section.

(4B) In any other case, the date specified in the notice as mentioned in subsection (3)(b) above shall not be earlier than the expiry of the period of two weeks from the date of the service of the notice.".

CHAPTER III

INJUNCTIONS AGAINST ANTI-SOCIAL BEHAVIOUR

152.—(1) The High Court or a county court may, on an application by a local authority, grant an injunction prohibiting a person from—

(a) engaging in or threatening to engage in conduct causing or likely to cause a nuisance or annoyance to a person residing in, visiting or otherwise engaging in a lawful activity in residential premises to which this section applies or in the locality of such premises,

(b) using or threatening to use residential premises to which this section applies for immoral or illegal purposes, or

(c) entering residential premises to which this section applies or being found in the locality of any such premises.

(2) This section applies to residential premises of the following descriptions—

(a) dwelling-houses held under secure or introductory tenancies from the local authority;

(b) accommodation provided by that authority under Part VII of this Act or Part III of the Housing Act 1985 (homelessness).

(3) The court shall not grant an injunction under this section unless it is of the opinion that—

(a) the respondent has used or threatened to use violence against any person of a description mentioned in subsection (1)(a), and

(b) there is a significant risk of harm to that person or a person of a similar description if the injunction is not granted.

(4) An injunction under this section may—

(a) in the case of an injunction under subsection (1)(a) or (b), relate to particular acts or to conduct, or types of conduct, in general or to both, and

(b) in the case of an injunction under subsection (1)(c), relate to particular premises or a particular locality;

and may be made for a specified period or until varied or discharged.

(5) An injunction under this section may be varied or discharged by the court on an application by—

(a) the respondent, or

Power to grant injunctions against anti-social behaviour.

1985 c. 68.

(b) the local authority which made the original application.

(6) The court may attach a power of arrest to one or more of the provisions of an injunction which it intends to grant under this section.

(7) The court may, in any case where it considers that it is just and convenient to do so, grant an injunction under this section, or vary such an injunction, even though the respondent has not been given such notice of the proceedings as would otherwise be required by rules of court.

If the court does so, it must afford the respondent an opportunity to make representations relating to the injunction or variation as soon as just and convenient at a hearing of which notice has been given to all the parties in accordance with rules of court.

(8) In this section "local authority" has the same meaning as in the Housing Act 1985.

153.—(1) In the circumstances set out in this section, the High Court or a county court may attach a power of arrest to one or more of the provisions of an injunction which it intends to grant in relation to a breach or anticipated breach of the terms of a tenancy.

(2) The applicant is—

(a) a local housing authority,

(b) a housing action trust,

(c) a registered social landlord, or

(d) a charitable housing trust,

acting in its capacity as landlord of the premises which are subject to the tenancy.

(3) The respondent is the tenant or a joint tenant under the tenancy agreement.

(4) The tenancy is one by virtue of which—

(a) a dwelling-house is held under an introductory, secure or assured tenancy, or

(b) accommodation is provided under Part VII of this Act or Part III of the Housing Act 1985 (homelessness).

(5) The breach or anticipated breach of the terms of the tenancy consists of the respondent—

(a) engaging in or threatening to engage in conduct causing or likely to cause a nuisance or annoyance to a person residing, visiting or otherwise engaging in a lawful activity in the locality,

(b) using or threatening to use the premises for immoral or illegal purposes, or

(c) allowing any sub-tenant or lodger of his or any other person residing (whether temporarily or otherwise) on the premises or visiting them to act as mentioned in paragraph (a) or (b).

(6) The court is of the opinion that—

(a) the respondent or any person mentioned in subsection (5)(c) has used or threatened violence against a person residing, visiting or otherwise engaging in a lawful activity in the locality, and

(b) there is a significant risk of harm to that person or a person of a similar description if the power of arrest is not attached to one or more provisions of the injunction immediately.

(7) Nothing in this section prevents the grant of an injunction relating to other matters, in addition to those mentioned above, in relation to which no power of arrest is attached.

154.—(1) In determining whether to exercise its power under section 152(6) or section 153 to attach a power of arrest to an injunction which it intends to grant on an ex-parte application, the High Court or a county court shall have regard to all the circumstances including—

> Powers of arrest: ex-parte applications for injunctions.

(a) whether it is likely that the applicant will be deterred or prevented from seeking the exercise of the power if the power is not exercised immediately, and

(b) whether there is reason to believe that the respondent is aware of the proceedings for the injunction but is deliberately evading service and that the applicant or any person of a description mentioned in 152(1)(a) or section 153(5)(a) (as the case may be) will be seriously prejudiced if the decision as to whether to exercise the power were delayed until substituted service is effected.

(2) Where the court exercises its power as mentioned in subsection (1), it shall afford the respondent an opportunity to make representations relating to the exercise of the power as soon as just and convenient at a hearing of which notice has been given to all the parties in accordance with rules of court.

155.—(1) If a power of arrest is attached to certain provisions of an injunction by virtue of section 152(6) or section 153, a constable may arrest without warrant a person whom he has reasonable cause for suspecting to be in breach of any such provision or otherwise in contempt of court in relation to a breach of any such provision.

> Arrest and remand.

A constable shall after making any such arrest forthwith inform the person on whose application the injunction was granted.

(2) Where a person is arrested under subsection (1)—

(a) he shall be brought before the relevant judge within the period of 24 hours beginning at the time of his arrest, and

(b) if the matter is not then disposed of forthwith, the judge may remand him.

In reckoning for the purposes of this subsection any period of 24 hours no account shall be taken of Christmas Day, Good Friday or any Sunday.

(3) If the court has granted an injunction in circumstances such that a power of arrest could have been attached under section 152(6) or section 153 but—

(a) has not attached a power of arrest under the section in question to any provisions of the injunction, or

(b) has attached that power only to certain provisions of the injunction,

then, if at any time the applicant considers that the respondent has failed to comply with the injunction, he may apply to the relevant judge for the issue of a warrant for the arrest of the respondent.

(4) The relevant judge shall not issue a warrant on an application under subsection (3) unless—

(a) the application is substantiated on oath, and

(b) he has reasonable grounds for believing that the respondent has failed to comply with the injunction.

(5) If a person is brought before a court by virtue of a warrant issued under subsection (4) and the court does not dispose of the matter forthwith, the court may remand him.

1980 c. 43.

(6) Schedule 15 (which makes provision corresponding to that applying in magistrates' courts in civil cases under sections 128 and 129 of the Magistrates' Courts Act 1980) applies in relation to the powers of the High Court and a county court to remand a person under this section.

(7) If a person remanded under this section is granted bail by virtue of subsection (6), he may be required by the relevant judge to comply, before release on bail or later, with such requirements as appear to the judge to be necessary to secure that he does not interfere with witnesses or otherwise obstruct the course of justice.

Remand for medical examination and report.

156.—(1) If the relevant judge has reason to consider that a medical report will be required, any power to remand a person under section 155 may be exercised for the purpose of enabling a medical examination and report to be made.

(2) If such a power is so exercised the adjournment shall not be for more than 4 weeks at a time unless the judge remands the accused in custody.

(3) If the judge so remands the accused, the adjournment shall not be for more than 3 weeks at a time.

(4) If there is reason to suspect that a person who has been arrested—

(a) under section 155(1), or

(b) under a warrant issued under section 155(4),

1983 c. 20.

is suffering from mental illness or severe mental impairment, the relevant judge shall have the same power to make an order under section 35 of the Mental Health Act 1983 (remand for report on accused's mental condition) as the Crown Court has under section 35 of that Act in the case of an accused person within the meaning of that section.

Powers of arrest: supplementary provisions.

157.—(1) If in exercise of its power under section 152(6) or section 153 the High Court or a county court attaches a power of arrest to any provisions of an injunction, it may provide that the power of arrest is to have effect for a shorter period than the other provisions of the injunction.

(2) Any period specified for the purposes of subsection (1) may be extended by the court (on one or more occasions) on an application to vary or discharge the injunction.

(3) If a power of arrest has been attached to certain provisions of an injunction by virtue of section 152(6) or section 153, the court may vary or discharge the injunction in so far as it confers a power of arrest (whether or not any application has been made to vary or discharge any other provision of the injunction).

(4) An injunction may be varied or discharged under subsection (3) on an application by the respondent or the person on whose application the injunction was made.

158.—(1) For the purposes of this Chapter—

Interpretation: Chapter III.

"charitable housing trust" means a housing trust, within the meaning of the Housing Associations Act 1985, which is a charity within the meaning of the Charities Act 1993;

1985 c. 69.
1993 c. 10.

"child" means a person under the age of 18 years;

"harm"—

　　(a) in relation to a person who has reached the age of 18 years, means ill-treatment or the impairment of health, and

　　(b) in relation to a child, means ill-treatment or the impairment of health or development;

"health" includes physical or mental health;

"ill-treatment", in relation to a child, includes sexual abuse and forms of ill-treatment which are not physical;

"relevant judge", in relation to an injunction, means—

　　(a) where the injunction was granted by the High Court, a judge of that court,

　　(b) where the injunction was granted by a county court, a judge or district judge of that or any other county court;

"tenancy" includes a licence, and "tenant" and "landlord" shall be construed accordingly.

(2) Where the question of whether harm suffered by a child is significant turns on the child's health or development, his health or development shall be compared with that which could reasonably be expected of a similar child.

PART VI

ALLOCATION OF HOUSING ACCOMMODATION

Introductory

159.—(1) A local housing authority shall comply with the provisions of this Part in allocating housing accommodation.

Allocation of housing accommodation.

(2) For the purposes of this Part a local housing authority allocate housing accommodation when they—

　(a) select a person to be a secure or introductory tenant of housing accommodation held by them,

　(b) nominate a person to be a secure or introductory tenant of housing accommodation held by another person, or

　(c) nominate a person to be an assured tenant of housing accommodation held by a registered social landlord.

(3) The reference in subsection (2)(a) to selecting a person to be a secure tenant includes deciding to exercise any power to notify an existing tenant or licensee that his tenancy or licence is to be a secure tenancy.

(4) The references in subsection (2)(b) and (c) to nominating a person include nominating a person in pursuance of any arrangements (whether legally enforceable or not) to require that housing accommodation, or a specified amount of housing accommodation, is made available to a person or one of a number of persons nominated by the authority.

(5) The provisions of this Part do not apply to the allocation of housing accommodation by a local housing authority to a person who is already—

(a) a secure or introductory tenant,

(b) an assured tenant (otherwise than under an assured shorthold tenancy) of housing accommodation held by a registered social landlord, or

(c) an assured tenant of housing accommodation allocated to him by a local housing authority.

(6) The provisions of this Part do not apply to the allocation of housing accommodation by a local housing authority to two or more persons jointly if—

(a) one or more of them is a person within subsection (5)(a), (b) or (c), and

(b) none of the others is excluded from being a qualifying person by section 161(2) or regulations under section 161(3).

(7) Subject to the provisions of this Part, a local housing authority may allocate housing accommodation in such manner as they consider appropriate.

Cases where provisions about allocation do not apply.

1985 c. 68.

160.—(1) The provisions of this Part about the allocation of housing accommodation do not apply in the following cases.

(2) They do not apply where a secure tenancy—

(a) vests under section 89 of the Housing Act 1985 (succession to periodic secure tenancy on death of tenant),

(b) remains a secure tenancy by virtue of section 90 of that Act (devolution of term certain of secure tenancy on death of tenant),

(c) is assigned under section 92 of that Act (assignment of secure tenancy by way of exchange),

(d) is assigned to a person who would be qualified to succeed the secure tenant if the secure tenant died immediately before the assignment, or

(e) vests or is otherwise disposed of in pursuance of an order made under—

1973 c. 18.

(i) section 24 of the Matrimonial Causes Act 1973 (property adjustment orders in connection with matrimonial proceedings),

1984 c. 42.

(ii) section 17(1) of the Matrimonial and Family Proceedings Act 1984 (property adjustment orders after overseas divorce, &c.), or

(iii) paragraph 1 of Schedule 1 to the Children Act 1989 (orders for financial relief against parents). 1989 c. 41.

(3) They do not apply where an introductory tenancy—

  (a) becomes a secure tenancy on ceasing to be an introductory tenancy,

  (b) vests under section 133(2) (succession to introductory tenancy on death of tenant),

  (c) is assigned to a person who would be qualified to succeed the introductory tenant if the introductory tenant died immediately before the assignment, or

  (d) vests or is otherwise disposed of in pursuance of an order made under—

    (i) section 24 of the Matrimonial Causes Act 1973 (property adjustment orders in connection with matrimonial proceedings), 1973 c. 18.

    (ii) section 17(1) of the Matrimonial and Family Proceedings Act 1984 (property adjustment orders after overseas divorce, &c.), or 1984 c. 42.

    (iii) paragraph 1 of Schedule 1 to the Children Act 1989 (orders for financial relief against parents).

(4) They do not apply in such other cases as the Secretary of State may prescribe by regulations.

(5) The regulations may be framed so as to make the exclusion of the provisions of this Part about the allocation of housing accommodation subject to such restrictions or conditions as may be specified.

In particular, those provisions may be excluded—

  (a) in relation to specified descriptions of persons, or

  (b) in relation to housing accommodation of a specified description or a specified proportion of housing accommodation of any specified description.

The housing register

161.—(1) A local housing authority shall allocate housing accommodation only to persons ("qualifying persons") who are qualified to be allocated housing accommodation by that authority. Allocation only to qualifying persons.

(2) A person subject to immigration control within the meaning of the Asylum and Immigration Act 1996 is not qualified to be allocated housing accommodation by any authority in England and Wales unless he is of a class prescribed by regulations made by the Secretary of State. 1996 c. 49.

(3) The Secretary of State may by regulations prescribe other classes of persons who are, or are not, qualifying persons in relation to local housing authorities generally or any particular local housing authority.

(4) Subject to subsection (2) and any regulations under subsection (3) a local housing authority may decide what classes of persons are, or are not, qualifying persons.

(5) The prohibition in subsection (1) extends to the allocation of housing accommodation to two or more persons jointly if any of them is excluded from being a qualifying person by subsection (2) or regulations under subsection (3).

(6) The prohibition does not otherwise extend to the allocation of housing accommodation to two or more persons jointly if one or more of them are qualifying persons.

The housing register.

162.—(1) Every local housing authority shall establish and maintain a register of qualifying persons (their "housing register").

(2) An authority's housing register may be kept in such form as the authority think fit.

(3) It may, in particular, be kept as part of a register maintained for other housing purposes or maintained in common by the authority and one or more other landlords, provided the entries constituting the authority's housing register can be distinguished.

(4) An authority's housing register shall contain such information about the persons on it and other relevant matters as the Secretary of State may prescribe by regulations.

(5) Subject to any such regulations, the authority may decide what information is to be contained in the register.

Operation of housing register.

163.—(1) A person shall be put on a local housing authority's housing register if he applies to be put on and it appears to the authority that he is a qualifying person.

(2) A local housing authority may put a person on their housing register without any application, if it appears to them that he is a qualifying person.

(3) When a local housing authority put a person on their housing register (on his application or otherwise), they shall notify him that they have done so.

(4) A local housing authority may amend an entry on their housing register in such circumstances as they think fit.

If they do so, they shall notify the person concerned of the amendment.

(5) A local housing authority may remove a person from their housing register in such circumstances as they think fit.

(6) They shall do so—

　(a) if it appears to them that he has never been a qualifying person or is no longer such a person, or

　(b) if he requests them to do so and he is not owed any duty under section 193 or 195(2) (main housing duties owed to persons who are homeless or threatened with homelessness).

(7) Before removing a person from the register, a local housing authority shall comply with such requirements, as to notification or otherwise, as the Secretary of State may prescribe by regulations.

164.—(1) If a local housing authority decide—

(a) not to put a person on their housing register who has applied to be put on, or

(b) to remove a person from their housing register otherwise than at his request,

they shall notify him of their decision and of the reasons for it.

(2) The notice shall also inform him of his right to request a review of the decision and of the time within which such a request must be made.

(3) A request for review must be made before the end of the period of 21 days beginning with the day on which he is notified of the authority's decision and reasons, or such longer period as the authority may in writing allow.

(4) There is no right to request a review of the decision reached on an earlier review.

(5) On a request being duly made to them, the authority shall review their decision.

(6) Notice required to be given to a person under this section shall be given in writing and, if not received by him, shall be treated as having been given if it is made available at the authority's office for a reasonable period for collection by him.

165.—(1) The Secretary of State may make provision by regulations as to the procedure to be followed in connection with a review under section 164.

Nothing in the following provisions affects the generality of this power.

(2) Provision may be made by regulations—

(a) requiring the decision on review to be made by a person of appropriate seniority who was not involved in the original decision, and

(b) as to the circumstances in which the person concerned is entitled to an oral hearing, and whether and by whom he may be represented at such a hearing.

(3) The authority shall notify the person concerned of the decision on the review.

(4) If the decision is to confirm the original decision, they shall also notify him of the reasons for the decision.

(5) Provision may be made by regulations as to the period within which the review must be carried out and notice given of the decision.

(6) Notice required to be given to a person under this section shall be given in writing and, if not received by him, shall be treated as having been given if it is made available at the authority's office for a reasonable period for collection by him.

166.—(1) A person on the housing register of a local housing authority is entitled—

(a) to see the entry relating to himself and to receive a copy of it free of charge, and

(b) to be given such general information as will enable him to assess how long it is likely to be before housing accommodation appropriate to his needs becomes available for allocation to him.

(2) The fact that a person is on an authority's housing register, and the information about him included in the register, shall not be divulged to any other member of the public.

The allocation scheme

Allocation in accordance with allocation scheme.

167.—(1) Every local housing authority shall have a scheme (their "allocation scheme") for determining priorities, and as to the procedure to be followed, in allocating housing accommodation.

For this purpose "procedure" includes all aspects of the allocation process, including the persons or descriptions of persons by whom decisions are to be taken.

(2) As regards priorities, the scheme shall be framed so as to secure that reasonable preference is given to—

(a) people occupying insanitary or overcrowded housing or otherwise living in unsatisfactory housing conditions,

(b) people occupying housing accommodation which is temporary or occupied on insecure terms,

(c) families with dependent children,

(d) households consisting of or including someone who is expecting a child,

(e) households consisting of or including someone with a particular need for settled accommodation on medical or welfare grounds, and

(f) households whose social or economic circumstances are such that they have difficulty in securing settled accommodation.

The scheme shall also be framed so as to secure that additional preference is given to households within paragraph (e) consisting of someone with a particular need for settled accommodation on medical or welfare grounds who cannot reasonably be expected to find settled accommodation for themselves in the foreseeable future.

(3) The Secretary of State may by regulations—

(a) specify further descriptions of people to whom preference is to be given as mentioned in subsection (2), or

(b) amend or repeal any part of subsection (2).

(4) The Secretary of State may by regulations specify factors which a local housing authority shall not take into account in allocating housing accommodation.

(5) As regards the procedure to be followed, the scheme shall be framed in accordance with such principles as the Secretary of State may prescribe by regulations.

(6) Subject to the above provisions, and to any regulations made under them, the authority may decide on what principles the scheme is to be framed.

(7) Before adopting an allocation scheme, or making an alteration to their scheme reflecting a major change of policy, a local housing authority shall—

   (a) send a copy of the draft scheme, or proposed alteration, to every registered social landlord with which they have nomination arrangements (see section 159(4)), and

   (b) afford those persons a reasonable opportunity to comment on the proposals.

(8) A local housing authority shall not allocate housing accommodation except in accordance with their allocation scheme.

168.—(1) A local housing authority shall publish a summary of their allocation scheme and provide a copy of the summary free of charge to any member of the public who asks for one.

(2) The authority shall make the scheme available for inspection at their principal office and shall provide a copy of the scheme, on payment of a reasonable fee, to any member of the public who asks for one.

(3) When the authority make an alteration to their scheme reflecting a major change of policy, they shall within a reasonable period of time notify everyone on their housing register, explaining in general terms the effect of the change.

Information about allocation scheme.

Supplementary

169.—(1) In the exercise of their functions under this Part, local housing authorities shall have regard to such guidance as may from time to time be given by the Secretary of State.

(2) The Secretary of State may give guidance generally or to specified descriptions of authorities.

Guidance to authorities by the Secretary of State.

170. Where a local housing authority so request, a registered social landlord shall co-operate to such extent as is reasonable in the circumstances in offering accommodation to people with priority on the authority's housing register.

Co-operation between registered social landlords and local housing authorities.

171.—(1) A person commits an offence if, in connection with the exercise by a local housing authority of their functions under this Part—

   (a) he knowingly or recklessly makes a statement which is false in a material particular, or

   (b) he knowingly withholds information which the authority have reasonably required him to give in connection with the exercise of those functions.

(2) A person guilty of an offence under this section is liable on summary conviction to a fine not exceeding level 5 on the standard scale.

False statements and withholding information.

172.—(1) Regulations under this Part shall be made by statutory instrument.

(2) No regulations shall be made under section 167(3) (regulations amending provisions about priorities in allocating housing accommodation) unless a draft of the regulations has been laid before and approved by a resolution of each House of Parliament.

Regulations.

PART VI

(3) Any other regulations under this Part shall be subject to annulment in pursuance of a resolution of either House of Parliament.

(4) Regulations under this Part may contain such incidental, supplementary and transitional provisions as appear to the Secretary of State appropriate, and may make different provision for different cases including different provision for different areas.

Consequential amendments: Part VI.

173. The enactments mentioned in Schedule 16 have effect with the amendments specified there which are consequential on the provisions of this Part.

Index of defined expressions: Part VI.

174. The following Table shows provisions defining or otherwise explaining expressions used in this Part (other than provisions defining or explaining an expression used in the same section)—

allocation (of housing)	section 159(2)
allocation scheme	section 167
assured tenancy	section 230
housing register	section 162
introductory tenancy and introductory tenant	sections 230 and 124
local housing authority	section 230
qualifying person (in relation to housing register)	section 161
registered social landlord	sections 230 and 2
secure tenancy and secure tenant	section 230

PART VII

HOMELESSNESS

Homelessness and threatened homelessness

Homelessness and threatened homelessness.

175.—(1) A person is homeless if he has no accommodation available for his occupation, in the United Kingdom or elsewhere, which he—

(a) is entitled to occupy by virtue of an interest in it or by virtue of an order of a court,

(b) has an express or implied licence to occupy, or

(c) occupies as a residence by virtue of any enactment or rule of law giving him the right to remain in occupation or restricting the right of another person to recover possession.

(2) A person is also homeless if he has accommodation but—

(a) he cannot secure entry to it, or

(b) it consists of a moveable structure, vehicle or vessel designed or adapted for human habitation and there is no place where he is entitled or permitted both to place it and to reside in it.

(3) A person shall not be treated as having accommodation unless it is accommodation which it would be reasonable for him to continue to occupy.

(4) A person is threatened with homelessness if it is likely that he will become homeless within 28 days.

Meaning of accommodation available for occupation.

176. Accommodation shall be regarded as available for a person's occupation only if it is available for occupation by him together with—

(a) any other person who normally resides with him as a member of his family, or

(b) any other person who might reasonably be expected to reside with him.

References in this Part to securing that accommodation is available for a person's occupation shall be construed accordingly.

177.—(1) It is not reasonable for a person to continue to occupy accommodation if it is probable that this will lead to domestic violence against him, or against—

(a) a person who normally resides with him as a member of his family, or

(b) any other person who might reasonably be expected to reside with him.

For this purpose "domestic violence", in relation to a person, means violence from a person with whom he is associated, or threats of violence from such a person which are likely to be carried out.

(2) In determining whether it would be, or would have been, reasonable for a person to continue to occupy accommodation, regard may be had to the general circumstances prevailing in relation to housing in the district of the local housing authority to whom he has applied for accommodation or for assistance in obtaining accommodation.

(3) The Secretary of State may by order specify—

(a) other circumstances in which it is to be regarded as reasonable or not reasonable for a person to continue to occupy accommodation, and

(b) other matters to be taken into account or disregarded in determining whether it would be, or would have been, reasonable for a person to continue to occupy accommodation.

Whether it is reasonable to continue to occupy accommodation.

178.—(1) For the purposes of this Part, a person is associated with another person if—

(a) they are or have been married to each other;

(b) they are cohabitants or former cohabitants;

(c) they live or have lived in the same household;

(d) they are relatives;

(e) they have agreed to marry one another (whether or not that agreement has been terminated);

(f) in relation to a child, each of them is a parent of the child or has, or has had, parental responsibility for the child.

Meaning of associated person.

(2) If a child has been adopted or has been freed for adoption by virtue of any of the enactments mentioned in section 16(1) of the Adoption Act 1976, two persons are also associated with each other for the purposes of this Part if—

1976 c. 36.

(a) one is a natural parent of the child or a parent of such a natural parent, and

(b) the other is the child or a person—

(i) who has become a parent of the child by virtue of an adoption order or who has applied for an adoption order, or

(ii) with whom the child has at any time been placed for adoption.

(3) In this section—

"adoption order" has the meaning given by section 72(1) of the Adoption Act 1976;

"child" means a person under the age of 18 years;

"cohabitants" means a man and a woman who, although not married to each other, are living together as husband and wife, and "former cohabitants" shall be construed accordingly;

"parental responsibility" has the same meaning as in the Children Act 1989; and

1989 c. 41.

"relative" , in relation to a person, means—

(a) the father, mother, stepfather, stepmother, son, daughter, stepson, stepdaughter, grandmother, grandfather, grandson or granddaughter of that person or of that person's spouse or former spouse, or

(b) the brother, sister, uncle, aunt, niece or nephew (whether of the full blood or of the half blood or by affinity) of that person or of that person's spouse or former spouse,

and includes, in relation to a person who is living or has lived with another person as husband and wife, a person who would fall within paragraph (a) or (b) if the parties were married to each other.

General functions in relation to homelessness or threatened homelessness

Duty of local housing authority to provide advisory services.

179.—(1) Every local housing authority shall secure that advice and information about homelessness, and the prevention of homelessness, is available free of charge to any person in their district.

(2) The authority may give to any person by whom such advice and information is provided on behalf of the authority assistance by way of grant or loan.

(3) A local housing authority may also assist any such person—

(a) by permitting him to use premises belonging to the authority,

(b) by making available furniture or other goods, whether by way of gift, loan or otherwise, and

(c) by making available the services of staff employed by the authority.

Assistance for voluntary organisations.

180.—(1) The Secretary of State or a local housing authority may give assistance by way of grant or loan to voluntary organisations concerned with homelessness or matters relating to homelessness.

(2) A local housing authority may also assist any such organisation—

(a) by permitting them to use premises belonging to the authority,

(b) by making available furniture or other goods, whether by way of gift, loan or otherwise, and

   (c) by making available the services of staff employed by the authority.

   (3) A "voluntary organisation" means a body (other than a public or local authority) whose activities are not carried on for profit.

181.—(1) This section has effect as to the terms and conditions on which assistance is given under section 179 or 180.

   (2) Assistance shall be on such terms, and subject to such conditions, as the person giving the assistance may determine.

   (3) No assistance shall be given unless the person to whom it is given undertakes—

     (a) to use the money, furniture or other goods or premises for a specified purpose, and

     (b) to provide such information as may reasonably be required as to the manner in which the assistance is being used.

The person giving the assistance may require such information by notice in writing, which shall be complied with within 21 days beginning with the date on which the notice is served.

   (4) The conditions subject to which assistance is given shall in all cases include conditions requiring the person to whom the assistance is given—

     (a) to keep proper books of account and have them audited in such manner as may be specified,

     (b) to keep records indicating how he has used the money, furniture or other goods or premises, and

     (c) to submit the books of account and records for inspection by the person giving the assistance.

   (5) If it appears to the person giving the assistance that the person to whom it was given has failed to carry out his undertaking as to the purpose for which the assistance was to be used, he shall take all reasonable steps to recover from that person an amount equal to the amount of the assistance.

   (6) He must first serve on the person to whom the assistance was given a notice specifying the amount which in his opinion is recoverable and the basis on which that amount has been calculated.

Terms and conditions of assistance.

182.—(1) In the exercise of their functions relating to homelessness and the prevention of homelessness, a local housing authority or social services authority shall have regard to such guidance as may from time to time be given by the Secretary of State.

   (2) The Secretary of State may give guidance either generally or to specified descriptions of authorities.

Guidance by the Secretary of State.

Application for assistance in case of homelessness or threatened homelessness

183.—(1) The following provisions of this Part apply where a person applies to a local housing authority for accommodation, or for assistance in obtaining accommodation, and the authority have reason to believe that he is or may be homeless or threatened with homelessness.

   (2) In this Part—

Application for assistance.

"applicant" means a person making such an application,

"assistance under this Part" means the benefit of any function under the following provisions of this Part relating to accommodation or assistance in obtaining accommodation, and

"eligible for assistance" means not excluded from such assistance by section 185 (persons from abroad not eligible for housing assistance) or section 186 (asylum seekers and their dependants).

(3) Nothing in this section or the following provisions of this Part affects a person's entitlement to advice and information under section 179 (duty to provide advisory services).

Inquiry into cases of homelessness or threatened homelessness.

184.—(1) If the local housing authority have reason to believe that an applicant may be homeless or threatened with homelessness, they shall make such inquiries as are necessary to satisfy themselves—

(a) whether he is eligible for assistance, and

(b) if so, whether any duty, and if so what duty, is owed to him under the following provisions of this Part.

(2) They may also make inquiries whether he has a local connection with the district of another local housing authority in England, Wales or Scotland.

(3) On completing their inquiries the authority shall notify the applicant of their decision and, so far as any issue is decided against his interests, inform him of the reasons for their decision.

(4) If the authority have notified or intend to notify another local housing authority under section 198 (referral of cases), they shall at the same time notify the applicant of that decision and inform him of the reasons for it.

(5) A notice under subsection (3) or (4) shall also inform the applicant of his right to request a review of the decision and of the time within which such a request must be made (see section 202).

(6) Notice required to be given to a person under this section shall be given in writing and, if not received by him, shall be treated as having been given to him if it is made available at the authority's office for a reasonable period for collection by him or on his behalf.

Eligibility for assistance

Persons from abroad not eligible for housing assistance.

1996 c. 49.

185.—(1) A person is not eligible for assistance under this Part if he is a person from abroad who is ineligible for housing assistance.

(2) A person who is subject to immigration control within the meaning of the Asylum and Immigration Act 1996 is not eligible for housing assistance unless he is of a class prescribed by regulations made by the Secretary of State.

(3) The Secretary of State may make provision by regulations as to other descriptions of persons who are to be treated for the purposes of this Part as persons from abroad who are ineligible for housing assistance.

(4) A person from abroad who is not eligible for housing assistance shall be disregarded in determining for the purposes of this Part whether another person—

   (a) is homeless or threatened with homelessness, or

   (b) has a priority need for accommodation.

186.—(1) An asylum-seeker, or a dependant of an asylum-seeker who is not by virtue of section 185 a person from abroad who is ineligible for housing assistance, is not eligible for assistance under this Part if he has any accommodation in the United Kingdom, however temporary, available for his occupation.

(2) For the purposes of this section a person who makes a claim for asylum—

   (a) becomes an asylum-seeker at the time when his claim is recorded by the Secretary of State as having been made, and

   (b) ceases to be an asylum-seeker at the time when his claim is recorded by the Secretary of State as having been finally determined or abandoned.

(3) For the purposes of this section a person—

   (a) becomes a dependant of an asylum-seeker at the time when he is recorded by the Secretary of State as being a dependant of the asylum-seeker, and

   (b) ceases to be a dependant of an asylum-seeker at the time when the person whose dependant he is ceases to be an asylum-seeker or, if it is earlier, at the time when he is recorded by the Secretary of State as ceasing to be a dependant of the asylum-seeker.

(4) In relation to an asylum-seeker, "dependant" means a person—

   (a) who is his spouse or a child of his under the age of eighteen, and

   (b) who has neither a right of abode in the United Kingdom nor indefinite leave under the Immigration Act 1971 to enter or remain in the United Kingdom.

(5) In this section a "claim for asylum" means a claim made by a person that it would be contrary to the United Kingdom's obligations under the Convention relating to the Status of Refugees done at Geneva on 28th July 1951 and the Protocol to that Convention for him to be removed from, or required to leave, the United Kingdom.

187.—(1) The Secretary of State shall, at the request of a local housing authority, provide the authority with such information as they may require—

   (a) as to whether a person is or has become an asylum-seeker, or a dependant of an asylum-seeker, and

   (b) to enable them to determine whether such a person is eligible for assistance under this Part under section 185 (persons from abroad not eligible for housing assistance).

(2) Where that information is given otherwise than in writing, the Secretary of State shall confirm it in writing if a written request is made to him by the authority.

(3) If it appears to the Secretary of State that any application, decision or other change of circumstances has affected the status of a person about whom information was previously provided by him to a local housing

Marginal notes:

Asylum-seekers and their dependants.

1971 c. 77.

Provision of information by Secretary of State.

authority under this section, he shall inform the authority in writing of that fact, the reason for it and the date on which the previous information became inaccurate.

Interim duty to accommodate

Interim duty to accommodate in case of apparent priority need.

188.—(1) If the local housing authority have reason to believe that an applicant may be homeless, eligible for assistance and have a priority need, they shall secure that accommodation is available for his occupation pending a decision as to the duty (if any) owed to him under the following provisions of this Part.

(2) The duty under this section arises irrespective of any possibility of the referral of the applicant's case to another local housing authority (see sections 198 to 200).

(3) The duty ceases when the authority's decision is notified to the applicant, even if the applicant requests a review of the decision (see section 202).

The authority may continue to secure that accommodation is available for the applicant's occupation pending a decision on a review.

Priority need for accommodation.

189.—(1) The following have a priority need for accommodation—

(a) a pregnant woman or a person with whom she resides or might reasonably be expected to reside;

(b) a person with whom dependent children reside or might reasonably be expected to reside;

(c) a person who is vulnerable as a result of old age, mental illness or handicap or physical disability or other special reason, or with whom such a person resides or might reasonably be expected to reside;

(d) a person who is homeless or threatened with homelessness as a result of an emergency such as flood, fire or other disaster.

(2) The Secretary of State may by order—

(a) specify further descriptions of persons as having a priority need for accommodation, and

(b) amend or repeal any part of subsection (1).

(3) Before making such an order the Secretary of State shall consult such associations representing relevant authorities, and such other persons, as he considers appropriate.

(4) No such order shall be made unless a draft of it has been approved by resolution of each House of Parliament.

Duties to persons found to be homeless or threatened with homelessness

Duties to persons becoming homeless intentionally.

190.—(1) This section applies where the local housing authority are satisfied that an applicant is homeless and is eligible for assistance but are also satisfied that he became homeless intentionally.

(2) If the authority are satisfied that the applicant has a priority need, they shall—

   (a) secure that accommodation is available for his occupation for such period as they consider will give him a reasonable opportunity of securing accommodation for his occupation, and

   (b) provide him with advice and such assistance as they consider appropriate in the circumstances in any attempts he may make to secure that accommodation becomes available for his occupation.

(3) If they are not satisfied that he has a priority need, they shall provide him with advice and such assistance as they consider appropriate in the circumstances in any attempts he may make to secure that accommodation becomes available for his occupation.

191.—(1) A person becomes homeless intentionally if he deliberately does or fails to do anything in consequence of which he ceases to occupy accommodation which is available for his occupation and which it would have been reasonable for him to continue to occupy.

Becoming homeless intentionally.

(2) For the purposes of subsection (1) an act or omission in good faith on the part of a person who was unaware of any relevant fact shall not be treated as deliberate.

(3) A person shall be treated as becoming homeless intentionally if—

   (a) he enters into an arrangement under which he is required to cease to occupy accommodation which it would have been reasonable for him to continue to occupy, and

   (b) the purpose of the arrangement is to enable him to become entitled to assistance under this Part,

and there is no other good reason why he is homeless.

(4) A person who is given advice or assistance under section 197 (duty where other suitable alternative accommodation available), but fails to secure suitable accommodation in circumstances in which it was reasonably to be expected that he would do so, shall, if he makes a further application under this Part, be treated as having become homeless intentionally.

192.—(1) This section applies where the local housing authority—

   (a) are satisfied that an applicant is homeless and eligible for assistance, and

   (b) are not satisfied that he became homeless intentionally,

but are not satisfied that he has a priority need.

Duty to persons not in priority need who are not homeless intentionally.

(2) The authority shall provide the applicant with advice and such assistance as they consider appropriate in the circumstances in any attempts he may make to secure that accommodation becomes available for his occupation.

193.—(1) This section applies where the local housing authority are satisfied that an applicant is homeless, eligible for assistance and has a priority need, and are not satisfied that he became homeless intentionally.

Duty to persons with priority need who are not homeless intentionally.

This section has effect subject to section 197 (duty where other suitable accommodation available).

(2) Unless the authority refer the application to another local housing authority (see section 198), they shall secure that accommodation is available for occupation by the applicant.

(3) The authority are subject to the duty under this section for a period of two years ("the minimum period"), subject to the following provisions of this section.

After the end of that period the authority may continue to secure that accommodation is available for occupation by the applicant, but are not obliged to do so (see section 194).

(4) The minimum period begins with—

(a) if the applicant was occupying accommodation made available under section 188 (interim duty to accommodate), the day on which he was notified of the authority's decision that the duty under this section was owed to him;

(b) if the applicant was occupying accommodation made available to him under section 200(3) (interim duty where case considered for referral but not referred), the date on which he was notified under subsection (2) of that section of the decision that the conditions for referral were not met;

(c) in any other case, the day on which accommodation was first made available to him in pursuance of the duty under this section.

(5) The local housing authority shall cease to be subject to the duty under this section if the applicant, having been informed by the authority of the possible consequence of refusal, refuses an offer of accommodation which the authority are satisfied is suitable for him and the authority notify him that they regard themselves as having discharged their duty under this section.

(6) The local housing authority shall cease to be subject to the duty under this section if the applicant—

(a) ceases to be eligible for assistance,

(b) becomes homeless intentionally from the accommodation made available for his occupation,

(c) accepts an offer of accommodation under Part VI (allocation of housing), or

(d) otherwise voluntarily ceases to occupy as his only or principal home the accommodation made available for his occupation.

(7) The local housing authority shall also cease to be subject to the duty under this section if—

(a) the applicant, having been informed of the possible consequence of refusal, refuses an offer of accommodation under Part VI, and

(b) the authority are satisfied that the accommodation was suitable for him and that it was reasonable for him to accept it and notify him accordingly within 21 days of the refusal.

(8) For the purposes of subsection (7) an applicant may reasonably be expected to accept an offer of accommodation under Part VI even though

he is under contractual or other obligations in respect of his existing accommodation, provided he is able to bring those obligations to an end before he is required to take up the offer.

(9) A person who ceases to be owed the duty under this section may make a fresh application to the authority for accommodation or assistance in obtaining accommodation.

194.—(1) Where a local housing authority have been subject to the duty under section 193 in relation to a person until the end of the minimum period, they may continue to secure that accommodation is available for his occupation.

(2) They shall not do so unless they are satisfied on a review under this section that—

  (a) he has a priority need,

  (b) there is no other suitable accommodation available for occupation by him in their district, and

  (c) he wishes the authority to continue securing that accommodation is available for his occupation;

and they shall not continue to do so for more than two years at a time unless they are satisfied on a further review under this section as to those matters.

The review shall be carried out towards the end of the minimum period, or subsequent two year period, with a view to enabling the authority to make an assessment of the likely situation at the end of that period.

(3) They shall cease to do so if events occur such that, by virtue of section 193(6) or (7), they would cease to be subject to any duty under that section.

(4) Where an authority carry out a review under this section they shall make such inquiries as they consider appropriate to determine—

  (a) whether they are satisfied as to the matters mentioned in subsection (2)(a) to (c), and

  (b) whether any of the events referred to in subsection (3) has occurred;

and on completing the review they shall notify the applicant of their determination and of whether they propose to exercise, or continue to exercise, their power under this section.

(5) The authority may at any time, whether in consequence of a review or otherwise, give notice to the person concerned that they propose to cease exercising their power under this section in his case.

(6) The notice must specify—

  (a) the day on which they will cease exercising their power under this section, and

  (b) any action that they intend to take as a result,

and must be given not less than the prescribed period before the day so specified.

195.—(1) This section applies where the local housing authority are satisfied that an applicant is threatened with homelessness and is eligible for assistance.

Power exercisable after minimum period of duty under s. 193.

Duties in case of threatened homelessness.

(2) If the authority—

  (a) are satisfied that he has a priority need, and

  (b) are not satisfied that he became threatened with homelessness intentionally,

they shall take reasonable steps to secure that accommodation does not cease to be available for his occupation.

This subsection has effect subject to section 197 (duty where other suitable accommodation available).

(3) Subsection (2) does not affect any right of the authority, whether by virtue of a contract, enactment or rule of law, to secure vacant possession of any accommodation.

(4) Where in pursuance of the duty under subsection (2) the authority secure that accommodation other than that occupied by the applicant when he made his application is available for occupation by him, the provisions of section 193(3) to (9) (period for which duty owed) and section 194 (power exercisable after minimum period of duty) apply, with any necessary modifications, in relation to the duty under this section as they apply in relation to the duty under section 193.

(5) If the authority—

  (a) are not satisfied that the applicant has a priority need, or

  (b) are satisfied that he has a priority need but are also satisfied that he became threatened with homelessness intentionally,

they shall furnish him with advice and such assistance as they consider appropriate in the circumstances in any attempts he may make to secure that accommodation does not cease to be available for his occupation.

Becoming threatened with homelessness intentionally.

196.—(1) A person becomes threatened with homelessness intentionally if he deliberately does or fails to do anything the likely result of which is that he will be forced to leave accommodation which is available for his occupation and which it would have been reasonable for him to continue to occupy.

(2) For the purposes of subsection (1) an act or omission in good faith on the part of a person who was unaware of any relevant fact shall not be treated as deliberate.

(3) A person shall be treated as becoming threatened with homelessness intentionally if—

  (a) he enters into an arrangement under which he is required to cease to occupy accommodation which it would have been reasonable for him to continue to occupy, and

  (b) the purpose of the arrangement is to enable him to become entitled to assistance under this Part,

and there is no other good reason why he is threatened with homelessness.

(4) A person who is given advice or assistance under section 197 (duty where other suitable alternative accommodation available), but fails to secure suitable accommodation in circumstances in which it was reasonably to be expected that he would do so, shall, if he makes a further application under this Part, be treated as having become threatened with homelessness intentionally.

Duty where other suitable accommodation available

197.—(1) This section applies if the local housing authority would be under a duty under this Part—

    (a) to secure that accommodation is available for occupation by an applicant, or

    (b) to secure that accommodation does not cease to be available for his occupation,

but are satisfied that other suitable accommodation is available for occupation by him in their district.

(2) In that case, their duty is to provide the applicant with such advice and assistance as the authority consider is reasonably required to enable him to secure such accommodation.

(3) The duty ceases if the applicant fails to take reasonable steps to secure such accommodation.

(4) In deciding what advice and assistance to provide under this section, and whether the applicant has taken reasonable steps, the authority shall have regard to all the circumstances including—

    (a) the characteristics and personal circumstances of the applicant, and

    (b) the state of the local housing market and the type of accommodation available.

(5) For the purposes of this section accommodation shall not be regarded as available for occupation by the applicant if it is available only with assistance beyond what the authority consider is reasonable in the circumstances.

(6) Subsection (1) does not apply to the duty of a local housing authority under—

    section 188 (interim duty to accommodate in case of apparent priority need),

    section 190(2)(a) (limited duty to person becoming homeless intentionally), or

    section 200(1), (3) or (4) (interim duties where case is considered for referral or referred).

Duty where other suitable accommodation available.

Referral to another local housing authority

198.—(1) If the local housing authority would be subject to the duty under section 193 (accommodation for those with priority need who are not homeless intentionally) but consider that the conditions are met for referral of the case to another local housing authority, they may notify that other authority of their opinion.

The authority need not consider under section 197 whether other suitable accommodation is available before proceeding under this section.

(2) The conditions for referral of the case to another authority are met if—

    (a) neither the applicant nor any person who might reasonably be expected to reside with him has a local connection with the district of the authority to whom his application was made,

Referral of case to another local housing authority.

(b) the applicant or a person who might reasonably be expected to reside with him has a local connection with the district of that other authority, and

(c) neither the applicant nor any person who might reasonably be expected to reside with him will run the risk of domestic violence in that other district.

(3) For this purpose a person runs the risk of domestic violence—

(a) if he runs the risk of violence from a person with whom he is associated, or

(b) if he runs the risk of threats of violence from such a person which are likely to be carried out.

(4) The conditions for referral of the case to another authority are also met if—

(a) the applicant was on a previous application made to that other authority placed (in pursuance of their functions under this Part) in accommodation in the district of the authority to whom his application is now made, and

(b) the previous application was within such period as may be prescribed of the present application.

(5) The question whether the conditions for referral of a case are satisfied shall be decided by agreement between the notifying authority and the notified authority or, in default of agreement, in accordance with such arrangements as the Secretary of State may direct by order.

(6) An order may direct that the arrangements shall be—

(a) those agreed by any relevant authorities or associations of relevant authorities, or

(b) in default of such agreement, such arrangements as appear to the Secretary of State to be suitable, after consultation with such associations representing relevant authorities, and such other persons, as he thinks appropriate.

(7) No such order shall be made unless a draft of the order has been approved by a resolution of each House of Parliament.

Local connection.   **199.**—(1) A person has a local connection with the district of a local housing authority if he has a connection with it—

(a) because he is, or in the past was, normally resident there, and that residence is or was of his own choice,

(b) because he is employed there,

(c) because of family associations, or

(d) because of special circumstances.

(2) A person is not employed in a district if he is serving in the regular armed forces of the Crown.

(3) Residence in a district is not of a person's own choice if—

(a) he becomes resident there because he, or a person who might reasonably be expected to reside with him, is serving in the regular armed forces of the Crown, or

(b) he, or a person who might reasonably be expected to reside with him, becomes resident there because he is detained under the authority of an Act of Parliament.

(4) In subsections (2) and (3) "regular armed forces of the Crown" means the Royal Navy, the regular forces as defined by section 225 of the Army Act 1955, the regular air force as defined by section 223 of the Air Force Act 1955 and Queen Alexandra's Royal Naval Nursing Service.

1955 c. 18.
1955 c. 19.

(5) The Secretary of State may by order specify other circumstances in which—

(a) a person is not to be treated as employed in a district, or

(b) residence in a district is not to be treated as of a person's own choice.

200.—(1) Where a local housing authority notify an applicant that they intend to notify or have notified another local housing authority of their opinion that the conditions are met for the referral of his case to that other authority—

Duties to applicant whose case is considered for referral or referred.

(a) they cease to be subject to any duty under section 188 (interim duty to accommodate in case of apparent priority need), and

(b) they are not subject to any duty under section 193 (the main housing duty),

but they shall secure that accommodation is available for occupation by the applicant until he is notified of the decision whether the conditions for referral of his case are met.

(2) When it has been decided whether the conditions for referral are met, the notifying authority shall notify the applicant of the decision and inform him of the reasons for it.

The notice shall also inform the applicant of his right to request a review of the decision and of the time within which such a request must be made.

(3) If it is decided that the conditions for referral are not met, the notifying authority shall secure that accommodation is available for occupation by the applicant until they have considered whether other suitable accommodation is available for his occupation in their district.

If they are satisfied that other suitable accommodation is available for his occupation in their district, section 197(2) applies; and if they are not so satisfied, they are subject to the duty under section 193 (the main housing duty).

(4) If it is decided that the conditions for referral are met, the notified authority shall secure that accommodation is available for occupation by the applicant until they have considered whether other suitable accommodation is available for his occupation in their district.

If they are satisfied that other suitable accommodation is available for his occupation in their district, section 197(2) applies; and if they are not so satisfied, they are subject to the duty under section 193 (the main housing duty).

(5) The duty under subsection (1), (3) or (4) ceases as provided in that subsection even if the applicant requests a review of the authority's decision (see section 202).

The authority may continue to secure that accommodation is available for the applicant's occupation pending the decision on a review.

(6) Notice required to be given to an applicant under this section shall be given in writing and, if not received by him, shall be treated as having been given to him if it is made available at the authority's office for a reasonable period for collection by him or on his behalf.

Application of referral provisions to cases arising in Scotland.

1987 c. 26.

201. Sections 198 and 200 (referral of application to another local housing authority and duties to applicant whose case is considered for referral or referred) apply—

(a) to applications referred by a local authority in Scotland in pursuance of sections 33 and 34 of the Housing (Scotland) Act 1987, and

(b) to persons whose applications are so transferred,

as they apply to cases arising under this Part (the reference in section 198 to this Part being construed as a reference to Part II of that Act).

Right to request review of decision

Right to request review of decision.

202.—(1) An applicant has the right to request a review of—

(a) any decision of a local housing authority as to his eligibility for assistance,

(b) any decision of a local housing authority as to what duty (if any) is owed to him under sections 190 to 193 and 195 to 197 (duties to persons found to be homeless or threatened with homelessness),

(c) any decision of a local housing authority to notify another authority under section 198(1) (referral of cases),

(d) any decision under section 198(5) whether the conditions are met for the referral of his case,

(e) any decision under section 200(3) or (4) (decision as to duty owed to applicant whose case is considered for referral or referred), or

(f) any decision of a local housing authority as to the suitability of accommodation offered to him in discharge of their duty under any of the provisions mentioned in paragraph (b) or (e).

(2) There is no right to request a review of the decision reached on an earlier review.

(3) A request for review must be made before the end of the period of 21 days beginning with the day on which he is notified of the authority's decision or such longer period as the authority may in writing allow.

(4) On a request being duly made to them, the authority or authorities concerned shall review their decision.

Procedure on a review.

203.—(1) The Secretary of State may make provision by regulations as to the procedure to be followed in connection with a review under section 202.

Nothing in the following provisions affects the generality of this power.

(2) Provision may be made by regulations—

  (a) requiring the decision on review to be made by a person of appropriate seniority who was not involved in the original decision, and

  (b) as to the circumstances in which the applicant is entitled to an oral hearing, and whether and by whom he may be represented at such a hearing.

(3) The authority, or as the case may be either of the authorities, concerned shall notify the applicant of the decision on the review.

(4) If the decision is—

  (a) to confirm the original decision on any issue against the interests of the applicant, or

  (b) to confirm a previous decision—

        (i) to notify another authority under section 198 (referral of cases), or

        (ii) that the conditions are met for the referral of his case,

they shall also notify him of the reasons for the decision.

(5) In any case they shall inform the applicant of his right to appeal to a county court on a point of law, and of the period within which such an appeal must be made (see section 204).

(6) Notice of the decision shall not be treated as given unless and until subsection (5), and where applicable subsection (4), is complied with.

(7) Provision may be made by regulations as to the period within which the review must be carried out and notice given of the decision.

(8) Notice required to be given to a person under this section shall be given in writing and, if not received by him, shall be treated as having been given if it is made available at the authority's office for a reasonable period for collection by him or on his behalf.

204.—(1) If an applicant who has requested a review under section 202— Right of appeal to county court on point of law.

  (a) is dissatisfied with the decision on the review, or

  (b) is not notified of the decision on the review within the time prescribed under section 203,

he may appeal to the county court on any point of law arising from the decision or, as the case may be, the original decision.

(2) An appeal must be brought within 21 days of his being notified of the decision or, as the case may be, of the date on which he should have been notified of a decision on review.

(3) On appeal the court may make such order confirming, quashing or varying the decision as it thinks fit.

(4) Where the authority were under a duty under section 188, 190 or 200 to secure that accommodation is available for the applicant's occupation, they may continue to secure that accommodation is so available—

  (a) during the period for appealing under this section against the authority's decision, and

  (b) if an appeal is brought, until the appeal (and any further appeal) is finally determined.

Supplementary provisions

Discharge of
functions:
introductory.

205.—(1) The following sections have effect in relation to the discharge by a local housing authority of their functions under this Part to secure that accommodation is available for the occupation of a person—

section 206 (general provisions),

section 207 (provision of accommodation by authority),

section 208 (out-of-area placements),

section 209 (arrangements with private landlord).

(2) In those sections those functions are referred to as the authority's "housing functions under this Part".

Discharge of
functions by local
housing
authorities.

206.—(1) A local housing authority may discharge their housing functions under this Part only in the following ways—

(a) by securing that suitable accommodation provided by them is available,

(b) by securing that he obtains suitable accommodation from some other person, or

(c) by giving him such advice and assistance as will secure that suitable accommodation is available from some other person.

(2) A local housing authority may require a person in relation to whom they are discharging such functions—

(a) to pay such reasonable charges as they may determine in respect of accommodation which they secure for his occupation (either by making it available themselves or otherwise), or

(b) to pay such reasonable amount as they may determine in respect of sums payable by them for accommodation made available by another person.

Discharge of
functions:
provision of
accommodation
by the authority.
1985 c. 68.

207.—(1) A local housing authority shall not under section 206(1)(a) discharge their housing functions under this Part by providing accommodation other than—

(a) accommodation in a hostel within the meaning of section 622 of the Housing Act 1985, or

(b) accommodation leased to the authority as mentioned in subsection (2) below,

for more than two years (continuously or in aggregate) in any period of three years.

This applies irrespective of the number of applications for accommodation or assistance in obtaining accommodation made by the person concerned.

(2) The accommodation referred to in subsection (1)(b) is accommodation—

(a) leased to the authority with vacant possession for use as temporary housing accommodation on terms which include provision for the lessor to obtain vacant possession from the authority on the expiry of a specified period or when required by the lessor,

(b) the lessor of which is not an authority or body within section 80(1) of the Housing Act 1985 (the landlord condition for secure tenancies), and

(c) in which the authority have no interest other than under the lease in question or as a mortgagee.

(3) The authority shall not discharge such functions in relation to a person who—

(a) normally resides with another person as a member of his family, or

(b) might reasonably be expected to reside with another person,

in such a way that subsection (1) would be contravened if the functions were discharged in relation to that other person.

(4) The Secretary of State may, on the application of a local housing authority, by direction exclude or modify the operation of subsection (1) in relation to that authority if it appears to him that the authority will not otherwise be able reasonably to discharge their housing functions under this Part.

(5) Any such direction shall have effect only—

(a) with respect to applicants of a description specified in the direction, and

(b) for a period specified in the direction, which shall not exceed one year,

and may be expressed to have effect subject to any conditions specified in the direction.

(6) Where the Secretary of State gives or has given a direction under subsection (4), he may give the authority such directions as he considers appropriate as to the discharge of their housing functions under this Part in cases affected by the direction having or ceasing to have effect.

208.—(1) So far as reasonably practicable a local housing authority shall in discharging their housing functions under this Part secure that accommodation is available for the occupation of the applicant in their district. *Discharge of functions: out-of-area placements.*

(2) If they secure that accommodation is available for the occupation of the applicant outside their district, they shall give notice to the local housing authority in whose district the accommodation is situated.

(3) The notice shall state—

(a) the name of the applicant,

(b) the number and description of other persons who normally reside with him as a member of his family or might reasonably be expected to reside with him,

(c) the address of the accommodation,

(d) the date on which the accommodation was made available to him, and

(e) which function under this Part the authority was discharging in securing that the accommodation is available for his occupation.

(4) The notice must be in writing, and must be given before the end of the period of 14 days beginning with the day on which the accommodation was made available to the applicant.

Discharge of functions: arrangements with private landlord.

209.—(1) This section applies where in pursuance of any of their housing functions under this Part a local housing authority make arrangements with a private landlord to provide accommodation.

1985 c. 68.

For this purpose a "private landlord" means a landlord who is not within section 80(1) of the Housing Act 1985 (the landlord condition for secure tenancies).

(2) If the housing function arises under section 188, 190, 200, or 204(4) (interim duties), a tenancy granted in pursuance of the arrangements to a person specified by the authority cannot be an assured tenancy before the end of the period of twelve months beginning with—

(a) the date on which the applicant was notified of the authority's decision under section 184(3) or 198(5), or

(b) if there is a review of that decision under section 202 or an appeal to the court under section 204, the date on which he is notified of the decision on review or the appeal is finally determined,

unless, before or during that period, the tenant is notified by the landlord (or, in the cases of joint landlords, at least one of them) that the tenancy is to be regarded as an assured shorthold tenancy or an assured tenancy other than an assured shorthold tenancy.

A registered social landlord cannot serve such a notice making such a tenancy an assured tenancy other than an assured shorthold tenancy.

(3) Where in any other case a tenancy is granted in pursuance of the arrangements by a registered social landlord to a person specified by the authority—

(a) the tenancy cannot be an assured tenancy unless it is an assured shorthold tenancy, and

(b) the landlord cannot convert the tenancy to an assured tenancy unless the accommodation is allocated to the tenant under Part VI.

Suitability of accommodation.

210.—(1) In determining for the purposes of this Part whether accommodation is suitable for a person, the local housing authority shall have regard to Parts IX, X and XI of the Housing Act 1985 (slum clearance; overcrowding; houses in multiple occupation).

(2) The Secretary of State may by order specify—

(a) circumstances in which accommodation is or is not to be regarded as suitable for a person, and

(b) matters to be taken into account or disregarded in determining whether accommodation is suitable for a person.

Protection of property of homeless persons and persons threatened with homelessness.

211.—(1) This section applies where a local housing authority have reason to believe that—

(a) there is danger of loss of, or damage to, any personal property of an applicant by reason of his inability to protect it or deal with it, and

(b) no other suitable arrangements have been or are being made.

(2) If the authority have become subject to a duty towards the applicant under—

section 188 (interim duty to accommodate),

section 190, 193 or 195 (duties to persons found to be homeless or threatened with homelessness), or

section 200 (duties to applicant whose case is considered for referral or referred),

then, whether or not they are still subject to such a duty, they shall take reasonable steps to prevent the loss of the property or prevent or mitigate damage to it.

(3) If they have not become subject to such a duty, they may take any steps they consider reasonable for that purpose.

(4) The authority may decline to take action under this section except upon such conditions as they consider appropriate in the particular case, which may include conditions as to—

(a) the making and recovery by the authority of reasonable charges for the action taken, or

(b) the disposal by the authority, in such circumstances as may be specified, of property in relation to which they have taken action.

(5) References in this section to personal property of the applicant include personal property of any person who might reasonably be expected to reside with him.

(6) Section 212 contains provisions supplementing this section.

212.—(1) The authority may for the purposes of section 211 (protection of property of homeless persons or persons threatened with homelessness)—

Protection of property: supplementary provisions.

(a) enter, at all reasonable times, any premises which are the usual place of residence of the applicant or which were his last usual place of residence, and

(b) deal with any personal property of his in any way which is reasonably necessary, in particular by storing it or arranging for its storage.

(2) Where the applicant asks the authority to move his property to a particular location nominated by him, the authority—

(a) may, if it appears to them that his request is reasonable, discharge their responsibilities under section 211 by doing as he asks, and

(b) having done so, have no further duty or power to take action under that section in relation to that property.

If such a request is made, the authority shall before complying with it inform the applicant of the consequence of their doing so.

(3) If no such request is made (or, if made, is not acted upon) the authority cease to have any duty or power to take action under section 211 when, in their opinion, there is no longer any reason to believe that there is a danger of loss of or damage to a person's personal property by reason of his inability to protect it or deal with it.

But property stored by virtue of their having taken such action may be kept in store and any conditions upon which it was taken into store continue to have effect, with any necessary modifications.

(4) Where the authority—

(a) cease to be subject to a duty to take action under section 211 in respect of an applicant's property, or

(b) cease to have power to take such action, having previously taken such action,

they shall notify the applicant of that fact and of the reason for it.

(5) The notification shall be given to the applicant—

(a) by delivering it to him, or

(b) by leaving it, or sending it to him, at his last known address.

(6) References in this section to personal property of the applicant include personal property of any person who might reasonably be expected to reside with him.

Co-operation between relevant housing authorities and bodies.

213.—(1) Where a local housing authority—

(a) request another relevant housing authority or body, in England, Wales or Scotland, to assist them in the discharge of their functions under this Part, or

(b) request a social services authority, in England, Wales or Scotland, to exercise any of their functions in relation to a case which the local housing authority are dealing with under this Part,

the authority or body to whom the request is made shall co-operate in rendering such assistance in the discharge of the functions to which the request relates as is reasonable in the circumstances.

(2) In subsection (1)(a) "relevant housing authority or body" means—

(a) in relation to England and Wales, a local housing authority, a new town corporation, a registered social landlord or a housing action trust;

(b) in relation to Scotland, a local authority, a development corporation, a registered housing association or Scottish Homes.

1985 c. 68.
1987 c. 26.

Expressions used in paragraph (a) have the same meaning as in the Housing Act 1985; and expressions used in paragraph (b) have the same meaning as in the Housing (Scotland) Act 1987.

(3) Subsection (1) above applies to a request by a local authority in Scotland under section 38 of the Housing (Scotland) Act 1987 as it applies to a request by a local housing authority in England and Wales (the references to this Part being construed, in relation to such a request, as references to Part II of that Act).

General provisions

214.—(1) It is an offence for a person, with intent to induce a local housing authority to believe in connection with the exercise of their functions under this Part that he or another person is entitled to accommodation or assistance in accordance with the provisions of this Part, or is entitled to accommodation or assistance of a particular description—

    (a) knowingly or recklessly to make a statement which is false in a material particular, or

    (b) knowingly to withhold information which the authority have reasonably required him to give in connection with the exercise of those functions.

(2) If before an applicant receives notification of the local housing authority's decision on his application there is any change of facts material to his case, he shall notify the authority as soon as possible.

The authority shall explain to every applicant, in ordinary language, the duty imposed on him by this subsection and the effect of subsection (3).

(3) A person who fails to comply with subsection (2) commits an offence unless he shows that he was not given the explanation required by that subsection or that he had some other reasonable excuse for non-compliance.

(4) A person guilty of an offence under this section is liable on summary conviction to a fine not exceeding level 5 on the standard scale.

False statements, withholding information and failure to disclose change of circumstances.

215.—(1) In this Part "prescribed" means prescribed by regulations of the Secretary of State.

(2) Regulations or an order under this Part may make different provision for different purposes, including different provision for different areas.

(3) Regulations or an order under this Part shall be made by statutory instrument.

(4) Unless required to be approved in draft, regulations or an order under this Part shall be subject to annulment in pursuance of a resolution of either House of Parliament.

Regulations and orders.

216.—(1) The provisions of this Part have effect in place of the provisions of Part III of the Housing Act 1985 (housing the homeless) and shall be construed as one with that Act.

(2) Subject to any transitional provision contained in an order under section 232(4) (power to include transitional provision in commencement order), the provisions of this Part do not apply in relation to an applicant whose application for accommodation or assistance in obtaining accommodation was made before the commencement of this Part.

(3) The enactments mentioned in Schedule 17 have effect with the amendments specified there which are consequential on the provisions of this Part.

Transitional and consequential matters.

1985 c. 68.

PART VII
Minor definitions:
Part VII.

1970 c. 42.

1988 c. 43.

1968 c. 49.

Index of defined
expressions: Part
VII.

217.—(1) In this Part, subject to subsection (2)—

"relevant authority" means a local housing authority or a social services authority; and

"social services authority" means a local authority for the purposes of the Local Authority Social Services Act 1970, as defined in section 1 of that Act.

(2) In this Part, in relation to Scotland—

(a) "local housing authority" means a local authority within the meaning of the Housing (Scotland) Act 1988, and

(b) "social services authority" means a local authority for the purposes of the Social Work (Scotland) Act 1968.

(3) References in this Part to the district of a local housing authority—

(a) have the same meaning in relation to an authority in England or Wales as in the Housing Act 1985, and

(b) in relation to an authority in Scotland, mean the area of the local authority concerned.

218. The following Table shows provisions defining or otherwise explaining expressions used in this Part (other than provisions defining or explaining an expression used in the same section)—

accommodation available for occupation	section 176
applicant	section 183(2)
assistance under this Part	section 183(2)
associated (in relation to a person)	section 178
assured tenancy and assured shorthold tenancy	section 230
district (of local housing authority)	section 217(3)
eligible for assistance	section 183(2)
homeless	section 175(1)
housing functions under this Part (in sections 206 to 209)	section 205(2)
intentionally homeless	section 191
intentionally threatened with homelessness	section 196
local connection	section 199
local housing authority—	
-in England and Wales	section 230
-in Scotland	section 217(2)(a)
minimum period (for purposes of section 193)	section 193(3) and (4)
prescribed	section 215(1)
priority need	section 189
reasonable to continue to occupy accommodation	section 177
registered social landlord	section 230
relevant authority	section 217(1)
social services authority	section 217(1) and (2)(b)
threatened with homelessness	section 175(4)

PART VIII

MISCELLANEOUS AND GENERAL PROVISIONS

Miscellaneous

219.—(1) The Secretary of State may give directions to social landlords about the making of service charges in respect of works of repair, maintenance or improvement—

Directions as to certain charges by social landlords.

    (a) requiring or permitting the waiver or reduction of charges where relevant assistance is given by the Secretary of State, and

    (b) permitting the waiver or reduction of charges in such other circumstances as may be specified in the directions.

(2) A direction shall not require the waiver or reduction of charges by reference to assistance for which application was made before the date on which the direction was given, but subject to that directions may relate to past charges or works to such extent as appears to the Secretary of State to be appropriate.

(3) Directions which require or permit the waiver or reduction of charges have corresponding effect—

    (a) in relation to charges already demanded so as to require or permit the non-enforcement of the charges, and

    (b) in relation to charges already paid so as to require or permit a refund.

(4) For the purposes of this section "social landlord" means—

    (a) an authority or body within section 80(1) of the Housing Act 1985 (the landlord condition for secure tenancies), other than a housing co-operative, or

1985 c. 68.

    (b) a registered social landlord.

(5) In this section "assistance" means grant or other financial assistance of any kind; and directions may specify what assistance is relevant for the purposes of this section, and to what buildings or other land any assistance is to be regarded as relevant.

(6) The provisions of section 220 supplement this section.

220.—(1) Directions under section 219 may make different provision for different cases or descriptions of case.

Directions as to certain charges: supplementary provisions.

This includes power to make—

    (a) different provision for different social landlords or descriptions of social landlords, and

    (b) different provision for different areas.

(2) Directions under section 219 requiring the reduction of a service charge may specify the amount (or proportion) of the reduction or provide for its determination in such manner as may be specified.

(3) Directions under section 219 permitting the waiver or reduction of a service charge may specify criteria to which the social landlord is to have regard in deciding whether to do so or to what extent.

(4) The Secretary of State shall publish any direction under section 219 relating to all social landlords or any description of social landlords in such manner as he considers appropriate for bringing it to the notice of the landlords concerned.

(5) For the purposes of section 219 "service charge" means an amount payable by a lessee of a dwelling—

(a) which is payable, directly or indirectly, for repairs, maintenance or improvements, and

(b) the whole or part of which varies or may vary according to the relevant costs.

(6) The relevant costs are the costs or estimated costs incurred or to be incurred by or on behalf of the social landlord, or a superior landlord, in connection with the matters for which the service charge is payable.

For this purpose costs are relevant costs in relation to a service charge whether they are incurred, or to be incurred, in the period for which the service charge is payable or in an earlier or later period.

(7) In this section—

"costs" includes overheads, and

"dwelling" means a building or part of a building occupied or intended to be occupied as a separate dwelling.

Exercise of compulsory purchase powers in relation to Crown land.

221.—(1) This section applies to any power to acquire land compulsorily under—

(a) the Housing Act 1985,

(b) the Housing Associations Act 1985,

(c) Part III of the Housing Act 1988 (housing action trust areas), or

1985 c. 69.
1988 c. 50.
1989 c. 42.

(d) Part VII of the Local Government and Housing Act 1989 (renewal areas).

(2) Any power to which this section applies may be exercised in relation to an interest in Crown land which is for the time being held otherwise than by or on behalf of the Crown, but only with the consent of the appropriate authority.

(3) In this section "Crown land" means land in which there is a Crown interest or a Duchy interest.

For this purpose—

"Crown interest" means an interest belonging to Her Majesty in right of the Crown or belonging to a government department or held in trust for Her Majesty for the purposes of a government department; and

"Duchy interest" means an interest belonging to Her Majesty in right of the Duchy of Lancaster or belonging to the Duchy of Cornwall.

(4) For the purposes of this section "the appropriate authority", in relation to Crown land, is—

(a) in the case of land belonging to Her Majesty in right of the Crown and forming part of the Crown Estate, the Crown Estate Commissioners;

(b) in relation to any other land belonging to Her Majesty in right of the Crown, the government department having the management of that land;

(c) in relation to land belonging to Her Majesty in right of the Duchy of Lancaster, the Chancellor of the Duchy;

(d) in relation to land belonging to the Duchy of Cornwall, such person as the Duke of Cornwall, or the possessor for the time being of the Duchy of Cornwall, appoints;

(e) in the case of land belonging to a government department or held in trust for Her Majesty for the purposes of a government department, that department.

(5) If any question arises as to what authority is the appropriate authority in relation to any land, that question shall be referred to the Treasury, whose decision shall be final.

222. The enactments mentioned in Schedule 18 have effect with the amendments specified there, which are miscellaneous minor amendments relating to housing.

> Part I relates to housing management.
>
> Part II relates to housing finance.
>
> Part III relates to orders in relation to property in family and matrimonial proceedings, &c.
>
> Part IV relates to other housing provisions.

Miscellaneous minor amendments.

General

223.—(1) Where an offence under this Act committed by a body corporate is proved to have been committed with the consent or connivance of a director, manager, secretary or other similar officer of the body corporate, or a person purporting to act in such a capacity, he as well as the body corporate is guilty of an offence and liable to be proceeded against and punished accordingly.

Offences by body corporate.

(2) Where the affairs of a body corporate are managed by its members, subsection (1) applies in relation to the acts and defaults of a member in connection with his functions of management as if he were a director of the body corporate.

224.—(1) The Common Council of the City of London may appoint a committee, consisting of so many persons as they think fit, for any purposes of this Act which in their opinion may be better regulated and managed by means of a committee.

The Common Council of the City of London.

(2) A committee so appointed—

(a) shall consist as to a majority of its members of members of the Common Council, and

(b) shall not be authorised to borrow money or to make a rate,

and shall be subject to any regulations and restrictions which may be imposed by the Common Council.

(3) A person is not, by reason only of the fact that he occupies a house at a rental from the Common Council, disqualified from being elected or being a member of that Council or any committee of that Council; but no

person shall vote as a member of that Council, or any such committee, on a resolution or question which is proposed or arises in pursuance of this Act and relates to land in which he is beneficially interested.

(4) A person who votes in contravention of subsection (3) commits a summary offence and is liable on conviction to a fine not exceeding level 4 on the standard scale; but the fact of his giving the vote does not invalidate any resolution or proceeding of the authority.

The Isles of Scilly.

225.—(1) This Act applies to the Isles of Scilly subject to such exceptions, adaptations and modifications as the Secretary of State may by order direct.

(2) An order shall be made by statutory instrument which shall be subject to annulment in pursuance of a resolution of either House of Parliament.

Corresponding provision for Northern Ireland.
1974 c. 28.

226. An Order in Council under paragraph 1(1)(b) of Schedule 1 to the Northern Ireland Act 1974 (legislation for Northern Ireland in the interim period) which states that it is made only for purposes corresponding to those of section 120 (payment of housing benefit to third parties)—

(a) shall not be subject to paragraph 1(4) and (5) of that Schedule (affirmative resolution of both Houses of Parliament), but

(b) shall be subject to annulment in pursuance of a resolution of either House of Parliament.

Repeals.

227. The enactments specified in Schedule 19 are repealed to the extent specified.

Financial provisions.

228.—(1) There shall be paid out of money provided by Parliament—

(a) any expenses of the Secretary of State incurred in consequence of this Act, and

(b) any increase attributable to this Act in the sums payable out of money so provided under any other enactment.

(2) There shall be paid out of the National Loans Fund any increase attributable to this Act in the sums so payable under any other enactment.

(3) Any sums received by the Secretary of State under this Act shall be paid into the Consolidated Fund.

Meaning of "lease" and "tenancy" and related expressions.

229.—(1) In this Act "lease" and "tenancy" have the same meaning.

(2) Both expressions include—

(a) a sub-lease or a sub-tenancy, and

(b) an agreement for a lease or tenancy (or sub-lease or sub-tenancy).

(3) The expressions "lessor" and "lessee" and "landlord" and "tenant", and references to letting, to the grant of a lease or to covenants or terms, shall be construed accordingly.

230. In this Act—

"assured tenancy", "assured shorthold tenancy" and "assured agricultural occupancy" have the same meaning as in Part I of the Housing Act 1988;

"enactment" includes an enactment comprised in subordinate legislation (within the meaning of the Interpretation Act 1978);

"housing action trust" has the same meaning as in the Housing Act 1988;

"housing association" has the same meaning as in the Housing Associations Act 1985;

"introductory tenancy" and "introductory tenant" have the same meaning as in Chapter I of Part V of this Act;

"local housing authority" has the same meaning as in the Housing Act 1985;

"registered social landlord" has the same meaning as in Part I of this Act;

"secure tenancy" and "secure tenant" have the same meaning as in Part IV of the Housing Act 1985.

Final provisions

231.—(1) The provisions of this Act extend to England and Wales, and only to England and Wales, subject as follows.

(2) The following provisions also extend to Scotland—

Part IV (housing benefit and related matters), and

the provisions of this Part so far as relating to Part IV.

(3) Section 226 (power to make corresponding provision for Northern Ireland) also extends to Northern Ireland.

(4) Any amendment or repeal by this Act of an enactment has the same extent as the enactment amended or repealed, except that—

(a) amendments or repeals of provisions of the Housing Associations Act 1985, other than in consequence of paragraph 1 of Schedule 18 to this Act (repeal of Part IV of the Housing Act 1988), do not extend to Scotland,

(b) amendments or repeals of provisions of the Housing Act 1988 relating to registered housing associations do not extend to Scotland,

(c) amendments or repeals of provisions of the Asylum and Immigration Appeals Act 1993 or the Asylum and Immigration Act 1996 do not extend to Scotland or Northern Ireland, and

(d) repeals of the following provisions do not extend to Scotland—

(i) section 24(5)(a) and (c) of the Local Government Act 1988,

(ii) section 182 of the Local Government and Housing Act 1989,

(iii) paragraph 21(3) of Schedule 6 to the Charities Act 1993, and

(iv) provisions in Schedule 26 to the Local Government, Planning and Land Act 1980.

(5) Any power conferred by this Act to make consequential amendments or repeals of enactments may be exercised in relation to enactments as they extend to any part of the United Kingdom.

Commencement.

232.—(1) The following provisions of this Act come into force on Royal Assent—

> section 110 (new leases: valuation principles),
>
> section 120 (payment of housing benefit to third parties), and
>
> sections 223 to 226 and 228 to 233 (general provisions).

(2) The following provisions of this Act come into force at the end of the period of two months beginning with the date on which this Act is passed—

> sections 81 and 82 (restriction on termination of tenancy for failure to pay service charge),
>
> section 85 (appointment of manager by the court),
>
> section 94 (provision of general legal advice about residential tenancies),
>
> section 95 (jurisdiction of county courts),
>
> section 221 (exercise of compulsory purchase powers in relation to Crown land),
>
> paragraph 24 (powers of local housing authorities to acquire land for housing purposes), paragraph 26 (preserved right to buy) and paragraphs 27 to 29 of Schedule 18 (local authority assistance in connection with mortgages), and
>
> sections 222 and 227, and Schedule 19 (consequential repeals), in so far as they relate to those paragraphs.

(3) The other provisions of this Act come into force on a day appointed by order of the Secretary of State, and different days may be appointed for different areas and different purposes.

(4) An order under subsection (3) shall be made by statutory instrument and may contain such transitional provisions and savings as appear to the Secretary of State to be appropriate.

Short title.

233. This Act may be cited as the Housing Act 1996.

SCHEDULES

SCHEDULE 1   Section 7.

REGISTERED SOCIAL LANDLORDS: REGULATION

PART I

CONTROL OF PAYMENTS TO MEMBERS, &C

Payments by way of gift, dividend or bonus

1.—(1) A registered social landlord shall not make a gift or pay a sum by way of dividend or bonus to—

  (a) a person who is or has been a member of the body,

  (b) a person who is a member of the family of a person within paragraph (a), or

  (c) a company of which a person within paragraph (a) or (b) is a director,

except as permitted by this paragraph.

  (2) The following are permitted—

  (a) the payment of a sum which, in accordance with the constitution or rules of the body, is paid as interest on capital lent to the body or subscribed by way of shares in the body;

  (b) the payment by a fully mutual housing association to a person who has ceased to be a member of the association of a sum which is due to him either under his tenancy agreement with the association or under the terms of the agreement under which he became a member of the association.

  (3) Where an industrial and provident society or a company registered under the Companies Act 1985 pays a sum or makes a gift in contravention of this paragraph, the society or company may recover the sum or the value of the gift, and proceedings for its recovery shall be taken if the Corporation so directs.

1985 c. 6.

Payments and benefits to officers and employees, &c.

2.—(1) A registered social landlord which is an industrial and provident society or a company registered under the Companies Act 1985 shall not make a payment or grant a benefit to—

  (a) an officer or employee of the society or company,

  (b) a person who at any time within the preceding twelve months has been a person within paragraph (a),

  (c) a close relative of a person within paragraph (a) or (b), or

  (d) a business trading for profit of which a person falling within paragraph (a), (b) or (c) is a principal proprietor or in the management of which such a person is directly concerned,

except as permitted by this paragraph.

  (2) The following are permitted—

  (a) payments made or benefits granted to an officer or employee of the society or company under his contract of employment with the society or company;

  (b) the payment of remuneration or expenses to an officer of the society or company who does not have a contract of employment with the society or company;

(c) any such payment as may be made in accordance with paragraph 1(2) (interest payable in accordance with the rules and certain sums payable by a fully mutual housing association to a person who has ceased to be a member);

(d) the grant or renewal of a tenancy by a co-operative housing association;

(e) where a tenancy of a house has been granted to, or to a close relative of, a person who later became an officer or employee, the grant to that tenant of a new tenancy whether of the same or another house;

(f) payments made or benefits granted in accordance with any determination made by the Corporation.

(3) A determination for the purposes of sub-paragraph (2)(f) may specify the class or classes of case in which a payment may be made or benefit granted and specify the maximum amount.

(4) Where a society or company pays a sum or grants a benefit in contravention of this paragraph, the society or company may recover the sum or value of the benefit; and proceedings for its recovery shall be taken if the Corporation so directs.

Maximum amounts payable by way of fees, expenses, &c.

3.—(1) The Corporation may from time to time specify the maximum amounts which may be paid by a registered social landlord which is an industrial and provident society or a company registered under the Companies Act 1985—

(a) by way of fees or other remuneration, or by way of expenses, to a member of the society or company who is not an officer or employee of the society or company, or

(b) by way of remuneration or expenses to an officer of the society or company who does not have a contract of employment with the society or company.

(2) Different amounts may be so specified for different purposes.

(3) Where a society or company makes a payment in excess of the maximum permitted under this paragraph, the society or company may recover the excess, and proceedings for its recovery shall be taken if the Corporation so directs.

Part II

Constitution, change of rules, amalgamation and dissolution

General power to remove director, trustee, &c.

4.—(1) The Corporation may, in accordance with the following provisions, by order remove—

(a) a director or trustee of a registered social landlord which is a registered charity,

(b) a committee member of a registered social landlord which is an industrial and provident society, or

(c) a director of a registered social landlord which is a company registered under the Companies Act 1985.

(2) The Corporation may make an order removing any such person if—

(a) he has been adjudged bankrupt or has made an arrangement with his creditors;

1986 c. 46.

(b) he is subject to a disqualification order under the Company Directors Disqualification Act 1986;

1986 c. 45.

(c) he is subject to an order under section 429(2) of the Insolvency Act 1986 (failure to pay under county court administration order);

(d) he is disqualified under section 72 of the Charities Act 1993 from being a charity trustee;

(e) he is incapable of acting by reason of mental disorder;

(f) he has not acted; or

(g) he cannot be found or does not act and his absence or failure to act is impeding the proper management of the registered social landlord's affairs.

(3) Before making an order the Corporation shall give at least 14 days' notice of its intention to do so to the person whom it intends to remove, and to the registered social landlord.

(4) That notice may be given by post, and if so given to the person whom the Corporation intend to remove may be addressed to his last known address in the United Kingdom.

(5) A person who is ordered to be removed under this paragraph may appeal against the order to the High Court.

Restriction on power of removal in case of registered charity

5.—(1) The Corporation may make an order under paragraph 4 removing a director or trustee of a registered charity only if the charity has, at any time before the power is exercised—

(a) received financial assistance under section 24 of the Local Government Act 1988 (assistance for privately let housing accommodation),

(b) had property transferred to it on a qualifying disposal under section 135 of the Leasehold Reform, Housing and Urban Development Act 1993, or

(c) received a grant or loan under any of the following provisions.

(2) The provisions are—

section 18 of this Act (social housing grants),

section 22 of this Act or section 58 of the Housing Associations Act 1985 (grants or loans by local authorities),

section 50 of the Housing Act 1988, section 41 of the Housing Associations Act 1985 or any enactment replaced by that section (housing association grant),

section 51 of the Housing Act 1988 or section 54 or 55 of the Housing Associations Act 1985 (revenue deficit grant or hostel deficit grant),

section 79 of the Housing Associations Act 1985 (loans by Housing Corporation),

section 31 of the Housing Act 1974 (management grants), or

any enactment mentioned in paragraph 2 or 3 of Schedule 1 to the Housing Associations Act 1985 (pre-1974 grants and certain loans).

Registered charity: power to appoint new director or trustee

6.—(1) The Corporation may by order appoint a person to be a director or trustee of a registered social landlord which is a registered charity—

(a) in place of a person removed by the Corporation,

(b) where there are no directors or no trustees, or

(c) where the Corporation is of the opinion that it is necessary for the proper management of the charity's affairs to have an additional director or trustee.

The power conferred by paragraph (c) may be exercised notwithstanding that it will cause the maximum number of directors or trustees permissible under the charity's constitution to be exceeded.

(2) The Corporation shall only exercise its power under sub-paragraph (1) if—

> (a) the charity has, at any time before the power is exercised, received financial assistance, had property transferred to it, or received a grant or loan as mentioned in paragraph 5, and
>
> (b) the Corporation has consulted the Charity Commissioners.

(3) A person may be so appointed notwithstanding any restrictions on appointment in the charity's constitution or rules.

(4) A person appointed under this paragraph shall hold office for such period and on such terms as the Corporation may specify; and on the expiry of the appointment the Corporation may renew the appointment for such period as it may specify.

This does not prevent a person appointed under this paragraph from retiring in accordance with the charity's constitution or rules.

(5) A person appointed under this paragraph as director or trustee of a registered charity is entitled—

> (a) to attend, speak and vote at any general meeting of the charity and to receive all notices of and other communications relating to any such meeting which a member is entitled to receive,
>
> (b) to move a resolution at any general meeting of the charity, and
>
> (c) to require a general meeting of the charity to be convened within 21 days of a request to that effect made in writing to the directors or trustees.

Company: power to appoint new director

7.—(1) The Corporation may by order appoint a person to be a director of a registered social landlord which is a company registered under the Companies Act 1985—

> (a) in place of a director removed by the Corporation,
>
> (b) where there are no directors, or
>
> (c) where the Corporation is of the opinion that it is necessary for the proper management of the company's affairs to have an additional director.

(2) A person may be so appointed whether or not he is a member of the company and notwithstanding anything in the company's articles of association.

(3) Where a person is appointed under this paragraph—

> (a) he shall hold office for such period and on such terms as the Corporation may specify, and
>
> (b) on the expiry of the appointment the Corporation may renew the appointment for such period as it may specify.

This does not prevent a person from retiring in accordance with the company's articles of association.

(4) A person appointed under this paragraph is entitled—

> (a) to attend, speak and vote at any general meeting of the company and to receive all notices of and other communications relating to any general meeting which a member of the company is entitled to receive,
>
> (b) to move a resolution at any general meeting of the company, and

(c) to require an extraordinary general meeting of the company to be convened within 21 days of a request to that effect made in writing to the directors of the company.

Industrial and provident society: power to appoint new committee member

8.—(1) The Corporation may by order appoint a person to be a committee member of a registered social landlord which is an industrial and provident society—

(a) in place of a person removed by the Corporation,

(b) where there are no members of the committee, or

(c) where the Corporation is of the opinion that it is necessary for the proper management of the society's affairs to have an additional committee member.

The power conferred by paragraph (c) may be exercised notwithstanding that it will cause the maximum number of committee members permissible under the society's constitution to be exceeded.

(2) A person may be so appointed whether or not he is a member of the society and, if he is not, notwithstanding that the rules of the society restrict appointment to members.

(3) A person appointed under this paragraph shall hold office for such period and on such terms as the Corporation may specify; and on the expiry of the appointment the Corporation may renew the appointment for such period as it may specify.

This does not prevent a person appointed under this paragraph from retiring in accordance with the rules of the society.

(4) A person appointed under this paragraph is entitled—

(a) to attend, speak and vote at any general meeting of the society and to receive all notices of and other communications relating to any general meeting which a member of the society is entitled to receive,

(b) to move a resolution at any general meeting of the society, and

(c) to require a general meeting of the society to be convened within 21 days of a request to that effect made in writing to the committee of the society.

Change of rules, &c. by industrial and provident society

9.—(1) This paragraph applies to an industrial and provident society whose registration as a social landlord has been recorded by the appropriate registrar.

(2) Notice shall be sent to the Corporation of any change of the society's name or of the situation of its registered office.

(3) Any other amendment of the society's rules is not valid without the Corporation's consent given by order under the seal of the Corporation.

(4) A copy of that consent shall be sent with the copies of the amendment required by section 10(1) of the Industrial and Provident Societies Act 1965 to be sent to the appropriate registrar.

1965 c. 12.

(5) The Industrial and Provident Societies Act 1965 applies in relation to the provisions of this paragraph as if they were contained in section 10 of that Act (amendment of registered rules).

Change of objects by certain charities

10.—(1) This paragraph applies to a registered social landlord—

1985 c. 6.

(a) which is a registered charity and is not a company incorporated under the Companies Act 1985, and

(b) whose registration under this Part of this Act has been recorded by the Charity Commissioners in accordance with section 3(3).

(2) No power contained in the provisions establishing the registered social landlord as a charity, or regulating its purposes or administration, to vary or add to its objects may be exercised without the consent of the Charity Commissioners.

Before giving their consent the Charity Commissioners shall consult the Corporation.

Change of memorandum or articles of association of company

11.—(1) This paragraph applies to a company registered under the Companies Act 1985 (including such a company which is also a registered charity) whose registration as a social landlord has been recorded by the registrar of companies.

(2) Notice shall be sent to the Corporation of any change of the company's name or of the address of its registered office.

(3) Any other alteration of the company's memorandum or articles of which notice is required to be given to the registrar of companies is not valid without the Corporation's consent given by order under the seal of the Corporation.

(4) A copy of that consent shall be sent with any copy of the alterations required to be sent to the registrar of companies under the Companies Act 1985.

Amalgamation and dissolution &c. of industrial and provident society

12.—(1) This paragraph applies to an industrial and provident society whose registration as a social landlord has been recorded by the appropriate registrar.

(2) The registrar shall not register a special resolution which is passed for the purposes of—

1965 c. 12.

(a) section 50 of the Industrial and Provident Societies Act 1965 (amalgamation of societies),

(b) section 51 of that Act (transfer of engagements between societies), or

(c) section 52 of that Act (power of a society to convert itself into, amalgamate with or transfer its engagements to a company registered under the Companies Act 1985),

unless, together with the copy of the resolution, there is sent to him a copy of the Corporation's consent to the amalgamation, transfer or conversion.

(3) Any new body created by the amalgamation or conversion or, in the case of a transfer of engagements, the transferee, shall be deemed to be registered as a social landlord forthwith upon the amalgamation, conversion or transfer taking effect.

1986 c. 45.

(4) If the society resolves by special resolution that it be wound up voluntarily under the Insolvency Act 1986, the resolution has no effect unless—

(a) before the resolution was passed the Corporation gave its consent to its passing, and

(b) a copy of the consent is forwarded to the appropriate registrar together with a copy of the resolution required to be so forwarded in accordance with the Companies Act 1985.

(5) If the society is to be dissolved by instrument of dissolution, the appropriate registrar shall not—

(a) register the instrument in accordance with section 58(5) of the Industrial and Provident Societies Act 1965, or

1965 c. 12.

(b) cause notice of the dissolution to be advertised in accordance with section 58(6) of that Act,

unless together with the instrument there is sent to him a copy of the Corporation's consent to its making.

(6) The references in this paragraph to the Corporation's consent are to consent given by order under the seal of the Corporation.

Arrangement, reconstruction, &c. of company

13.—(1) This paragraph applies to a company registered under the Companies Act 1985 whose registration as a social landlord has been recorded by the registrar of companies.

1985 c. 6.

(2) An order of the court given for the purposes of section 425 of the Companies Act 1985 (compromise or arrangement with creditors or members) is not effective unless the Corporation has given its consent.

A copy of the consent shall be sent to the registrar of companies along with the office copy of the order delivered to him under that section.

(3) An order of the court given for the purposes of section 427 of the Companies Act 1985 (transfer of undertaking or property for purposes of reconstruction or amalgamation) is not effective unless the Corporation has given its consent.

A copy of the consent shall be sent to the registrar of companies along with the office copy of the order delivered to him under that section.

(4) The registrar of companies shall not register any resolution under section 53 of the Industrial and Provident Societies Act 1965 (conversion of company into industrial and provident society), unless, together with the copy of the resolution, there is sent to him a copy of the Corporation's consent to the conversion.

(5) Where a director, administrator or liquidator of the company proposes to make a voluntary arrangement with the company's creditors under section 1 of the Insolvency Act 1986, the arrangement shall not take effect under section 5 (effect of approval by members and creditors) of that Act unless the Corporation has given its consent to the voluntary arrangement.

1986 c. 45.

(6) If the company resolves by special resolution that it be wound up voluntarily under the Insolvency Act 1986, the resolution has no effect unless—

(a) before the resolution was passed the Corporation gave its consent to its passing, and

(b) a copy of the consent is forwarded to the registrar of companies together with a copy of the resolution required to be so forwarded in accordance with section 380 of the Companies Act 1985.

(7) The references in this paragraph to the Corporation's consent are to consent given by order under the seal of the Corporation.

(8) Where sub-paragraph (3) or (4) applies, the transferee or, as the case may be, any new body created by the conversion shall be deemed to be registered as a social landlord forthwith upon the transfer or conversion taking effect.

Corporation's power to petition for winding up

14.—(1) The Corporation may present a petition for the winding up under the Insolvency Act 1986 of a registered social landlord which is—

(a) a company incorporated under the Companies Act 1985 (including such a company which is also a registered charity), or

1986 c. 45.
1965 c. 12.

(b) an industrial and provident society (to which the winding up provisions of the Insolvency Act 1986 apply in accordance with section 55(a) of the Industrial and Provident Societies Act 1965),

on either of the following grounds.

(2) The grounds are—

(a) that the landlord is failing properly to carry out its purposes or objects, or

(b) that the landlord is unable to pay its debts within the meaning of section 123 of the Insolvency Act 1986.

Transfer of net assets on dissolution or winding up

15.—(1) This paragraph applies—

(a) where a registered social landlord which is an industrial and provident society is dissolved as mentioned in section 55(a) or (b) of the Industrial and Provident Societies Act 1965 (winding-up under the Insolvency Act 1986 or by instrument of dissolution), and

1985 c. 6.

(b) where a registered social landlord which is a company registered under the Companies Act 1985 is wound up under the Insolvency Act 1986.

(2) On such a dissolution or winding-up, so much of the property of the society or company as remains after meeting the claims of its creditors and any other liabilities arising on or before the dissolution or winding-up shall be transferred to the Corporation or, if the Corporation so directs, to a specified registered social landlord.

The above provision has effect notwithstanding anything in the Industrial and Provident Societies Act 1965, the Companies Act 1985 or the Insolvency Act 1986, or in the rules of the society or, as the case may be, in the memorandum or articles of association of the company.

(3) In order to avoid the necessity for the sale of land belonging to the registered social landlord and thereby secure the transfer of the land under this paragraph, the Corporation may, if it appears to it appropriate to do so, make payments to discharge such claims or liabilities as are referred to in sub-paragraph (2).

(4) Where the registered social landlord which is dissolved or wound up is a charity, the Corporation may dispose of property transferred to it by virtue of this paragraph only to another registered social landlord—

(a) which is also a charity, and

(b) the objects of which appear to the Corporation to be, as nearly as practicable, akin to those of the body which is dissolved or wound up.

(5) In any other case the Corporation may dispose of property transferred to it by virtue of this paragraph to a registered social landlord or to a subsidiary of the Corporation.

(6) Where property transferred to the Corporation by virtue of this paragraph includes land subject to an existing mortgage or charge (whether in favour of the Corporation or not), the Corporation may, in exercise of its powers under Part III of the Housing Associations Act 1985, dispose of the land either—

1985 c. 69.

(a) subject to that mortgage or charge, or

(b) subject to a new mortgage or charge in favour of the Corporation securing such amount as appears to the Corporation to be appropriate in the circumstances.

PART III

ACCOUNTS AND AUDIT

General requirements as to accounts and audit

16.—(1) The Corporation may from time to time determine accounting requirements for registered social landlords with a view to ensuring that the accounts of every registered social landlord—

(a) are prepared in a proper form, and

(b) give a true and fair view of—

(i) the state of affairs of the landlord, so far as its housing activities are concerned, and

(ii) the disposition of funds and assets which are, or at any time have been, in its hands in connection with those activities.

(2) The Corporation by a determination under sub-paragraph (1) may lay down a method by which a registered charity is to distinguish in its accounts between its housing activities and other activities.

(3) The accounts of every registered social landlord shall comply with the requirements laid down under this paragraph.

(4) The auditor's report shall state, in addition to any other matters which it is required to state, whether in the auditor's opinion the accounts do so comply.

(5) Every registered social landlord shall furnish to the Corporation a copy of its accounts and auditor's report within six months of the end of the period to which they relate.

Appointment of auditors by industrial and provident societies

17. Section 4 of the Friendly and Industrial and Provident Societies Act 1968 (obligation to appoint qualified auditors to audit accounts and balance sheet for each year of account) applies to every industrial and provident society which is a registered social landlord, without regard to the volume of its receipts and payments, the number of its members or the value of its assets.

1968 c. 55.

Accounting and audit requirements for charities

18.—(1) A registered social landlord which is a registered charity shall, in respect of its housing activities (and separately from its other activities, if any), be subject to the following provisions (which impose accounting and audit requirements corresponding to those imposed by the Friendly and Industrial and Provident Societies Act 1968).

This does not affect any obligation of the charity under sections 41 to 45 of the Charities Act 1993 (charity accounts).

1993 c. 10.

(2) The charity shall in respect of its housing activities—

(a) cause to be kept properly books of account showing its transactions and its assets and liabilities, and

(b) establish and maintain a satisfactory system of control of its books of accounts, its cash holdings and all its receipts and remittances.

The books of account must be such as to enable a true and fair view to be given of the state of affairs of the charity in respect of its housing activities, and to explain its transactions in the course of those activities.

(3) The charity shall for each period of account prepare—

(a) a revenue account giving a true and fair view of the charity's income and expenditure in the period, so far as arising in connection with its housing activities, and

(b) a balance sheet giving a true and fair view as at the end of the period of the state of the charity's affairs.

The revenue account and balance sheet must be signed by at least two directors or trustees of the charity.

(4) The charity shall in each period of account appoint a qualified auditor to audit the accounts prepared in accordance with sub-paragraph (3).

1989 c. 40.
1985 c. 6.

A qualified auditor means a person who is eligible for appointment as auditor of the charity under Part II of the Companies Act 1989 or who would be so eligible if the charity were a company registered under the Companies Act 1985.

(5) The auditor shall make a report to the charity on the accounts audited by him, stating whether in his opinion—

(a) the revenue account gives a true and fair view of the state of income and expenditure of the charity in respect of its housing activities and of any other matters to which it relates, and

(b) the balance sheet gives a true and fair view of the state of affairs of the charity as at the end of the period of account.

(6) The auditor in preparing his report shall carry out such investigations as will enable him to form an opinion as to the following matters—

(a) whether the association has kept, in respect of its housing activities, proper books of account in accordance with the requirements of this paragraph,

(b) whether the charity has maintained a satisfactory system of control over its transactions in accordance with those requirements, and

(c) whether the accounts are in agreement with the charity's books;

and if he is of opinion that the charity has failed in any respect to comply with this paragraph, or if the accounts are not in agreement with the books, he shall state that fact in his report.

(7) The auditor—

(a) has a right of access at all times to the books, deeds and accounts of the charity, so far as relating to its housing activities, and to all other documents relating to those activities, and

(b) is entitled to require from officers of the charity such information and explanations as he thinks necessary for the performance of his duties;

and if he fails to obtain all the information and explanations which, to the best of his knowledge and belief, are necessary for the purposes of his audit, he shall state that fact in his report.

(8) A period of account for the purposes of this paragraph is twelve months or such other period not less than six months or more than 18 months as the charity may, with the consent of the Corporation, determine.

Responsibility for securing compliance with accounting requirements

19.—(1) Every responsible person, that is to say, every person who—

(a) is directly concerned with the conduct and management of the affairs of a registered social landlord, and

(b) is in that capacity responsible for the preparation and audit of accounts,

shall ensure that paragraph 16 (general requirements as to accounts and audit) and, where applicable, paragraph 18 (accounting and audit requirements for charities) are complied with by the registered social landlord.

(2) If—

(a) paragraph 16(5) (furnishing of accounts and auditor's report) is not complied with,

(b) the accounts furnished to the Corporation under that provision do not comply with the accounting requirements laid down under paragraph 16(1),

(c) paragraph 18 (accounting and audit requirements for charities), where applicable, is not complied with,

(d) section 55(9) of the Housing Act 1988 (surplus rental income: power to require information) is not complied with, or   1988 c. 50.

(e) any notice under section 26 (information relating to disposal proceeds fund) is not complied with,

every responsible person, and the registered social landlord itself, commits a summary offence and is liable on conviction to a fine not exceeding level 3 on the standard scale.

(3) In proceedings for an offence under this paragraph it is a defence—

(a) for a responsible person to prove that he did everything that could reasonably have been expected of him by way of discharging the relevant duty;

(b) for a registered social landlord to prove that every responsible person did everything that could reasonably have been expected of him by way of discharging the relevant duty in relation to the registered social landlord.

(4) Proceedings for an offence under this paragraph may be brought only by or with the consent of the Corporation or the Director of Public Prosecutions.

Part IV

Inquiry into affairs of registered social landlords

Inquiry

20.—(1) The Corporation may direct an inquiry into the affairs of a registered social landlord if it appears to the Corporation that there may have been misconduct or mismanagement.

For this purpose "misconduct" includes any failure to comply with the requirements of this Part of this Act.

(2) Any such inquiry shall be conducted by one or more persons appointed by the Corporation.

(3) If one person is appointed he must be a person who is not a member or an employee of the Corporation and has not been such a member or employee within the previous five years; and if more than one person is appointed at least one of them must be such a person.

(4) If the Corporation so directs, or if during the course of the inquiry the person or persons conducting the inquiry consider it necessary, the inquiry shall extend to the affairs of any other body which at any material time is or was a subsidiary or associate of the registered social landlord.

(5) The person or persons conducting the inquiry may, if they think fit during the course of the inquiry, make one or more interim reports on such matters as appear to them to be appropriate.

(6) On completion of the inquiry the person or persons conducting the inquiry shall make a final report on such matters as the Corporation may specify.

(7) An interim or final report shall be in such form as the Corporation may specify.

Power of appointed person to obtain information

21.—(1) A person appointed by the Corporation under paragraph 20 to conduct an inquiry (or, if more than one person is so appointed, each of those persons) has, for the purposes of the inquiry, the same powers as are conferred on the Corporation by section 30 (general power to obtain information).

(2) Where by virtue of a notice under that section given by an appointed person any documents are produced to any person, the person to whom they are produced may take copies of or make extracts from them.

(3) Section 31 (enforcement of notice to provide information, &c.) applies in relation to a notice given under this paragraph by an appointed person as it applies in relation to a notice given under section 30 by the Corporation.

Extraordinary audit for purposes of inquiry

22.—(1) For the purposes of an inquiry under paragraph 20 the Corporation may require the accounts and balance sheet of the registered social landlord concerned, or such of them as the Corporation may specify, to be audited by a qualified auditor appointed by the Corporation.

(2) A person is a qualified auditor for this purpose if he would be eligible for appointment as auditor of the ordinary accounts of the registered social landlord.

(3) On completion of the audit the appointed auditor shall make a report to the Corporation on such matters and in such form as the Corporation may specify.

(4) The expenses of the audit, including the remuneration of the auditor, shall be paid by the Corporation.

(5) An audit under this paragraph is additional to, and does not affect, any audit made or to be made under any other enactment.

Powers exercisable on interim basis

23.—(1) The Corporation may make an order under this paragraph—

(a) where an inquiry has been directed under paragraph 20 and the Corporation has reasonable grounds to believe—

(i) that there has been misconduct or mismanagement in the affairs of the registered social landlord, and

(ii) that immediate action is needed to protect the interests of the tenants of the registered social landlord or to protect the assets of the landlord; or

(b) where an interim report has been made under paragraph 20(5) as a result of which the Corporation is satisfied that there has been misconduct or mismanagement in the affairs of a registered social landlord.

(2) The orders that may be made under this paragraph are—

(a) an order suspending any officer, employee or agent of the registered social landlord who appears to the Corporation to have been responsible for or privy to the misconduct or mismanagement or by his conduct to have contributed to or facilitated it;

(b) an order directing any bank or other person who holds money or securities on behalf of the registered social landlord not to part with the money or securities without the approval of the Corporation;

(c) an order restricting the transactions which may be entered into, or the nature or amount of the payments which may be made, by the registered social landlord without the approval of the Corporation.

(3) An order under this paragraph, if not previously revoked by the Corporation, shall cease to have effect six months after the making of the final report under paragraph 20(6) unless the Corporation renews it, which it may do for a further period of up to six months.

(4) A person suspended by an order under sub-paragraph (2)(a) may appeal against the order to the High Court.

(5) Where a person is suspended by such an order, the Corporation may give directions with respect to the performance of his functions and otherwise as to matters arising from his suspension.

The Corporation may, in particular, appoint a named person to perform his functions.

(6) A person who contravenes an order under sub-paragraph (2)(b) commits an offence and is liable on summary conviction to a fine not exceeding level 5 on the standard scale or imprisonment for a term not exceeding three months, or both.

Proceedings for such an offence may be brought only by or with the consent of the Corporation or the Director of Public Prosecutions.

Powers exercisable as a result of final report or audit

24.—(1) Where the Corporation is satisfied, as the result of an inquiry under paragraph 20 or an audit under paragraph 22, that there has been misconduct or mismanagement in the affairs of a registered social landlord, it may make an order under this paragraph.

(2) The orders that may be made under this paragraph are—

(a) an order removing any officer, employee or agent of the registered social landlord who appears to the Corporation to have been responsible for or privy to the misconduct or mismanagement or by his conduct to have contributed to or facilitated it;

(b) an order suspending any such person for up to six months, pending determination whether he should be removed;

(c) an order directing any bank or other person who holds money or securities on behalf of the registered social landlord not to part with the money or securities without the approval of the Corporation;

(d) an order restricting the transactions which may be entered into, or the nature or amount of the payments which may be made, by the registered social landlord without the approval of the Corporation.

(3) Before making an order under sub-paragraph (2)(a) the Corporation shall give at least 14 days' notice of its intention to do so—

(a) to the person it intends to remove, and

(b) to the registered social landlord concerned.

Notice under this sub-paragraph may be given by post, and if so given to the person whom the Corporation intends to remove may be addressed to his last known address in the United Kingdom.

(4) A person who is ordered to be removed under sub-paragraph (2)(a) or suspended under sub-paragraph (2)(b) may appeal against the order to the High Court.

(5) Where a person is suspended under sub-paragraph (2)(b), the Corporation may give directions with respect to the performance of his functions and otherwise as to matters arising from the suspension.

The Corporation may, in particular, appoint a named person to perform his functions.

(6) A person who contravenes an order under sub-paragraph (2)(c) commits an offence and is liable on summary conviction to a fine not exceeding level 5 on the standard scale or imprisonment for a term not exceeding three months, or both.

Proceedings for such an offence may be brought only by or with the consent of the Corporation or the Director of Public Prosecutions.

Disqualification as officer of registered social landlord.

25.—(1) A person is disqualified from being an officer of a registered social landlord if the Corporation has made an order against him under—

    (a) paragraph 24(2)(a) (removal for misconduct or mismanagement), or

1985 c. 69.
1974 c. 44.

    (b) section 30(1)(a) of the Housing Associations Act 1985 or section 20(1)(a) of the Housing Act 1974 (corresponding earlier provisions).

(2) The Corporation may, on the application of any such person, waive his disqualification either generally or in relation to a particular registered social landlord or particular class of registered social landlord.

(3) Any waiver shall be notified in writing to the person concerned.

(4) For the purposes of this paragraph the Corporation shall keep, in such manner as it thinks fit, a register of all persons who have been removed from office by the Corporation under the provisions mentioned in sub-paragraph (1).

(5) The register shall be available for public inspection at all reasonable times.

Persons acting as officer while disqualified.

26.—(1) A person who acts as an officer of a registered social landlord while he is disqualified under paragraph 25(1) commits an offence.

A person guilty of such an offence is liable—

    (a) on summary conviction, to imprisonment for a term not exceeding six months or to a fine not exceeding the statutory maximum, or both;

    (b) on conviction on indictment, to imprisonment for a term not exceeding two years or to a fine, or both.

(2) Proceedings for an offence under sub-paragraph (1) may be brought only by or with the consent of the Corporation or the Director of Public Prosecutions.

(3) Acts done as an officer of a registered social landlord by a person who is disqualified under paragraph 25(1) are not invalid by reason only of that disqualification.

(4) Where the Corporation is satisfied—

    (a) that a person has acted as an officer of a registered social landlord while disqualified under paragraph 25(1), and

    (b) that while so acting he has received from the registered social landlord any payments or benefits in connection with his so acting,

it may by order direct him to repay to the registered social landlord the whole or part of any such sums or, as the case may be, to pay to it the whole or part of the monetary value (as determined by it) of any such benefit.

Power to direct transfer of land

27.—(1) Where as a result of an inquiry under paragraph 20 or an audit under paragraph 22 the Corporation is satisfied as regards a registered social landlord—

    (a) that there has been misconduct or mismanagement in its administration, or

(b) that the management of its land would be improved if its land were transferred in accordance with the provisions of this paragraph,

the Corporation may, with the consent of the Secretary of State, direct the registered social landlord to make such a transfer.

(2) Where the registered social landlord concerned is a charity, the Corporation may only direct a transfer to be made to another registered social landlord—

(a) which is also a charity, and

(b) the objects of which appear to the Corporation to be, as nearly as practicable, akin to those of the registered social landlord concerned.

(3) In any other case the Corporation may direct a transfer to be made to the Corporation or to another registered social landlord.

(4) The transfer shall be on such terms as the Corporation may direct on the basis of principles determined by it.

The consent of the Secretary of State is required both for the terms of the transfer and for the determination of the principles on which it is based.

(5) The price shall not be less than the amount certified by the district valuer to be the amount the property would command if sold by a willing seller to another registered social landlord.

(6) The terms shall include provision as to the payment of debts and liabilities (including debts and liabilities secured on the land).

Availability of powers in relation to registered charities.

28.—(1) The Corporation may exercise its powers under paragraphs 20 to 26 in relation to a registered charity only if the charity has, at any time before the powers are exercised—

(a) received financial assistance under section 24 of the Local Government Act 1988 (assistance for privately let housing accommodation),   1988 c. 9.

(b) had property transferred to it on a qualifying disposal under section 135 of the Leasehold Reform, Housing and Urban Development Act 1993, or   1993 c. 28.

(c) received a grant or loan under any of the following provisions.

(2) The provisions are—

section 18 of this Act (social housing grant),

section 22 of this Act or section 58 of the Housing Associations Act 1985 (grants or loans by local authorities),   1985 c. 69.

section 50 of the Housing Act 1988, section 41 of the Housing Associations Act 1985 or any enactment replaced by that section (housing association grant),   1988 c. 50.

section 51 of the Housing Act 1988 or section 54 or 55 of the Housing Associations Act 1985 (revenue deficit grant or hostel deficit grant),

section 79 of the Housing Associations Act 1985 (loans by Housing Corporation),

section 31 of the Housing Act 1974 (management grants), or   1974 c. 44.

any enactment mentioned in paragraph 2 or 3 of Schedule 1 to the Housing Associations Act 1985 (pre-1974 grants and certain loans).

(3) In relation to a registered charity paragraphs 20 to 26 have effect with the following adaptations—

(a) references to its affairs are confined to its housing activities and such other activities (if any) as are incidental to or connected with its housing activities;

(b) references to its accounts do not include revenue accounts which do not relate to its housing activities, except so far as such accounts are necessary for the auditing of revenue accounts which do so relate or of the balance sheet;

(c) a person is a qualified auditor for the purpose of paragraph 22 (extraordinary audit) only if he is an auditor qualified for the purposes of paragraph 18 (accounting and audit requirements for charities).

(4) The Corporation shall notify the Charity Commissioners upon the exercise in relation to a registered charity of its powers under—

(a) paragraph 20(1) (inquiry into affairs of registered social landlord),

(b) paragraph 23(2)(a) (interim suspension of person in connection with misconduct or mismanagement), or

(c) paragraph 24(2)(a) or (b) (removal of person in connection with misconduct or mismanagement or suspension with a view to removal).

29. The Corporation may not exercise its powers under paragraph 27 in relation to a registered charity.

SCHEDULE 2

SOCIAL RENTED SECTOR: HOUSING COMPLAINTS

Social landlords required to be member of approved scheme

1.—(1) A social landlord must be a member of an approved scheme covering, or more than one approved scheme which together cover, all his housing activities.

(2) If a social landlord fails to comply with the duty imposed by this paragraph, the Secretary of State may apply to the High Court for an order directing him to comply within a specified period and the High Court may, if it thinks fit, make such an order.

(3) Nothing in this Schedule shall be construed as restricting membership of an approved scheme to social landlords.

Matters for which scheme must provide

2.—(1) A scheme shall not be approved for the purposes of this Schedule unless it makes provision for—

1. The establishment or appointment of an independent person to administer the scheme.

2. The criteria for membership for—

(a) social landlords under a duty to be members of an approved scheme, and

(b) other persons.

3. The manner of becoming or ceasing to be a member.

4. The matters about which complaints may be made under the scheme.

5. The grounds on which a matter may be excluded from investigation, including that the matter is the subject of court proceedings or was the subject of court proceedings where judgment on the merits was given.

6. The descriptions of individual who may make a complaint under the scheme.

7. The appointment of an independent individual to be the housing ombudsman under the scheme.

8. The appointment of staff to administer the scheme and to assist the housing ombudsman and the terms upon which they are appointed.

9. A duty of the housing ombudsman to investigate any complaint duly made and not withdrawn, and a power to investigate any complaint duly made but withdrawn, and where he investigates to make a determination.

10. A power of the housing ombudsman to propose alternative methods of resolving a dispute.

11. The powers of the housing ombudsman for the purposes of his investigations, and the procedure to be followed in the conduct of investigations.

12. The powers of the housing ombudsman on making a determination.

13. The making and publication of annual reports by the housing ombudsman on the discharge of his functions.

14. The manner in which determinations are to be—

(a) communicated to the complainant and the person against whom the complaint was made, and

(b) published.

15. The manner in which the expenses of the scheme are to be defrayed by the members.

16. The keeping and auditing of accounts and the submission of accounts to the Secretary of State.

17. The making of annual reports on the administration of the scheme.

18. The manner of amending the scheme.

(2) The Secretary of State may by order amend sub-paragraph (1) by adding to or deleting from it any item or by varying any item for the time being contained in it.

(3) An order under sub-paragraph (2) shall be made by statutory instrument which shall be subject to annulment in pursuance of a resolution of either House of Parliament.

Approval of scheme, or amendment, and withdrawal of approval

3.—(1) An application to the Secretary of State for approval of a scheme shall be made in such manner as the Secretary of State may determine, and shall be accompanied by such information as the Secretary of State may require.

(2) If it appears to the Secretary of State that the scheme—

(a) provides for the matters specified in paragraph 2, and

(b) is a satisfactory scheme for the purposes of this Schedule,

he shall approve the scheme.

(3) An amendment of an approved scheme is not effective unless approved by the Secretary of State.

Sub-paragraph (1) applies in relation to an application for approval of an amendment as it applies to an application for approval of a scheme; and the Secretary of State shall approve the amendment if it appears to him that the scheme as amended meets the conditions in sub-paragraph (2).

(4) The Secretary of State may withdraw his approval of a scheme.

(5) If the Secretary of State proposes to withdraw his approval of a scheme, he shall serve on the person administering the scheme and on the housing ombudsman under the scheme, a notice stating—

(a) that he proposes to withdraw his approval,

(b) the grounds for the proposed withdrawal of his approval, and

(c) that the person receiving the notice may make representations with respect to the proposed withdrawal of approval within such period of not less than 14 days as is specified in the notice;

and he shall, before reaching a decision on whether to withdraw approval, consider any representations duly made to him.

(6) The Secretary of State shall give notice of his decision on a proposal to withdraw approval of a scheme, together with his reasons, to every person on whom he served a notice under sub-paragraph (5).

(7) Withdrawal of approval by the Secretary of State has effect from such date as is specified in the notice of his decision.

(8) Where the person administering a scheme is given notice of a decision to withdraw approval of the scheme, he shall give notice of the decision to every member of the scheme.

Notice to be given of becoming a member of an approved scheme

4.—(1) A social landlord who—

(a) becomes a member of an approved scheme, or

(b) is a member of a scheme which becomes an approved scheme,

shall, within the period of 21 days beginning with the date of becoming a member or, as the case may be, of being informed of the Secretary of State's approval of the scheme, give notice of that fact to the Corporation.

(2) The Corporation, on receiving the notice, shall record his membership of an approved scheme.

(3) A person who fails to comply with sub-paragraph (1) commits an offence and is liable on summary conviction to a fine not exceeding level 4 on the standard scale.

Proceedings for such an offence may be brought only by or with the consent of the Corporation or the Director of Public Prosecutions.

Withdrawal from approved scheme

5.—(1) A social landlord wishing to withdraw from membership of an approved scheme shall send notice of his proposed withdrawal to the Corporation.

(2) The notice shall specify—

(a) the housing activities in relation to which he is subject to investigation under the scheme,

(b) the approved scheme or schemes of which he is also a member or will, on his withdrawal, become a member, and

(c) under which scheme or schemes the housing activities mentioned in paragraph (a) will be subject to investigation after his withdrawal.

(3) If the Corporation is satisfied that withdrawal by the landlord from the scheme will not result in a failure to comply with his duty under paragraph 1, it shall confirm the landlord's withdrawal from the scheme.

(4) If the Corporation is not so satisfied, it shall withhold confirmation of the landlord's withdrawal from the scheme; and the landlord shall continue to be a member of the scheme and bound and entitled under the scheme accordingly.

Register of approved schemes

6.—(1) The Corporation shall maintain a register of schemes approved by the Secretary of State for the purposes of this Schedule and of the social landlords who are members of those schemes.

(2) The Secretary of State shall give notice to the Corporation—

(a) when he grants or withdraws his approval of a scheme, and

(b) when he approves an amendment of a scheme,

and he shall supply the Corporation with copies of any approved scheme or any amendment to a scheme.

(3) A member of the public shall be entitled, upon payment of such fees as the Corporation may determine, to receive a copy of an approved scheme and a list of the social landlords who are members of it.

Determinations by housing ombudsman

7.—(1) A housing ombudsman under an approved scheme shall investigate any complaint duly made to him and not withdrawn, and may investigate any complaint duly made but withdrawn, and where he investigates a complaint he shall determine it by reference to what is, in his opinion, fair in all the circumstances of the case.

(2) He may in his determination—

(a) order the member of a scheme against whom the complaint was made to pay compensation to the complainant, and

(b) order that the member or the complainant shall not exercise or require the performance of any of the contractual or other obligations or rights existing between them.

(3) If the member against whom the complaint was made fails to comply with the determination within a reasonable time, the housing ombudsman may order him to publish in such manner as the ombudsman sees fit that he has failed to comply with the determination.

(4) Where the member is not a social landlord, the housing ombudsman may also order that the member—

(a) be expelled from the scheme, and

(b) publish in such manner as the housing ombudsman sees fit that he has been expelled and the reasons for his expulsion.

(5) If a person fails to comply with an order under sub-paragraph (3) or (4)(b), the housing ombudsman may take such steps as he thinks appropriate to publish what the member ought to have published and recover from the member the costs of doing so.

(6) A member who is ordered by the housing ombudsman to pay compensation or take any other steps has power to do so, except that a member which is also a charity shall not do anything contrary to its trusts.

Publication of determinations, &c.

8.—(1) A housing ombudsman under an approved scheme may publish—

(a) his determination on any complaint, and

(b) such reports as he thinks fit on the discharge of his functions.

(2) He may include in any such determination or report statements, communications, reports, papers or other documentary evidence obtained in the exercise of his functions.

(3) In publishing any determination or report, a housing ombudsman shall have regard to the need for excluding so far as practicable—

(a) any matter which relates to the private affairs of an individual, where publication would seriously and prejudicially affect the interests of that individual, and

(b) any matter which relates specifically to the affairs of a member of an approved scheme, where publication would seriously and prejudicially affect its interests, unless the inclusion of that matter is necessary for the purposes of the determination or report.

Absolute privilege for communications, &c.

9. For the purposes of the law of defamation absolute privilege attaches to—

(a) any communication between a housing ombudsman under an approved scheme and any person by or against whom a complaint is made to him,

(b) any determination by such an ombudsman, and

(c) the publication of such a determination or any report under paragraph 8.

Appointment and status of housing ombudsman

10.—(1) Where an approved scheme provides that it shall be administered by a body corporate, that body shall appoint on such terms as it thinks fit the housing ombudsman for the purposes of the scheme and the appointment and its terms shall be subject to the approval of the Secretary of State.

(2) Where an approved scheme does not so provide—

(a) the housing ombudsman for the purposes of the scheme shall be appointed by the Secretary of State on such terms as the Secretary of State thinks fit,

(b) the Secretary of State may by order provide that the housing ombudsman for the purposes of the scheme shall be a corporation sole, and

(c) the staff to administer the scheme and otherwise assist the ombudsman in the discharge of his functions shall be appointed and employed by him.

(3) The Secretary of State may at any time remove from office a housing ombudsman (whether appointed by him or otherwise).

(4) A housing ombudsman appointed by the Secretary of State or otherwise shall not be regarded as the servant or agent of the Crown or as enjoying any status, privilege or immunity of the Crown or as exempt from any tax, duty, rate, levy or other charge whatsoever, whether general or local, and any property held by him shall not be regarded as property of, or held on behalf of, the Crown.

Subscriptions payable in respect of approved schemes

11.—(1) Members of an approved scheme shall pay a subscription, calculated as set out in the scheme, to the person administering the scheme.

(2) If a social landlord fails to comply with his duty under paragraph 1, the Secretary of State may determine—

(a) which approved scheme or schemes he should have joined, and

(b) what sums by way of subscription he should have paid,

and may require him to pay those amounts to the person administering the scheme or schemes.

(3) The person administering an approved scheme may recover sums payable under sub-paragraph (1) or (2) as if they were debts due to him.

(4) The Secretary of State or the Corporation may pay grant and provide other financial assistance to—

(a) a body corporate administering an approved scheme, or

(b) in a case where paragraph 10(2) applies, to the housing ombudsman under an approved scheme,

for such purposes and upon such terms as the Secretary of State or, as the case may be, the Corporation thinks fit.

SCHEDULE 3

Social rented sector: minor amendments

Finance Act 1981 (c.35)

Section 55.

1.—(1) Section 107 of the Finance Act 1981 (stamp duty payable upon sale of houses at a discount) is amended as follows.

(2) After subsection (3)(e) insert—

"(ea) a registered social landlord within the meaning of Part I of the Housing Act 1996;".

(3) In subsection (3)(f) for the words from "registered" to the end substitute "registered—

(i) in Scotland, under the Housing Associations Act 1985, or

(ii) in Northern Ireland, under Part II of the Housing (Northern Ireland) Order 1992;".

(4) In subsection (3A) (exclusion of certain sub-sales), for "subsection (3)(f)" substitute "subsection (3)(ea) or (f)".

(5) After subsection (3B) insert—

"(3C) A grant under section 20 or 21 of the Housing Act 1996 (purchase grants in respect of disposals at a discount by registered social landlords) shall not be treated as part of the consideration for a conveyance or transfer to which this section applies made by a body falling within subsection (3)(ea) above.".

Local Government Finance Act 1982 (c.32)

2.—(1) In Part III of the Local Government Finance Act 1982 (establishment and functions of Audit Commission), after section 28A insert—

"General functions of Commission in relation to registered social landlords.

28B.—(1) The Corporation and the Commission may agree one or more programmes of comparative studies designed to enable the Commission to make recommendations for improving economy, efficiency and effectiveness of registered social landlords.

(2) Where the Corporation and the Commission fail to agree a programme proposed by either of them, either of them may refer the matter to the Secretary of State who may direct that the programme be carried out either without modifications or with modifications specified in the direction.

(3) Where a programme is agreed or is directed to be carried out, the Commission shall ensure that studies giving effect to the programme are carried out by it or on its behalf.

(4) It shall be a term of every such programme that the Corporation make good to the Commission the full costs incurred by the Commission in carrying out the programme.

(5) The Commission shall publish reports on the studies carried out under this section.

(6) Before publishing any such report the Commission shall show a draft of it to the Corporation and shall consider whether to revise the draft in the light of the comments made by the Corporation.

Provisions
supplementary to
s.28B.

28C.—(1) The Commission may, if authorised to do so by the Corporation—

    (a) require a registered social landlord, or any officer or member of a registered social landlord, to supply such information as the Commission may require for the purposes of any study under section 28B above; and

    (b) require a registered social landlord included in any such study to make available for inspection such documents as are reasonably required for the purposes of the study.

(2) The Commission may require the information to be supplied, or the documents to be made available, to the Commission or to a person authorised by the Commission for the purposes of this section.

(3) A person who without reasonable excuse fails to comply with a requirement under this section commits an offence and is liable on summary conviction to a fine not exceeding level 3 on the standard scale.

(4) Information obtained by the Commission, or by a person acting on behalf of the Commission, in the course of a study under section 28B above may be disclosed by the Commission to the Corporation notwithstanding anything in section 30 below (general restriction on disclosure of information relating to particular bodies or persons).

Functions of
Commission in
relation to audit
of accounts of
registered social
landlords.

28D.—(1) The Commission may provide the Corporation with consultancy services relating to the audit of accounts of registered social landlords.

(2) The Commission may recover from the Corporation such costs incurred in providing the services as may be agreed by the Corporation.

Meaning of "the
Corporation" and
"registered social
landlord".

28E. In sections 28B to 28D above "the Corporation" and "registered social landlord" have the same meaning as in Part I of the Housing Act 1996.".

(2) In paragraph 9 of Schedule 3 to the Local Government Finance Act 1982 (the Audit Commission: duty to balance income and expenditure), in sub-paragraph (2) (functions to be managed separately) after sub-paragraph (a) insert—

    "(aa) its functions under sections 28B and 28C relating to registered social landlords;

    (ab) its functions under section 28D relating to such landlords;".

Housing Associations Act 1985 (c.69)

3. Section 33 of the Housing Associations Act 1985 (recognition of central association) shall cease to have effect.

4. In section 69(1) of the Housing Associations Act 1985 (power to vary or terminate certain agreements with housing associations: agreements to which the section applies), omit paragraphs (e) and (g).

5. In section 75(1) of the Housing Associations Act 1985 (general functions of the Corporation) for paragraphs (a) to (c) substitute—

"(a) to facilitate the proper performance of the functions of registered social landlords;

(b) to maintain a register of social landlords and to exercise supervision and control over such persons;

(c) to promote and assist the development of self-build societies (other than registered social landlords) and to facilitate the proper performance of the functions, and to publicise the aims and principles, of such societies;".

6. In Part III of the Housing Associations Act 1985 (general provisions relating to the Housing Corporation and Housing for Wales), after section 76 (general power of Secretary of State to give directions to Corporation) insert—

"Realisation of value of Corporation's loans portfolio.

76A.—(1) The Corporation may, and if so directed by the Secretary of State (under section 76) shall, enter into arrangements of a description approved by the Secretary of State for the purpose of realising the value of the whole or part of its loans portfolio.

(2) The arrangements may provide for—

(a) the transfer of any estate or interest of the Corporation, or

(b) the creation or disposal of economic interests not involving a transfer of an estate or interest,

and may extend to such incidental or ancillary matters as the Corporation or the Secretary of State considers appropriate.

(3) In this section the Corporation's "loans portfolio" means the Corporation's rights and obligations in relation to any loans or related securities.

(4) Nothing in the terms of any loan or related transaction entered into by the Corporation shall be construed as impliedly prohibiting or restricting the Corporation from dealing with its loans portfolio in accordance with arrangements under this section.".

7. In section 87 of the Housing Associations Act 1985 (financial assistance for formation, management, &c. of housing associations), for subsection (1) substitute—

"(1) The Corporation may give financial assistance to any person to facilitate the proper performance of the functions of registered social landlords or co-operative housing associations.".

Income and Corporation Taxes Act 1988 (c.1)

8.—(1) The Income and Corporation Taxes Act 1988 is amended as follows.

(2) In section 488 (co-operative housing associations), after subsection (7) insert—

"(7A) The Secretary of State may delegate any of his functions under subsections (6) and (7)—

(a) to the Housing Corporation, in the case of a body registered as a social landlord in the register maintained by the Housing Corporation under Part I of the Housing Act 1996, and

(b) to Housing for Wales, in the case of a body registered as a social landlord in the register maintained under that Part by Housing for Wales,

to such extent and subject to such conditions as he may specify.".

(3) In section 489 (self-build societies), after subsection (5) insert—

"(5A) The Secretary of State may delegate any of his functions under subsections (4) and (5) to—

(a) the Housing Corporation, where the society has its registered office in England for the purposes of the Industrial and Provident Societies Act 1965, and

(b) Housing for Wales, where the society has its registered office in Wales for the purposes of that Act,

to such extent and subject to such conditions as he may specify.".

Housing (Scotland) Act 1988 (c.43)

9. After section 2 of the Housing (Scotland) Act 1988 (general functions of Scottish Homes) insert—

"Sale of Scottish Homes' loans portfolio.   2A.—(1) Subject to subsection (2) below, Scottish Homes may enter into arrangements of a description approved by the Secretary of State for the purpose of realising the value of the whole or part of its loans portfolio.

(2) Without prejudice to the power of the Secretary of State to give directions under section 2(10) above, the Secretary of State may direct Scottish Homes to enter into arrangements under this section and it shall be the duty of Scottish Homes to comply with any such direction.

(3) The arrangements may provide for—

(a) the transfer of any estate or interest of Scottish Homes, or

(b) the creation or disposal of economic interests not involving a transfer of an estate or interest,

and may extend to such incidental or ancillary matters as Scottish Homes or the Secretary of State considers appropriate.

(4) In this section, Scottish Homes' "loans portfolio" means Scottish Homes' rights and obligations in relation to any loans or related securities.

(5) Nothing in the terms of any loan or related transaction entered into by Scottish Homes shall be construed as impliedly prohibiting or restricting it from dealing with its loans portfolio in accordance with arrangements under this section.

(6) A direction given under subsection (2) above may be varied or revoked by a subsequent direction given by the Secretary of State.".

Housing Act 1988 (c.50)

10. Section 58 of the Housing Act 1988 (application of Housing Acts to certain transactions) shall cease to have effect.

11. In section 79(2) of the Housing Act 1988 (permitted disposals of land by housing action trusts) for paragraph (a) and the word "or" at the end of the paragraph substitute—

> "(a) to a registered social landlord (within the meaning of Part I of the Housing Act 1996), or".

SCHEDULE 4

RIGHTS EXERCISABLE BY SURVEYOR APPOINTED BY TENANTS' ASSOCIATION

Introductory

1.—(1) A surveyor appointed for the purposes of section 84 has the rights conferred by this Schedule.

(2) In this Schedule—

(a) "the tenants' association" means the association by whom the surveyor was appointed, and

(b) the surveyor's "functions" are his functions in connection with the matters in respect of which he was appointed.

Appointment of assistants

2.—(1) The surveyor may appoint such persons as he thinks fit to assist him in carrying out his functions.

(2) References in this Schedule to the surveyor in the context of—

(a) being afforded any such facilities as are mentioned in paragraph 3, or

(b) carrying out an inspection under paragraph 4,

include a person so appointed.

Right to inspect documents, &c.

3.—(1) The surveyor has a right to require the landlord or any other relevant person—

(a) to afford him reasonable facilities for inspecting any documents sight of which is reasonably required by him for the purposes of his functions, and

(b) to afford him reasonable facilities for taking copies of or extracts from any such documents.

(2) In sub-paragraph (1) "other relevant person" means a person other than the landlord who is or, in relation to a future service charge, will be—

(a) responsible for applying the proceeds of the service charge, or

(b) under an obligation to a tenant who pays the service charge in respect of any matter to which the charge relates.

(3) The rights conferred on the surveyor by this paragraph are exercisable by him by notice in writing given by him to the landlord or other person concerned.

Where a notice is given to a person other than the landlord, the surveyor shall give a copy of the notice to the landlord.

(4) The landlord or other person to whom notice is given shall, within the period of one week beginning with the date of the giving of the notice or as soon as reasonably practicable thereafter, either—

(a) afford the surveyor the facilities required by him for inspecting and taking copies or extracts of the documents to which the notice relates, or

(b) give the surveyor a notice stating that he objects to doing so for reasons specified in the notice.

(5) Facilities for the inspection of any documents required under sub-paragraph (1)(a) shall be made available free of charge.

This does not mean that the landlord cannot treat as part of his costs of management any costs incurred by him in connection with making the facilities available.

(6) A reasonable charge may be made for facilities for the taking of copies or extracts required under sub-paragraph (1)(b).

(7) A notice is duly given under this paragraph to the landlord of a tenant if it is given to a person who receives on behalf of the landlord the rent payable by that tenant.

A person to whom such a notice is so given shall forward it as soon as may be to the landlord.

Right to inspect premises

4.—(1) The surveyor also has the right to inspect any common parts comprised in relevant premises or any appurtenant property.

(2) In sub-paragraph (1)—

"common parts", in relation to a building or part of a building, includes the structure and exterior of the building or part and any common facilities within it;

"relevant premises" means so much of—

(i) the building or buildings containing the dwellings let to members of the tenants' association, and

(ii) any other building or buildings,

as constitute premises in relation to which management functions are discharged in respect of the costs of which service charges are payable by members of the association; and

"appurtenant property" means so much of any property not contained in relevant premises as constitutes property in relation to which any such management functions are discharged.

For the purposes of the above definitions "management functions" includes functions with respect to the provision of services, or the repair, maintenance or insurance of property.

(3) On being requested to do so, the landlord shall afford the surveyor reasonable access for the purposes of carrying out an inspection under this paragraph.

(4) Such reasonable access shall be afforded to the surveyor free of charge.

This does not mean that the landlord cannot treat as part of his costs of management any costs incurred by him in connection with affording reasonable access to the surveyor.

(5) A request is duly made under this paragraph to the landlord of a tenant if it is made to a person appointed by the landlord to deal with such requests or, if no such person has been appointed, to a person who receives on behalf of the landlord the rent payable by that tenant.

A person to whom such a request is made shall notify the landlord of the request as soon as may be.

Enforcement of rights by the court

5.—(1) If the landlord or other person to whom notice was given under paragraph 3 has not, by the end of the period of one month beginning with the date on which notice was given, complied with the notice, the court may, on the application of the surveyor, make an order requiring him to do so within such period as is specified in the order.

(2) If the landlord does not, within a reasonable period after the making of a request under paragraph 4, afford the surveyor reasonable access for the purposes of carrying out an inspection under that paragraph, the court may, on the application of the surveyor, make an order requiring the landlord to do so on such date as is specified in the order.

(3) An application for an order under this paragraph must be made before the end of the period of four months beginning with the date on which notice was given under paragraph 3 or the request was made under paragraph 4.

(4) An order under this paragraph may be made in general terms or may require the landlord or other person to do specific things, as the court thinks fit.

Documents held by superior landlord

6.—(1) Where a landlord is required by a notice under paragraph 3 to afford the surveyor facilities for inspection or taking copies or extracts in respect of any document which is in the custody or under the control of a superior landlord—

(a) the landlord shall on receiving the notice inform the surveyor as soon as may be of that fact and of the name and address of the superior landlord, and

(b) the surveyor may then give the superior landlord notice in writing requiring him to afford the facilities in question in respect of the document.

(2) Paragraphs 3 and 5(1) and (3) have effect, with any necessary modifications, in relation to a notice given to a superior landlord under this paragraph.

Effect of disposal by landlord

7.—(1) Where a notice under paragraph 3 has been given or a request under paragraph 4 has been made to a landlord, and at a time when any obligations arising out of the notice or request remain to be discharged by him—

(a) he disposes of the whole or part of his interest as landlord of any member of the tenants' association, and

(b) the person acquiring that interest ("the transferee") is in a position to discharge any of those obligations to any extent,

that person shall be responsible for discharging those obligations to that extent, as if he had been given the notice under paragraph 3 or had received the request under paragraph 4.

(2) If the landlord is, despite the disposal, still in a position to discharge those obligations, he remains responsible for doing so.

Otherwise, the transferee is responsible for discharging them to the exclusion of the landlord.

(3) In connection with the discharge of such obligations by the transferee, paragraphs 3 to 6 apply with the substitution for any reference to the date on which notice was given under paragraph 3 or the request was made under paragraph 4 of a reference to the date of the disposal.

(4) In this paragraph "disposal" means a disposal whether by the creation or transfer of an estate or interest, and includes the surrender of a tenancy; and references to the transferee shall be construed accordingly.

Effect of person ceasing to be a relevant person

8. Where a notice under paragraph 3 has been given to a person other than the landlord and, at a time when any obligations arising out of the notice remain to be discharged by him, he ceases to be such a person as is mentioned in paragraph 3(2), then, if he is still in a position to discharge those obligations to any extent he remains responsible for discharging those obligations, and the provisions of this Schedule continue to apply to him, to that extent.

Section 87.

SCHEDULE 5

Text of Part II of the Landlord and Tenant Act 1987, as amended

"Part II

Appointment of Managers by Leasehold Valuation Tribunal

Tenant's right to apply to tribunal for appointment of manager.

21.—(1) The tenant of a flat contained in any premises to which this Part applies may, subject to the following provisions of this Part, apply to a leasehold valuation tribunal for an order under section 24 appointing a manager to act in relation to those premises.

(2) Subject to subsection (3), this Part applies to premises consisting of the whole or part of a building if the building or part contains two or more flats.

(3) This Part does not apply to any such premises at a time when—

(a) the interest of the landlord in the premises is held by an exempt landlord or a resident landlord, or

(b) the premises are included within the functional land of any charity.

(4) An application for an order under section 24 may be made—

(a) jointly by tenants of two or more flats if they are each entitled to make such an application by virtue of this section, and

(b) in respect of two or more premises to which this Part applies;

and, in relation to any such joint application as is mentioned in paragraph (a), references in this Part to a single tenant shall be construed accordingly.

(5) Where the tenancy of a flat contained in any such premises is held by joint tenants, an application for an order under section 24 in respect of those premises may be made by any one or more of those tenants.

(6) An application to the court for it to exercise in relation to any premises any jurisdiction to appoint a receiver or manager shall not be made by a tenant (in his capacity as such) in any circumstances in which an application could be made by him for an order under section 24 appointing a manager to act in relation to those premises.

1954 c. 56.

(7) References in this Part to a tenant do not include references to a tenant under a tenancy to which Part II of the Landlord and Tenant Act 1954 applies.

Preliminary notice by tenant.

22.—(1) Before an application for an order under section 24 is made in respect of any premises to which this Part applies by a tenant of a flat contained in those premises, a notice under this section must (subject to subsection (3)) be served on the landlord by the tenant.

(2) A notice under this section must—

(a) specify the tenant's name, the address of his flat and an address in England and Wales (which may be the address of his flat) at which the landlord may serve notices, including notices in proceedings, on him in connection with this Part;

(b) state that the tenant intends to make an application for an order under section 24 to be made by a leasehold valuation tribunal in respect of such premises to which this Part applies as are specified in the notice, but (if paragraph (d) is applicable) that he will not do so if the landlord complies with the requirement specified in pursuance of that paragraph;

(c) specify the grounds on which the tribunal would be asked to make such an order and the matters that would be relied on by the tenant for the purpose of establishing those grounds;

(d) where those matters are capable of being remedied by the landlord, require the landlord, within such reasonable period as is specified in the notice, to take such steps for the purpose of remedying them as are so specified; and

(e) contain such information (if any) as the Secretary of State may by regulations prescribe.

(3) A leasehold valuation tribunal may (whether on the hearing of an application for an order under section 24 or not) by order dispense with the requirement to serve a notice under this section in a case where it is satisfied that it would not be reasonably practicable to serve such a notice on the landlord, but the tribunal may, when doing so, direct that such other notices are served, or such other steps are taken, as it thinks fit.

(4) In a case where—

(a) a notice under this section has been served on the landlord, and

(b) his interest in the premises specified in pursuance of subsection (2)(b) is subject to a mortgage,

the landlord shall, as soon as is reasonably practicable after receiving the notice, serve on the mortgagee a copy of the notice.

23.—(1) No application for an order under section 24 shall be made to a leasehold valuation tribunal unless—

(a) in a case where a notice has been served under section 22, either—

(i) the period specified in pursuance of paragraph (d) of subsection (2) of that section has expired without the landlord having taken the steps that he was required to take in pursuance of that provision, or

(ii) that paragraph was not applicable in the circumstances of the case; or

(b) in a case where the requirement to serve such a notice has been dispensed with by an order under subsection (3) of that section, either—

(i) any notices required to be served, and any other steps required to be taken, by virtue of the order have been served or (as the case may be) taken, or

(ii) no direction was given by the tribunal when making the order.

(2) Procedure regulations shall make provision—

(a) for requiring notice of an application for an order under section 24 in respect of any premises to be served on such descriptions of persons as may be specified in the regulations; and

(b) for enabling persons served with any such notice to be joined as parties to the proceedings.

Application to tribunal for appointment of manager.

24.—(1) A leasehold valuation tribunal may, on an application for an order under this section, by order (whether interlocutory or final) appoint a manager to carry out in relation to any premises to which this Part applies—

Appointment of manager by the tribunal.

(a) such functions in connection with the management of the premises, or

(b) such functions of a receiver,

or both, as the tribunal thinks fit.

(2) A leasehold valuation tribunal may only make an order under this section in the following circumstances, namely—

(a) where the tribunal is satisfied—

(i) that the landlord either is in breach of any obligation owed by him to the tenant under his tenancy and relating to the management of the premises in question or any part of them or (in the case of an obligation dependent on notice) would be in breach of any such obligation but for the fact that it has not been reasonably practicable for the tenant to give him the appropriate notice, and

(ii) that it is just and convenient to make the order in all the circumstances of the case;

(ab) where the tribunal is satisfied—

(i) that unreasonable service charges have been made, or are proposed or likely to be made, and

(iii) that it is just and convenient to make the order in all the circumstances of the case;

(ac) where the tribunal is satisfied—

1993 c. 28.

(i) that the landlord has failed to comply with any relevant provision of a code of practice approved by the Secretary of State under section 87 of the Leasehold Reform, Housing and Urban Development Act 1993 (codes of management practice), and

(ii) that it is just and convenient to make the order in all the circumstances of the case; or

(b) where the tribunal is satisfied that other circumstances exist which make it just and convenient for the order to be made.

(2A) For the purposes of subsection (2)(ab) a service charge shall be taken to be unreasonable—

(a) if the amount is unreasonable having regard to the items for which it is payable,

(b) if the items for which it is payable are of an unnecessarily high standard, or

(c) if the items for which it is payable are of an insufficient standard with the result that additional service charges are or may be incurred.

1985 c. 70.

In that provision and this subsection "service charge" means a service charge within the meaning of section 18(1) of the Landlord and Tenant Act 1985, other than one excluded from that section by section 27 of that Act (rent of dwelling registered and not entered as variable).

(3) The premises in respect of which an order is made under this section may, if the tribunal thinks fit, be either more or less extensive than the premises specified in the application on which the order is made.

(4) An order under this section may make provision with respect to—

(a) such matters relating to the exercise by the manager of his functions under the order, and

(b) such incidental or ancillary matters,

as the tribunal thinks fit; and, on any subsequent application made for the purpose by the manager, the tribunal may give him directions with respect to any such matters.

(5) Without prejudice to the generality of subsection (4), an order under this section may provide—

(a) for rights and liabilities arising under contracts to which the manager is not a party to become rights and liabilities of the manager;

(b) for the manager to be entitled to prosecute claims in respect of causes of action (whether contractual or tortious) accruing before or after the date of his appointment;

(c) for remuneration to be paid to the manager by the landlord, or by the tenants of the premises in respect of which the order is made or by all or any of those persons;

(d) for the manager's functions to be exercisable by him (subject to subsection (9)) either during a specified period or without limit of time.

(6) Any such order may be granted subject to such conditions as the tribunal thinks fit, and in particular its operation may be suspended on terms fixed by the tribunal.

(7) In a case where an application for an order under this section was preceded by the service of a notice under section 22, the tribunal may, if it thinks fit, make such an order notwithstanding—

(a) that any period specified in the notice in pursuance of subsection (2)(d) of that section was not a reasonable period, or

(b) that the notice failed in any other respect to comply with any requirement contained in subsection (2) of that section or in any regulations applying to the notice under section 54(3).

(8) The Land Charges Act 1972 and the Land Registration Act 1925 shall apply in relation to an order made under this section as they apply in relation to an order appointing a receiver or sequestrator of land.

1972 c. 61.
1925 c. 21.

(9) A leasehold valuation tribunal may, on the application of any person interested, vary or discharge (whether conditionally or unconditionally) an order made under this section; and if the order has been protected by an entry registered under the Land Charges Act 1972 or the Land Registration Act 1925, the tribunal may by order direct that the entry shall be cancelled.

(9A) The court shall not vary or discharge an order under subsection (9) on a landlord's application unless it is satisfied—

(a) that the variation or discharge of the order will not result in a recurrence of the circumstances which led to the order being made, and

(b) that it is just and convenient in all the circumstances of the case to vary or discharge the order.

(10) An order made under this section shall not be discharged by a leasehold valuation tribunal by reason only that, by virtue of section 21(3), the premises in respect of which the order was made have ceased to be premises to which this Part applies.

(11) References in this section to the management of any premises include references to the repair, maintenance or insurance of those premises.

24A.—(1) The jurisdiction conferred by this Part on a leasehold valuation tribunal is exercisable by a rent assessment committee constituted in accordance with Schedule 10 to the Rent Act 1977 which when so constituted for the purposes of exercising any such jurisdiction shall be known as a leasehold valuation tribunal.

Jurisdiction of leasehold valuation tribunal.
1977 c. 42.

(2) The power to make regulations under section 74(1)(b) of the Rent Act 1977 (procedure of rent assessment committees) extends to prescribing the procedure to be followed in connection with any proceedings before a leasehold valuation tribunal under this Part.

Such regulations are referred to in this Part as "procedure regulations".

(3) Any order made by a leasehold valuation tribunal under this Part may, with the leave of the court, be enforced in the same way as an order of the county court.

(4) No costs incurred by a party in connection with proceedings under this Part before a leasehold valuation tribunal shall be recoverable by order of any court.

(5) Paragraphs 2, 3 and 7 of Schedule 22 to the Housing Act 1980 (supplementary provisions relating to leasehold valuation tribunals: appeals and provision of information) apply to a leasehold valuation tribunal constituted for the purposes of this section.

(6) No appeal shall lie to the Lands Tribunal from a decision of a leasehold valuation tribunal under this Part without the leave of the leasehold valuation tribunal concerned or the Lands Tribunal.

(7) On an appeal to the Lands Tribunal from a decision of a leasehold valuation tribunal under this Part—

(a) the Lands Tribunal may exercise any power available to the leasehold valuation tribunal in relation to the original matter, and

(b) an order of the Lands Tribunal may be enforced in the same way as an order of the leasehold valuation tribunal.

Leasehold valuation tribunal: applications and fees.

24B.—(1) The Secretary of State may make provision by order as to the form of, or the particulars to be contained in, an application made to a leasehold valuation tribunal under this Part.

(2) The Secretary of State may make provision by order—

(a) requiring the payment of fees in respect of any such application, or in respect of any proceedings before, a leasehold valuation tribunal under this Part; and

(b) empowering a leasehold valuation tribunal to require a party to proceedings before it to reimburse any other party the amount of any fees paid by him.

(3) The fees payable shall be such as may be specified in or determined in accordance with the order subject to this limit, that the fees payable in respect of any one application or reference by the court together with any proceedings before the tribunal arising out of that application or reference shall not exceed £500 or such other amount as may be specified by order of the Secretary of State.

(4) An order under this section may make different provision for different cases or classes of case or for different areas.

(5) An order may, in particular, provide for the reduction or waiver of fees by reference to the financial resources of the party by whom they are to be paid or met.

Any such order may apply, subject to such modifications as may be specified in the order, any other statutory means-testing regime as it has effect from time to time.

(6) An order under this section shall be made by statutory instrument.

(7) No order altering the limit under subsection (3) shall be made unless a draft of the order has been laid before and approved by a resolution of each House of Parliament.

(8) Any other order under this section, unless it contains only such provision as is mentioned in subsection (1), shall be subject to annulment in pursuance of a resolution of either House of Parliament.".

SCHEDULE 6

AMENDMENTS OF PART I OF THE LANDLORD AND TENANT ACT 1987

PART I

RIGHTS OF FIRST REFUSAL

The following sections are substituted for sections 5 to 10 of the Landlord and Tenant Act 1987—

"Rights of first refusal

5.—(1) Where the landlord proposes to make a relevant disposal affecting premises to which this Part applies, he shall serve a notice under this section (an "offer notice") on the qualifying tenants of the flats contained in the premises (the "constituent flats").

Landlord required to serve offer notice on tenants.

(2) An offer notice must comply with the requirements of whichever is applicable of the following sections—

   section 5A (requirements in case of contract to be completed by conveyance, &c.),

   section 5B (requirements in case of sale at auction),

   section 5C (requirements in case of grant of option or right of pre-emption),

   section 5D (requirements in case of conveyance not preceded by contract, &c.);

and in the case of a disposal to which section 5E applies (disposal for non-monetary consideration) shall also comply with the requirements of that section.

(3) Where a landlord proposes to effect a transaction involving the disposal of an estate or interest in more than one building (whether or not involving the same estate or interest), he shall, for the purpose of complying with this section, sever the transaction so as to deal with each building separately.

(4) If, as a result of the offer notice being served on different tenants on different dates, the period specified in the notice as the period for accepting the offer would end on different dates, the notice shall have effect in relation to all the qualifying tenants on whom it is served as if it provided for that period to end with the latest of those dates.

(5) A landlord who has not served an offer notice on all of the qualifying tenants on whom it was required to be served shall nevertheless be treated as having complied with this section—

   (a) if he has served an offer notice on not less than 90% of the qualifying tenants on whom such a notice was required to be served, or

   (b) where the qualifying tenants on whom it was required to be served number less than ten, if he has served such a notice on all but one of them.

5A.—(1) The following requirements must be met in relation to an offer notice where the disposal consists of entering into a contract to create or transfer an estate or interest in land.

Offer notice: requirements in case of contract to be completed by conveyance, &c.

(2) The notice must contain particulars of the principal terms of the disposal proposed by the landlord, including in particular—

   (a) the property, and the estate or interest in that property, to which the contract relates,

   (b) the principal terms of the contract (including the deposit and consideration required).

(3) The notice must state that the notice constitutes an offer by the landlord to enter into a contract on those terms which may be accepted by the requisite majority of qualifying tenants of the constituent flats.

(4) The notice must specify a period within which that offer may be so accepted, being a period of not less than two months which is to begin with the date of service of the notice.

(5) The notice must specify a further period of not less than two months within which a person or persons may be nominated by the tenants under section 6.

(6) This section does not apply to the grant of an option or right of pre-emption (see section 5C).

Offer notice: requirements in case of sale by auction.

5B.—(1) The following requirements must be met in relation to an offer notice where the landlord proposes to make the disposal by means of a sale at a public auction held in England and Wales.

(2) The notice must contain particulars of the principal terms of the disposal proposed by the landlord, including in particular the property to which it relates and the estate or interest in that property proposed to be disposed of.

(3) The notice must state that the disposal is proposed to be made by means of a sale at a public auction.

(4) The notice must state that the notice constitutes an offer by the landlord, which may be accepted by the requisite majority of qualifying tenants of the constituent flats, for the contract (if any) entered into by the landlord at the auction to have effect as if a person or persons nominated by them, and not the purchaser, had entered into it.

(5) The notice must specify a period within which that offer may be so accepted, being a period of not less than two months beginning with the date of service of the notice.

(6) The notice must specify a further period of not less than 28 days within which a person or persons may be nominated by the tenants under section 6.

(7) The notice must be served not less than four months or more than six months before the date of the auction; and—

(a) the period specified in the notice as the period within which the offer may be accepted must end not less than two months before the date of the auction, and

(b) the period specified in the notice as the period within which a person may be nominated under section 6 must end not less than 28 days before the date of the auction.

(8) Unless the time and place of the auction and the name of the auctioneers are stated in the notice, the landlord shall, not less than 28 days before the date of the auction, serve on the requisite majority of qualifying tenants of the constituent flats a further notice stating those particulars.

Offer notice: requirements in case of grant or option or right of pre-emption.

5C.—(1) The following requirements must be met in relation to an offer notice where the disposal consists of the grant of an option or right of pre-emption.

(2) The notice must contain particulars of the principal terms of the disposal proposed by the landlord, including in particular—

(a) the property, and the estate or interest in that property, to which the option or right of pre-emption relates,

(b) the consideration required by the landlord for granting the option or right of pre-emption, and

(c) the principal terms on which the option or right of pre-emption would be exercisable, including the consideration payable on its exercise.

(3) The notice must state that the notice constitutes an offer by the landlord to grant an option or right of pre-emption on those terms which may be accepted by the requisite majority of qualifying tenants of the constituent flats.

(4) The notice must specify a period within which that offer may be so accepted, being a period of not less than two months which is to begin with the date of service of the notice.

(5) The notice must specify a further period of not less than two months within which a person or persons may be nominated by the tenants under section 6.

5D.—(1) The following requirements must be met in relation to an offer notice where the disposal is not made in pursuance of a contract, option or right of pre-emption binding on the landlord.

(2) The notice must contain particulars of the principal terms of the disposal proposed by the landlord, including in particular—

> (a) the property to which it relates and the estate or interest in that property proposed to be disposed of, and
>
> (b) the consideration required by the landlord for making the disposal.

(3) The notice must state that the notice constitutes an offer by the landlord to dispose of the property on those terms which may be accepted by the requisite majority of qualifying tenants of the constituent flats.

(4) The notice must specify a period within which that offer may be so accepted, being a period of not less than two months which is to begin with the date of service of the notice.

(5) The notice must specify a further period of not less than two months within which a person or persons may be nominated by the tenants under section 6.

Offer notice: requirements in case of conveyance not preceded by contract, &c.

5E.—(1) This section applies where, in any case to which section 5 applies, the consideration required by the landlord for making the disposal does not consist, or does not wholly consist, of money.

(2) The offer notice, in addition to complying with whichever is applicable of sections 5A to 5D, must state—

> (a) that an election may made under section 8C (explaining its effect), and
>
> (b) that, accordingly, the notice also constitutes an offer by the landlord, which may be accepted by the requisite majority of qualifying tenants of the constituent flats, for a person or persons nominated by them to acquire the property in pursuance of sections 11 to 17.

(3) The notice must specify a period within which that offer may be so accepted, being a period of not less than two months which is to begin with the date of service of the notice.

Offer notice: disposal for non-monetary consideration.

6.—(1) Where a landlord has served an offer notice, he shall not during—

> (a) the period specified in the notice as the period during which the offer may be accepted, or
>
> (b) such longer period as may be agreed between him and the requisite majority of the qualifying tenants of the constituent flats,

dispose of the protected interest except to a person or persons nominated by the tenants under this section.

(2) Where an acceptance notice is duly served on him, he shall not during the protected period (see subsection (4) below) dispose of the protected interest except to a person duly nominated for the purposes of this section by the requisite majority of qualifying tenants of the constituent flats (a "nominated person").

Acceptance of landlord's offer: general provisions.

(3) An "acceptance notice" means a notice served on the landlord by the requisite majority of qualifying tenants of the constituent flats informing him that the persons by whom it is served accept the offer contained in his notice.

An acceptance notice is "duly served" if it is served within—

(a) the period specified in the offer notice as the period within which the offer may be accepted, or

(b) such longer period as may be agreed between the landlord and the requisite majority of qualifying tenants of the constituent flats.

(4) The "protected period" is the period beginning with the date of service of the acceptance notice and ending with—

(a) the end of the period specified in the offer notice as the period for nominating a person under this section, or

(b) such later date as may be agreed between the landlord and the requisite majority of qualifying tenants of constituent flats.

(5) A person is "duly nominated" for the purposes of this section if he is nominated at the same time as the acceptance notice is served or at any time after that notice is served and before the end of—

(a) the period specified in the offer notice as the period for nomination, or

(b) such longer period as may be agreed between the landlord and the requisite majority of qualifying tenants of the constituent flats.

(6) A person nominated for the purposes of this section by the requisite majority of qualifying tenants of the constituent flats may be replaced by another person so nominated if, and only if, he has (for any reason) ceased to be able to act as a nominated person.

(7) Where two or more persons have been nominated and any of them ceases to act without being replaced, the remaining person or persons so nominated may continue to act.

Failure to accept landlord's offer or to make nomination.

7.—(1) Where a landlord has served an offer notice on the qualifying tenants of the constituent flats and—

(a) no acceptance notice is duly served on the landlord, or

(b) no person is nominated for the purposes of section 6 during the protected period,

the landlord may, during the period of 12 months beginning with the end of that period, dispose of the protected interest to such person as he thinks fit, but subject to the following restrictions.

(2) Where the offer notice was one to which section 5B applied (sale by auction), the restrictions are—

(a) that the disposal is made by means of a sale at a public auction, and

(b) that the other terms correspond to those specified in the offer notice.

(3) In any other case the restrictions are—

(a) that the deposit and consideration required are not less than those specified in the offer notice, and

(b) that the other terms correspond to those specified in the offer notice.

(4) The entitlement of a landlord, by virtue of this section or any other corresponding provision of this Part, to dispose of the protected interest during a specified period of 12 months extends only to a disposal of that interest, and accordingly the requirements of section 1(1) must be satisfied with respect to any other disposal by him during that period of 12 months (unless the disposal is not a relevant disposal affecting any premises to which at the time of the disposal this Part applies).

8.—(1) This section applies where a landlord serves an offer notice on the qualifying tenants of the constituent flat and—

    (a) an acceptance notice is duly served on him, and

    (b) a person is duly nominated for the purposes of section 6,

by the requisite majority of qualifying tenants of the constituent flats.

Landlord's obligations in case of acceptance and nomination.

(2) Subject to the following provisions of this Part, the landlord shall not dispose of the protected interest except to the nominated person.

(3) The landlord shall, within the period of one month beginning with the date of service of notice of nomination, either—

    (a) serve notice on the nominated person indicating an intention no longer to proceed with the disposal of the protected interest, or

    (b) be obliged to proceed in accordance with the following provisions of this Part.

(4) A notice under subsection (3)(a) is a notice of withdrawal for the purposes of section 9B(2) to (4) (consequences of notice of withdrawal by landlord).

(5) Nothing in this section shall be taken as prejudicing the application of the provisions of this Part to any further offer notice served by the landlord on the qualifying tenants of the constituent flats.

8A.—(1) This section applies where the landlord is obliged to proceed and the offer notice was not one to which section 5B applied (sale by auction).

Landlord's obligation: general provisions.

(2) The landlord shall, within the period of one month beginning with the date of service of the notice of nomination, send to the nominated person a form of contract for the acquisition of the protected interest on the terms specified in the landlord's offer notice.

(3) If he fails to do so, the following provisions of this Part apply as if he had given notice under section 9B (notice of withdrawal by landlord) at the end of that period.

(4) If the landlord complies with subsection (2), the nominated person shall, within the period of two months beginning with the date on which it is sent or such longer period beginning with that date as may be agreed between the landlord and that person, either—

    (a) serve notice on the landlord indicating an intention no longer to proceed with the acquisition of the protected interest, or

    (b) offer an exchange of contracts, that is to say, sign the contract and send it to the landlord, together with the requisite deposit.

In this subsection "the requisite deposit" means a deposit of an amount determined by or under the contract or an amount equal to 10 per cent. of the consideration, whichever is the less.

(5) If the nominated person—

    (a) serves notice in pursuance of paragraph (a) of subsection (4), or

    (b) fails to offer an exchange of contracts within the period specified in that subsection,

the following provisions of this Part apply as if he had given notice under section 9A (withdrawal by nominated person) at the same time as that notice or, as the case may be, at the end of that period.

(6) If the nominated person offers an exchange of contracts within the period specified in subsection (4), but the landlord fails to complete the exchange within the period of seven days beginning with the day on which he received that person's contract, the following provisions of this Part apply as if the landlord had given notice under section 9B (withdrawal by landlord) at the end of that period.

SCH. 6
Landlord's
obligation:
election in case of
sale at auction.

8B.—(1) This section applies where the landlord is obliged to proceed and the offer notice was one to which section 5B applied (sale by auction).

(2) The nominated person may, by notice served on the landlord not less than 28 days before the date of the auction, elect that the provisions of this section shall apply.

(3) If a contract for the disposal is entered into at the auction, the landlord shall, within the period of seven days beginning with the date of the auction, send a copy of the contract to the nominated person.

(4) If, within the period of 28 days beginning with the date on which such a copy is so sent, the nominated person—

    (a) serves notice on the landlord accepting the terms of the contract, and

    (b) fulfils any conditions falling to be fulfilled by the purchaser on entering into the contract,

the contract shall have effect as if the nominated person, and not the purchaser, had entered into the contract.

(5) Unless otherwise agreed, any time limit in the contract as it has effect by virtue of subsection (4) shall start to run again on the service of notice under that subsection; and nothing in the contract as it has effect by virtue of a notice under this section shall require the nominated person to complete the purchase before the end of the period of 28 days beginning with the day on which he is deemed to have entered into the contract.

(6) If the nominated person—

    (a) does not serve notice on the landlord under subsection (2) by the time mentioned in that subsection, or

    (b) does not satisfy the requirements of subsection (4) within the period mentioned in that subsection,

the following provisions of this Part apply as if he had given notice under section 9A (withdrawal by nominated person) at the end of that period.

Election in case of
disposal for non-
monetary
consideration.

8C.—(1) This section applies where an acceptance notice is duly served on the landlord indicating an intention to accept the offer referred to in section 5E (offer notice: disposal for non-monetary consideration).

(2) The requisite majority of qualifying tenants of the constituent flats may, by notice served on the landlord within—

    (a) the period specified in the offer notice for nominating a person or persons for the purposes of section 6, or

    (b) such longer period as may be agreed between the landlord and the requisite majority of qualifying tenants of the constituent flats,

elect that the following provisions shall apply.

(3) Where such an election is made and the landlord disposes of the protected interest on terms corresponding to those specified in his offer notice in accordance with section 5A, 5B, 5C or 5D, sections 11 to 17 shall have effect as if—

    (a) no notice under section 5 had been served;

    (b) in section 11A(3) (period for serving notice requiring information, &c.), the reference to four months were a reference to 28 days; and

    (c) in section 12A(2) and 12B(3) (period for exercise of tenants' rights against purchaser) each reference to six months were a reference to two months.

(4) For the purposes of sections 11 to 17 as they have effect by virtue of subsection (3) so much of the consideration for the original disposal as did not consist of money shall be treated as such amount in money as was equivalent to its value in the hands of the landlord.

The landlord or the nominated person may apply to have that amount determined by a leasehold valuation tribunal.

8D.—(1) Where—

(a) the original disposal was the grant of an option or right of pre-emption, and

(b) in pursuance of the option or right, the landlord makes another disposal affecting the premises ("the later disposal") before the end of the period specified in subsection (2),

Disposal in pursuance of option or right of pre-emption.

sections 11 to 17 shall have effect as if the later disposal, and not the original disposal, were the relevant disposal.

(2) The period referred to in subsection (1)(b) is the period of four months beginning with the date by which—

(a) notices under section 3A of the Landlord and Tenant Act 1985 (duty of new landlord to inform tenants of rights) relating to the original disposal, or

1985 c. 70.

(b) where that section does not apply, documents of any other description—

(i) indicating that the original disposal has taken place, and

(ii) alerting the tenants to the existence of their rights under this Part and the time within which any such rights must be exercised,

have been served on the requisite majority of qualifying tenants of the constituent flats.

8E.—(1) Where the landlord is obliged to proceed but is precluded by a covenant, condition or other obligation from disposing of the protected interest to the nominated person unless the consent of some other person is obtained—

Covenant, &c. affecting landlord's power to dispose.

(a) he shall use his best endeavours to secure that the consent of that person to that disposal is given, and

(b) if it appears to him that that person is obliged not to withhold his consent unreasonably but has nevertheless so withheld it, he shall institute proceedings for a declaration to that effect.

(2) Subsection (1) ceases to apply if a notice of withdrawal is served under section 9A or 9B (withdrawal of either party from transaction) or if notice is served under section 10 (lapse of landlord's offer: premises ceasing to be premises to which this Part applies).

(3) Where the landlord has discharged any duty imposed on him by subsection (1) but any such consent as is there mentioned has been withheld, and no such declaration as is there mentioned has been made, the landlord may serve a notice on the nominated person stating that to be the case.

When such a notice has been served, the landlord may, during the period of 12 months beginning with the date of service of the notice, dispose of the protected interest to such person as he thinks fit, but subject to the following restrictions.

(4) Where the offer notice was one to which section 5B applied (sale by auction), the restrictions are—

(a) that the disposal is made by means of a sale at a public auction, and

(b) that the other terms correspond to those specified in the offer notice.

(5) In any other case the restrictions are—

    (a) that the deposit and consideration required are not less than those specified in the offer notice or, if higher, those agreed between the landlord and the nominated person (subject to contract), and

    (b) that the other terms correspond to those specified in the offer notice.

    (6) Where notice is given under subsection (3), the landlord may recover from the nominated party and the qualifying tenants who served the acceptance notice any costs reasonably incurred by him in connection with the disposal between the end of the first four weeks of the nomination period and the time when that notice is served by him.

    Any such liability of the nominated person and those tenants is a joint and several liability.

Notice of withdrawal by nominated person.

    9A.—(1) Where the landlord is obliged to proceed, the nominated person may serve notice on the landlord (a "notice of withdrawal") indicating his intention no longer to proceed with the acquisition of the protected interest.

    (2) If at any time the nominated person becomes aware that the number of the qualifying tenants of the constituent flats desiring to proceed with the acquisition of the protected interest is less than the requisite majority of qualifying tenants of those flats, he shall forthwith serve a notice of withdrawal.

    (3) Where notice of withdrawal is given by the nominated person under this section, the landlord may, during the period of 12 months beginning with the date of service of the notice, dispose of the protected interest to such person as he thinks fit, but subject to the following restrictions.

    (4) Where the offer notice was one to which section 5B applied (sale by auction), the restrictions are—

    (a) that the disposal is made by means of a sale at a public auction, and

    (b) that the other terms correspond to those specified in the offer notice.

    (5) In any other case the restrictions are—

    (a) that the deposit and consideration required are not less than those specified in the offer notice or, if higher, those agreed between the landlord and the nominated person (subject to contract), and

    (b) that the other terms correspond to those specified in the offer notice.

    (6) If notice of withdrawal is served under this section before the end of the first four weeks of the nomination period specified in the offer notice, the nominated person and the qualifying tenants who served the acceptance notice are not liable for any costs incurred by the landlord in connection with the disposal.

    (7) If notice of withdrawal is served under this section after the end of those four weeks, the landlord may recover from the nominated person and the qualifying tenants who served the acceptance notice any costs reasonably incurred by him in connection with the disposal between the end of those four weeks and the time when the notice of withdrawal was served on him.

    Any such liability of the nominated person and those tenants is a joint and several liability.

    (8) This section does not apply after a binding contract for the disposal of the protected interest—

    (a) has been entered into by the landlord and the nominated person, or

    (b) has otherwise come into existence between the landlord and the nominated person by virtue of any provision of this Part.

9B.—(1) Where the landlord is obliged to proceed, he may serve notice on the nominated person (a "notice of withdrawal") indicating his intention no longer to proceed with the disposal of the protected interest.

Notice of withdrawal by landlord.

(2) Where a notice of withdrawal is given by the landlord, he is not entitled to dispose of the protected interest during the period of 12 months beginning with the date of service of the notice.

(3) If a notice of withdrawal is served before the end of the first four weeks of the nomination period specified in the offer notice, the landlord is not liable for any costs incurred in connection with the disposal by the nominated person and the qualifying tenants who served the acceptance notice.

(4) If a notice of withdrawal is served after the end of those four weeks, the nominated person and the qualifying tenants who served the acceptance notice may recover from the landlord any costs reasonably incurred by them in connection with the disposal between the end of those four weeks and the time when the notice of withdrawal was served.

(5) This section does not apply after a binding contract for the disposal of the protected interest—

(a) has been entered into by the landlord and the nominated person, or

(b) has otherwise come into existence between the landlord and the nominated person by virtue of any provision of this Part.

10.—(1) If after a landlord has served an offer notice the premises concerned cease to be premises to which this Part applies, the landlord may serve a notice on the qualifying tenants of the constituent flats stating—

Lapse of landlord's offer.

(a) that the premises have ceased to be premises to which this Part applies, and

(b) that the offer notice, and anything done in pursuance of it, is to be treated as not having been served or done;

and on the service of such a notice the provisions of this Part cease to have effect in relation to that disposal.

(2) A landlord who has not served such a notice on all of the qualifying tenants of the constituent flats shall nevertheless be treated as having duly served a notice under subsection (1)—

(a) if he has served such a notice on not less than 90% of those tenants, or

(b) where those qualifying tenants number less than ten, if he has served such a notice on all but one of them.

(3) Where the landlord is entitled to serve a notice under subsection (1) but does not do so, this Part shall continue to have effect in relation to the disposal in question as if the premises in question were still premises to which this Part applies.

(4) The above provisions of this section do not apply after a binding contract for the disposal of the protected interest—

(a) has been entered into by the landlord and the nominated person, or

(b) has otherwise come into existence between the landlord and the nominated person by virtue of any provision of this Part.

(5) Where a binding contract for the disposal of the protected interest has been entered into between the landlord and the nominated person but it has been lawfully rescinded by the landlord, the landlord may, during the period of 12 months beginning with the date of the rescission of the contract, dispose of that interest to such person (and on such terms) as he thinks fit.".

SCH. 6

PART II

ENFORCEMENT BY TENANTS OF RIGHTS AGAINST PURCHASER

1987 c. 31.

The following sections are substituted for sections 11 to 15 of the Landlord and Tenant Act 1987—

"Enforcement by tenants of rights against purchaser

Circumstances in which tenants' rights enforceable against purchaser.

11.—(1) The following provisions of this Part apply where a landlord has made a relevant disposal affecting premises to which at the time of the disposal this Part applied ("the original disposal"), and either—

(a) no notice was served by the landlord under section 5 with respect to that disposal, or

(b) the disposal was made in contravention of any provision of sections 6 to 10,

and the premises are still premises to which this Part applies.

(2) In those circumstances the requisite majority of the qualifying tenants of the flats contained in the premises affected by the relevant disposal (the "constituent flats") have the rights conferred by the following provisions—

section 11A (right to information as to terms of disposal, &c.),

section 12A (right of qualifying tenants to take benefit of contract),

section 12B (right of qualifying tenants to compel sale, &c. by purchaser), and

section 12C (right of qualifying tenants to compel grant of new tenancy by superior landlord).

(3) In those sections the transferee under the original disposal (or, in the case of the surrender of a tenancy, the superior landlord) is referred to as "the purchaser".

This shall not be read as restricting the operation of those provisions to disposals for consideration.

Right to information as to terms of disposal, &c.

11A.—(1) The requisite majority of qualifying tenants of the constituent flats may serve a notice on the purchaser requiring him—

(a) to give particulars of the terms on which the original disposal was made (including the deposit and consideration required) and the date on which it was made, and

(b) where the disposal consisted of entering into a contract, to provide a copy of the contract.

(2) The notice must specify the name and address of the person to whom (on behalf of the tenants) the particulars are to be given, or the copy of the contract provided.

(3) Any notice under this section must be served before the end of the period of four months beginning with the date by which—

1985 c. 70.

(a) notices under section 3A of the Landlord and Tenant Act 1985 (duty of new landlord to inform tenants of rights) relating to the original disposal, or

(b) where that section does not apply, documents of any other description—

(i) indicating that the original disposal has taken place, and

(ii) alerting the tenants to the existence of their rights under this Part and the time within which any such rights must be exercised,

have been served on the requisite majority of qualifying tenants of the constituent flats.

(4) A person served with a notice under this section shall comply with it within the period of one month beginning with the date on which it is served on him.

12A.—(1) Where the original disposal consisted of entering into a contract, the requisite majority of qualifying tenants of the constituent flats may by notice to the landlord elect that the contract shall have effect as if entered into not with the purchaser but with a person or persons nominated for the purposes of this section by the requisite majority of qualifying tenants of the constituent flats.

Right of qualifying tenants to take benefit of contract.

(2) Any such notice must be served before the end of the period of six months beginning—

    (a) if a notice was served on the purchaser under section 11A (right to information as to terms of disposal, &c.), with the date on which the purchaser complied with that notice;

    (b) in any other case, with the date by which documents of any description—

        (i) indicating that the original disposal has taken place, and

        (ii) alerting the tenants to the existence of their rights under this Part and the time within which any such rights must be exercised,

    have been served on the requisite majority of qualifying tenants of the constituent flats.

(3) The notice shall not have effect as mentioned in subsection (1) unless the nominated person—

    (a) fulfils any requirements as to the deposit required on entering into the contract, and

    (b) fulfils any other conditions required to be fulfilled by the purchaser on entering into the contract.

(4) Unless otherwise agreed, any time limit in the contract as it has effect by virtue of a notice under this section shall start to run again on the service of that notice; and nothing in the contract as it has effect by virtue of a notice under this section shall require the nominated person to complete the purchase before the end of the period of 28 days beginning with the day on which he is deemed to have entered into the contract.

(5) Where the original disposal related to other property in addition to premises to which this Part applied at the time of the disposal—

    (a) a notice under this section has effect only in relation to the premises to which this Part applied at the time of the original disposal, and

    (b) the terms of the contract shall have effect with any necessary modifications.

In such a case the notice under this section may specify the subject-matter of the disposal, and the terms on which the disposal is to be made (whether doing so expressly or by reference to the original disposal), or may provide for that estate or interest, or any such terms, to be determined by a leasehold valuation tribunal.

12B.—(1) This section applies where—

Right of qualifying tenants to compel sale, &c. by purchaser.

    (a) the original disposal consisted of entering into a contract and no notice has been served under section 12A (right of qualifying tenants to take benefit of contract), or

    (b) the original disposal did not consist of entering into a contract.

(2) The requisite majority of qualifying tenants of the constituent flats may serve a notice (a "purchase notice") on the purchaser requiring him to dispose of the estate or interest that was the subject-matter of the original disposal, on the

terms on which it was made (including those relating to the consideration payable), to a person or persons nominated for the purposes of this section by any such majority of qualifying tenants of those flats.

(3) Any such notice must be served before the end of the period of six months beginning—

    (a) if a notice was served on the purchaser under section 11A (right to information as to terms of disposal, &c.), with the date on which the purchaser complied with that notice;

    (b) in any other case, with the date by which—

1985 c. 70.

        (i) notices under section 3A of the Landlord and Tenant Act 1985 (duty of new landlord to inform tenants of rights) relating to the original disposal, or

        (ii) where that section does not apply, documents of any other description indicating that the original disposal has taken place, and alerting the tenants to the existence of their rights under this Part and the time within which any such rights must be exercised,

have been served on the requisite majority of qualifying tenants of the constituent flats.

(4) A purchase notice shall where the original disposal related to other property in addition to premises to which this Part applied at the time of the disposal—

    (a) require the purchaser only to make a disposal relating to those premises, and

    (b) require him to do so on the terms referred to in subsection (2) with any necessary modifications.

In such a case the purchase notice may specify the subject-matter of the disposal, and the terms on which the disposal is to be made (whether doing so expressly or by reference to the original disposal), or may provide for those matters to be determined by a leasehold valuation tribunal.

(5) Where the property which the purchaser is required to dispose of in pursuance of the purchase notice has since the original disposal become subject to any charge or other incumbrance, then, unless the court by order directs otherwise—

    (a) in the case of a charge to secure the payment of money or the performance of any other obligation by the purchaser or any other person, the instrument by virtue of which the property is disposed of by the purchaser to the person or persons nominated for the purposes of this section shall (subject to the provisions of Part I of Schedule 1) operate to discharge the property from that charge; and

    (b) in the case of any other incumbrance, the property shall be so disposed of subject to the incumbrance but with a reduction in the consideration payable to the purchaser corresponding to the amount by which the existence of the incumbrance reduces the value of the property.

(6) Subsection (5)(a) and Part I of Schedule 1 apply, with any necessary modifications, to mortgages and liens as they apply to charges; but nothing in those provisions applies to a rentcharge.

(7) Where the property which the purchaser is required to dispose of in pursuance of the purchase notice has since the original disposal increased in monetary value owing to any change in circumstances (other than a change in the value of money), the amount of the consideration payable to the purchaser for the disposal by him of the property in pursuance of the purchase notice shall be the amount that might reasonably have been obtained on a corresponding disposal made on the open market at the time of the original disposal if the change in circumstances had already taken place.

12C.—(1) This section applies where the original disposal consisted of the surrender by the landlord of a tenancy held by him ("the relevant tenancy").

(2) The requisite majority of qualifying tenants of the constituent flats may serve a notice on the purchaser requiring him to grant a new tenancy of the premises which were subject to the relevant tenancy, on the same terms as those of the relevant tenancy and so as to expire on the same date as that tenancy would have expired, to a person or persons nominated for the purposes of this section by any such majority of qualifying tenants of those flats.

(3) Any such notice must be served before the end of the period of six months beginning—

(a) if a notice was served on the purchaser under section 11A (right to information as to terms of disposal, &c.), with the date on which the purchaser complied with that notice;

(b) in any other case, with the date by which documents of any description—

(i) indicating that the original disposal has taken place, and

(ii) alerting the tenants to the existence of their rights under this Part and the time within which any such rights must be exercised,

have been served on the requisite majority of qualifying tenants of the constituent flats.

(4) If the purchaser paid any amount to the landlord as consideration for the surrender by him of that tenancy, the nominated person shall pay that amount to the purchaser.

(5) Where the premises subject to the relevant tenancy included premises other than premises to which this Part applied at the time of the disposal, a notice under this section shall—

(a) require the purchaser only to grant a new tenancy relating to the premises to which this Part then applied, and

(b) require him to do so on the terms referred to in subsection (2) subject to any necessary modifications.

(6) The purchase notice may specify the subject-matter of the disposal, and the terms on which the disposal is to be made (whether doing so expressly or by reference to the original disposal), or may provide for those matters to be determined by a leasehold valuation tribunal.

12D.—(1) The person or persons initially nominated for the purposes of section 12A, 12B or 12C shall be nominated in the notice under that section.

(2) A person nominated for those purposes by the requisite majority of qualifying tenants of the constituent flats may be replaced by another person so nominated if, and only if, he has (for any reason) ceased to be able to act as a nominated person.

(3) Where two or more persons have been nominated and any of them ceases to act without being replaced, the remaining person or persons so nominated may continue to act.

(4) Where, in the exercise of its power to award costs, the court or the Lands Tribunal makes, in connection with any proceedings arising under or by virtue of this Part, an award of costs against the person or persons so nominated, the liability for those costs is a joint and several liability of that person or those persons together with the qualifying tenants by whom the relevant notice was served.

Sch. 6

Determination of
questions by
leasehold
valuation tribunal.

13.—(1) A leasehold valuation tribunal has jurisdiction to hear and determine—

(a) any question arising in relation to any matters specified in a notice under section 12A, 12B or 12C, and

(b) any question arising for determination as mentioned in section 8C(4), 12A(5) or 12B(4) (matters left for determination by tribunal).

(2) On an application under this section the interests of the persons by whom the notice was served under section 12A, 12B or 12C shall be represented by the nominated person; and accordingly the parties to any such application shall not include those persons.

Withdrawal of
nominated person
from transaction
under s.12B or
12C.

14.—(1) Where notice has been duly served on the landlord under—

section 12B (right of qualifying tenants to compel sale, &c. by purchaser), or

section 12C (right of qualifying tenants to compel grant of new tenancy by superior landlord),

the nominated person may at any time before a binding contract is entered into in pursuance of the notice, serve notice under this section on the purchaser (a "notice of withdrawal") indicating an intention no longer to proceed with the disposal.

(2) If at any such time the nominated person becomes aware that the number of qualifying tenants of the constituent flats desiring to proceed with the disposal is less than the requisite majority of those tenants, he shall forthwith serve a notice of withdrawal.

(3) If a notice of withdrawal is served under this section the purchaser may recover from the nominated person any costs reasonably incurred by him in connection with the disposal down to the time when the notice is served on him.

(4) If a notice of withdrawal is served at a time when proceedings arising under or by virtue of this Part are pending before the court or the Lands Tribunal, the liability of the nominated person for any costs incurred by the purchaser as mentioned in subsection (3) shall be such as may be determined by the court or (as the case may be) by the Tribunal.

(5) The costs that may be recovered by the purchaser under this section do not include any costs incurred by him in connection with an application to a leasehold valuation tribunal.".

PART III

ENFORCEMENT OF RIGHTS AGAINST SUBSEQUENT PURCHASERS AND TERMINATION OF RIGHTS

1987 c. 31.

The following sections replace sections 16 and 17 of the Landlord and Tenant Act 1987—

"Enforcement by tenants of rights against subsequent purchasers

Rights of
qualifying tenants
against
subsequent
purchaser.

16.—(1) This section applies where, at the time when a notice is served on the purchaser under section 11A, 12A, 12B or 12C, he no longer holds the estate or interest that was the subject-matter of the original disposal.

(2) In the case of a notice under section 11A (right to information as to terms of disposal, &c.) the purchaser shall, within the period for complying with that notice—

(a) serve notice on the person specified in the notice as the person to whom particulars are to be provided of the name and address of the person to whom he has disposed of that estate or interest ("the subsequent purchaser"), and

(b) serve on the subsequent purchaser a copy of the notice under section 11A and of the particulars given by him in response to it.

(3) In the case of a notice under section 12A, 12B or 12C the purchaser shall forthwith—

(a) forward the notice to the subsequent purchaser, and

(b) serve on the nominated person notice of the name and address of the subsequent purchaser.

(4) Once the purchaser serves a notice in accordance with subsection (2)(a) or (3)(b), sections 12A to 14 shall, instead of applying to the purchaser, apply to the subsequent purchaser as if he were the transferee under the original disposal.

(5) Subsections (1) to (4) have effect, with any necessary modifications, in a case where, instead of disposing of the whole of the estate or interest referred to in subsection (1) to another person, the purchaser has disposed of it in part or in parts to one or more other persons.

In such a case, sections 12A to 14—

(a) apply to the purchaser in relation to any part of that estate or interest retained by him, and

(b) in relation to any part of that estate or interest disposed of to any other person, apply to that other person instead as if he were (as respects that part) the transferee under the original disposal.

Termination of rights against purchasers or subsequent purchasers

17.—(1) If, at any time after a notice has been served under section 11A, 12A, 12B or 12C, the premises affected by the original disposal cease to be premises to which this Part applies, the purchaser may serve a notice on the qualifying tenants of the constituent flats stating—

Termination of rights against purchaser or subsequent purchaser.

(a) that the premises have ceased to be premises to which this Part applies, and

(b) that any such notice served on him, and anything done in pursuance of it, is to be treated as not having been served or done.

(2) A landlord who has not served such a notice on all of the qualifying tenants of the constituent flats shall nevertheless be treated as having duly served a notice under subsection (1)—

(a) if he has served such a notice on not less than 90% of those tenants, or

(b) where those qualifying tenants number less than ten, if he has served such a notice on all but one of them.

(3) Where a period of three months beginning with the date of service of a notice under section 12A, 12B or 12C on the purchaser has expired—

(a) without any binding contract having been entered into between the purchaser and the nominated person, and

(b) without there having been made any application in connection with the notice to the court or to a leasehold valuation tribunal,

the purchaser may serve on the nominated person a notice stating that the notice, and anything done in pursuance of it, is to be treated as not having been served or done.

(4) Where any such application as is mentioned in subsection (3)(b) was made within the period of three months referred to in that subsection, but—

(a) a period of two months beginning with the date of the determination of that application has expired,

(b) no binding contract has been entered into between the purchaser and the nominated person, and

(c) no other such application as is mentioned in subsection (3)(b) is pending,

the purchaser may serve on the nominated person a notice stating that any notice served on him under section 12A, 12B or 12C, and anything done in pursuance of any such notice, is to be treated as not having been served or done.

(5) Where the purchaser serves a notice in accordance with subsection (1), (3) or (4), this Part shall cease to have effect in relation to him in connection with the original disposal.

(6) Where a purchaser is entitled to serve a notice under subsection (1) but does not do so, this Part shall continue to have effect in relation to him in connection with the original disposal as if the premises in question were still premises to which this Part applies.

(7) References in this section to the purchaser include a subsequent purchaser to whom sections 12A to 14 apply by virtue of section 16(4) or (5).".

PART IV

CONSEQUENTIAL AMENDMENTS

1987 c. 31.   1. In section 4(2) of the Landlord and Tenant Act 1987 (relevant disposals: excluded disposals), in paragraph (aa) (disposals by way of security for a loan) omit the words "consisting of the creation of an estate or interest".

2. Before section 19 of the Landlord and Tenant Act 1987, under the heading "*Supplementary provisions*", insert—

"The requisite majority of qualifying tenants.

18A.—(1) In this Part "the requisite majority of qualifying tenants of the constituent flats" means qualifying tenants of constituent flats with more than 50 per cent. of the available votes.

(2) The total number of available votes shall be determined as follows—

(a) where an offer notice has been served under section 5, that number is equal to the total number of constituent flats let to qualifying tenants on the date when the period specified in that notice as the period for accepting the offer expires;

(b) where a notice is served under section 11A without a notice having been previously served under section 5, that number is equal to the total number of constituent flats let to qualifying tenants on the date of service of the notice under section 11A;

(c) where a notice is served under section 12A, 12B or 12C without a notice having been previously served under section 5 or section 11A, that number is equal to the total number of constituent flats let to qualifying tenants on the date of service of the notice under section 12A, 12B or 12C, as the case may be.

(3) There is one available vote in respect of each of the flats so let on the date referred to in the relevant paragraph of subsection (2), which shall be attributed to the qualifying tenant to whom it is let.

(4) The persons constituting the requisite majority of qualifying tenants for one purpose may be different from the persons constituting such a majority for another purpose.".

3.—(1) Section 20(1) of the Landlord and Tenant Act 1987 (interpretation of   1987 c. 31.
Part I) is amended as follows.

(2) For the definition of "acceptance notice" substitute—

""acceptance notice" has the meaning given by section 6(3);".

(3) For the definition of "constituent flat" substitute—

""constituent flat" shall be construed in accordance with section 5(1)
or 11(2), as the case may require;".

(4) Omit the definition of "the new landlord".

(5) After that definition insert—

""the nominated person" means the person or persons for the time
being nominated by the requisite majority of the qualifying
tenants of the constituent flats for the purposes of section 6, 12A,
12B or 12C, as the case may require;".

(6) For the definition of "the protected interest" substitute—

""the protected interest" means the estate, interest or other subject-
matter of an offer notice;".

(7) After that definition insert—

""the protected period" has the meaning given by section 6(4);".

(8) For the definition of "purchase notice" substitute—

""purchase notice" has the meaning given by section 12B(2);".

(9) After that definition insert—

""purchaser" has the meaning given by section 11(3);".

(10) In the definition of "the requisite majority" for "section 5(6) and (7)"
substitute "section 18A".

4. In section 20(2) of the Landlord and Tenant Act 1987, omit the words "or
counter-offer" in each place where they occur.

5. In Part III of the Landlord and Tenant Act 1987 (compulsory acquisition
by tenants of their landlord's interest), in section 31 (determination of terms by
rent assessment committees)—

(a) for "rent assessment committee", wherever occurring, substitute
"leasehold valuation tribunal";

(b) for "such a committee" or "the committee", wherever occurring,
substitute "the tribunal"; and

(c) omit subsection (5).

6. In section 52(1) of the Landlord and Tenant Act 1987 (jurisdiction of county
courts) for "rent assessment committee" substitute "leasehold valuation
tribunal".

7. After section 52 of the Landlord and Tenant Act 1987 insert—

"Jurisdiction of   52A.—(1) Any jurisdiction conferred by Part I or III of this
leasehold   Act on a leasehold valuation tribunal is exercisable by a rent
valuation tribunal   assessment committee constituted in accordance with Schedule
under Part I or   10 to the Rent Act 1977 which when so constituted for the   1977 c. 42.
III.   purposes of exercising any such jurisdiction shall be known as
                      a leasehold valuation tribunal.

(2) The power to make regulations under section 74(1)(b) of
the Rent Act 1977 (procedure of rent assessment committees)

extends to prescribing the procedure to be followed in connection with any proceedings before a leasehold valuation tribunal under this Act.

(3) Any application under this Act to a leasehold valuation tribunal must be in such form, and contain such particulars, as the Secretary of State may by regulations prescribe.

(4) Any costs incurred by a party to any such application in connection with the application shall be borne by that party.

1980 c. 51.

(5) Paragraphs 1, 2, 3 and 7 of Schedule 22 to the Housing Act 1980 (supplementary provisions relating to leasehold valuation tribunals: constitution, appeals and provision of information) apply to a leasehold valuation tribunal constituted for the purposes of this section.".

1987 c. 31.

8. In section 53(2)(b) of the Landlord and Tenant Act 1987 (regulations subject to negative resolution), for the words from "section 13(2)" to "section 31" substitute "section 52A(3)".

9. In section 54(4) of the Landlord and Tenant Act 1987 (saving for power under section 20(4)) for "either of the periods specified in section 5(2)" substitute "any of the periods specified in section 5A(4) or (5), 5B(5) or (6), 5C(4) or (5), 5D(4) or (5) or 5E(3)".

10. In section 60(1) of the Landlord and Tenant Act 1987 (general interpretation), omit the definition of "rent assessment committee".

11.—(1) In Schedule 1 to the Landlord and Tenant Act 1987 (discharge of mortgages, &c), in paragraph 1 (construction of provisions relating to discharge in pursuance of purchase notice)—

(a) for the words "the new landlord" wherever they appear substitute "the purchaser";

(b) in the definition of "consideration payable"—

(i) for the words "section 12(4)" substitute "section 12B(7)", and

(ii) for the words "section 16(2) or (3)" substitute "section 16(4) or (5)";

(c) in the definition of "nominated person", for the words "section 12(1)" substitute "section 12B(2)".

(2) In paragraphs 2, 4 and 5 of that Schedule (duty of nominated person to redeem mortgages, payments into court and savings)—

(a) for the words "section 12(4)(a)" wherever they appear substitute "section 12B(5)(a)";

(b) for the words "the new landlord" or "the new landlord's" wherever they appear substitute "the purchaser" or "the purchaser's".

SCHEDULE 7

Assured tenancies: schedule inserted after Schedule 2 to the Housing Act 1988

"SCHEDULE 2A

Assured Tenancies: Non-Shortholds

Tenancies excluded by notice

1.—(1) An assured tenancy in respect of which a notice is served as mentioned in sub-paragraph (2) below.

(2) The notice referred to in sub-paragraph (1) above is one which—

(a) is served before the assured tenancy is entered into,

(b) is served by the person who is to be the landlord under the assured tenancy on the person who is to be the tenant under that tenancy, and

(c) states that the assured tenancy to which it relates is not to be an assured shorthold tenancy.

2.—(1) An assured tenancy in respect of which a notice is served as mentioned in sub-paragraph (2) below.

(2) The notice referred to in sub-paragraph (1) above is one which—

(a) is served after the assured tenancy has been entered into,

(b) is served by the landlord under the assured tenancy on the tenant under that tenancy, and

(c) states that the assured tenancy to which it relates is no longer an assured shorthold tenancy.

Tenancies containing exclusionary provision

3. An assured tenancy which contains a provision to the effect that the tenancy is not an assured shorthold tenancy.

Tenancies under section 39

4. An assured tenancy arising by virtue of section 39 above, other than one to which subsection (7) of that section applies.

Former secure tenancies

5. An assured tenancy which became an assured tenancy on ceasing to be a secure tenancy.

Tenancies under Schedule 10 to the Local Government and Housing Act 1989

6. An assured tenancy arising by virtue of Schedule 10 to the Local Government and Housing Act 1989 (security of tenure on ending of long residential tenancies).   1989 c. 42.

Tenancies replacing non-shortholds

7.—(1) An assured tenancy which—

(a) is granted to a person (alone or jointly with others) who, immediately before the tenancy was granted, was the tenant (or, in the case of joint tenants, one of the tenants) under an assured tenancy other than a shorthold tenancy ("the old tenancy"),

(b) is granted (alone or jointly with others) by a person who was at that time the landlord (or one of the joint landlords) under the old tenancy, and

    (c) is not one in respect of which a notice is served as mentioned in sub-paragraph (2) below.

  (2) The notice referred to in sub-paragraph (1)(c) above is one which—

    (a) is in such form as may be prescribed,

    (b) is served before the assured tenancy is entered into,

    (c) is served by the person who is to be the tenant under the assured tenancy on the person who is to be the landlord under that tenancy (or, in the case of joint landlords, on at least one of the persons who are to be joint landlords), and

    (d) states that the assured tenancy to which it relates is to be a shorthold tenancy.

8. An assured tenancy which comes into being by virtue of section 5 above on the coming to an end of an assured tenancy which is not a shorthold tenancy.

Assured agricultural occupancies

9.—(1) An assured tenancy—

    (a) in the case of which the agricultural worker condition is, by virtue of any provision of Schedule 3 to this Act, for the time being fulfilled with respect to the dwelling-house subject to the tenancy, and

    (b) which does not fall within sub-paragraph (2) or (4) below.

  (2) An assured tenancy falls within this sub-paragraph if—

    (a) before it is entered into, a notice—

        (i) in such form as may be prescribed, and

        (ii) stating that the tenancy is to be a shorthold tenancy,

    is served by the person who is to be the landlord under the tenancy on the person who is to be the tenant under it, and

    (b) it is not an excepted tenancy.

  (3) For the purposes of sub-paragraph (2)(b) above, an assured tenancy is an excepted tenancy if—

    (a) the person to whom it is granted or, as the case may be, at least one of the persons to whom it is granted was, immediately before it is granted, a tenant or licensee under an assured agricultural occupancy, and

    (b) the person by whom it is granted or, as the case may be, at least one of the persons by whom it is granted was, immediately before it is granted, a landlord or licensor under the assured agricultural occupancy referred to in paragraph (a) above.

  (4) An assured tenancy falls within this sub-paragraph if it comes into being by virtue of section 5 above on the coming to an end of a tenancy falling within sub-paragraph (2) above.".

SCHEDULE 8

ASSURED TENANCIES: CONSEQUENTIAL AMENDMENTS

Housing Act 1985 (c.68)

1. In section 553(2) of the Housing Act 1985, for paragraph (c) there shall be substituted—

> "(c) the tenancy is not by virtue of any provision of Part I of the Housing Act 1988 an assured shorthold tenancy;".

Housing Act 1988 (c.50)

2.—(1) The Housing Act 1988 shall be amended as follows.

(2) In section 14, there shall be inserted at the end—

> "(9) This section shall apply in relation to an assured shorthold tenancy as if in subsection (1) the reference to an assured tenancy were a reference to an assured shorthold tenancy.".

(3) In section 20, for the side-note and subsection (1) there shall be substituted—

"Assured shorthold tenancies: pre-Housing Act 1996 tenancies.

20.—(1) Subject to subsection (3) below, an assured tenancy which is not one to which section 19A above applies is an assured shorthold tenancy if—

> (a) it is a fixed term tenancy granted for a term certain of not less than six months,
>
> (b) there is no power for the landlord to determine the tenancy at any time earlier than six months from the beginning of the tenancy, and
>
> (c) a notice in respect of it is served as mentioned in subsection (2) below.".

(4) In that section, after subsection (5) there shall be inserted—

> "(5A) Subsections (3) and (4) above do not apply where the new tenancy is one to which section 19A above applies.".

(5) In section 22, in subsection (1), the words from "in respect of" to "above" shall be omitted.

(6) In that section, after subsection (5) there shall be inserted—

> "(5A) Where—
>
> (a) an assured tenancy ceases to be an assured shorthold tenancy by virtue of falling within paragraph 2 of Schedule 2A to this Act, and
>
> (b) at the time when it so ceases to be an assured shorthold tenancy there is pending before a rent assessment committee an application in relation to it under this section,
>
> the fact that it so ceases to be an assured shorthold tenancy shall, in relation to that application, be disregarded for the purposes of this section.".

(7) In section 34(3), after "whether or not" there shall be inserted ", in the case of a tenancy to which the provision applies,".

(8) In section 39(7), after "whether or not" there shall be inserted ", in the case of a tenancy to which the provision applies,".

Section 106.

SCHEDULE 9

LOW RENT TEST: EXTENSION OF RIGHTS

Right to enfranchisement

1967 c. 88.

1. In the Leasehold Reform Act 1967, after section 1A there shall be inserted—

"Additional right to enfranchisement only in case of houses whose rent exceeds applicable limit under section 4.

1AA.—(1) Where—

(a) section 1(1) above would apply in the case of the tenant of a house but for the fact that the tenancy is not a tenancy at a low rent, and

(b) the tenancy falls within subsection (2) below and is not an excluded tenancy,

this Part of this Act shall have effect to confer on the tenant the same right to acquire the freehold of the house and premises as would be conferred by section 1(1) above if it were a tenancy at a low rent.

(2) A tenancy falls within this subsection if—

(a) it is granted for a term of years certain exceeding thirty-five years, whether or not it is (or may become) terminable before the end of that term by notice given by or to the tenant or by re-entry, forfeiture or otherwise,

(b) it is for a term fixed by law under a grant with a covenant or obligation for perpetual renewal, unless it is a tenancy by sub-demise from one which is not a tenancy which falls within this subsection,

1925 c. 20.

(c) it is a tenancy taking effect under section 149(6) of the Law of Property Act 1925 (leases terminable after a death or marriage), or

(d) it is a tenancy which—

(i) is or has been granted for a term of years certain not exceeding thirty-five years, but with a covenant or obligation for renewal without payment of a premium (but not for perpetual renewal), and

(ii) is or has been once or more renewed so as to bring to more than thirty-five years the total of the terms granted (including any interval between the end of a tenancy and the grant of a renewal).

(3) A tenancy is an excluded tenancy for the purposes of subsection (1) above if—

(a) the house which the tenant occupies under the tenancy is in an area designated for the purposes of this provision as a rural area by order made by the Secretary of State,

(b) the freehold of that house is owned together with adjoining land which is not occupied for residential purposes and has been owned together with such land since the coming into force of section 106 of the Housing Act 1996, and

(c) the tenancy was granted on or before the day on which that section came into force.

(4) Where this Part of this Act applies as if there were a single tenancy of property comprised in two or more separate tenancies, then, if each of the separate tenancies falls within subsection (2) above, this section shall apply as if the single tenancy did so.

(5) The power to make an order under subsection (3) above shall be exercisable by statutory instrument which shall be subject to annulment in pursuance of a resolution of either House of Parliament.".

2.—(1) In consequence of paragraph 1 above, the Leasehold Reform Act 1967 shall be amended as follows. 1967 c. 88.

(2) In section 1(3A)(b) (extension of rights not to apply to existing lettings by charitable housing trusts), after "1A" there shall be inserted ", 1AA".

(3) In section 3(3) (provision for aggregation of successive tenancies), after "this Part of this Act" there shall be inserted ", except section 1AA,".

(4) In section 9(1C) (price payable by tenant on enfranchisement by virtue of section 1A or 1B), after "1A" there shall be inserted ", 1AA".

(5) In section 9A(1) (compensation payable where right to enfranchisement arises by virtue of section 1A or 1B), after "1A" there shall be inserted ", 1AA".

(6) In section 32A(1)(b) (extensions to right to enfranchisement not to apply in relation to existing tenancies of property transferred for public benefit), at the end there shall be inserted "or if section 1AA above were not in force".

(7) In section 37(4) (treatment for the purposes of Part I of tenancy granted to continue as a periodical tenancy after the expiration of a term of years certain), after "this Part of this Act" there shall be inserted ", except section 1AA,".

(8) In Part II of Schedule 3 (procedural provisions), in paragraph 6 (which makes provision about the contents of a tenant's notice under Part I), after sub-paragraph (1) there shall be inserted—

"(1A) Where the tenant gives the notice by virtue of section 1AA of this Act, sub-paragraph (1) above shall have effect with the substitution for paragraph (b) of—

"(b) such particulars of the tenancy as serve to identify the instrument creating the tenancy and show that the tenancy is one in relation to which section 1AA(1) of this Act has effect to confer a right to acquire the freehold of the house and premises;".".

(9) In that Part of that Schedule, in paragraph 7(4) (admission in landlord's notice of tenant's right to have freehold to be binding on landlord, so far as relating to matters mentioned in section 1(1)(a) and (b)), for "mentioned in section 1(1)(a) and (b) of this Act" there shall be substituted "relevant to the existence of that right".

Right to collective enfranchisement

3.—(1) Chapter I of Part I of the Leasehold Reform, Housing and Urban Development Act 1993 (collective enfranchisement in case of tenants of flats) shall be amended as follows. 1993 c. 28.

(2) Section 5 (qualifying tenants) shall be amended as follows—

   (a) in subsection (1) (which defines a qualifying tenant as a tenant of a flat under a long lease at a low rent), for "at a low rent" there shall be substituted "which is at a low rent or for a particularly long term", and

(b) in subsection (2)(c) (which excludes from the definition a tenant under a lease granted in breach of the terms of a superior lease which is not a long lease at a low rent), after "rent" there shall be inserted "or for a particularly long term".

(3) After section 8 there shall be inserted—

"Meaning of "particularly long term".   8A.—(1) For the purposes of this Chapter a long lease is for a particularly long term if—

(a) it is granted for a term of years certain exceeding 35 years, whether or not it is (or may become) terminable before the end of that term by notice given by or to the tenant or by re-entry, forfeiture or otherwise,

(b) it is for a term fixed by law under a grant with a covenant or obligation for perpetual renewal (other than a lease by sub-demise from one which is not for a particularly long term),

1925 c. 20.   (c) it takes effect under section 149(6) of the Law of Property Act 1925 (leases terminable after a death or marriage), or

(d) it is a lease which—

(i) is or has been granted for a term of years certain not exceeding 35 years, but with a covenant or obligation for renewal without payment of a premium (but not for perpetual renewal), and

(ii) is or has been renewed on one or more occasions so as to bring to more than 35 years the total of the terms granted (including any interval between the end of a lease and the grant of a renewal).

(2) A long lease which does not fall within subsection (1) above shall nonetheless be treated for the purposes of this Chapter as being for a particularly long term if it is a long lease by virtue of paragraph (c) or (d) of section 7(1).

(3) Where this Chapter applies as if there were a single lease of property comprised in two or more separate leases, then, if each of the separate leases is for a particularly long term, this Chapter shall apply as if the single lease were for such a term.".

(4) In section 13(3)(e) (particulars to be included in initial notice which relevant to whether person a qualifying tenant), in sub-paragraph (ii), for "a lease at a low rent" there shall be substituted "at a low rent or for a particularly long term".

Right to new lease

4.—(1) Chapter II of that Part (individual right of tenant of flat to acquire new lease) shall be amended as follows.

(2) In section 39(3) (provisions of Chapter I which apply for the purposes of Chapter II), at the end of paragraph (c) there shall be inserted ", and

(d) section 8A,".

(3) In section 42(3) (particulars to be included in notice by qualifying tenant of claim to exercise right), in paragraph (b)(iii), there shall be inserted at the end "or, in accordance with section 8A (as that section so applies), a lease for a particularly long term".

5.—(1) In Chapter VII of that Part (general), section 94 (Crown land) shall be amended as follows.

(2) In subsection (3) (disapplication of restriction imposed by section 3(2) of the Crown Estate Act 1961 on term for which lease may be granted by Crown Estate Commissioners), in paragraph (a), for "at a low rent" there shall be substituted "which is at a low rent or for a particularly long term".

(3) In subsection (4) (power to shadow statutory rights), for "at a low rent" there shall be substituted "which is at a low rent or for a particularly long term".

(4) For subsection (12) there shall be substituted—

"(12) For the purposes of this section "long lease which is at a low rent or for a particularly long term" shall be construed in accordance with sections 7, 8 and 8A.".

SCHEDULE 10

SECTION 107: CONSEQUENTIAL AMENDMENTS

1. Chapter I of Part I of the Leasehold Reform, Housing and Urban Development Act 1993 shall be amended as follows.

2. In section 1(4) (right to acquire additional property satisfied by grant of rights over that property or other property)—

(a) in paragraph (a), for "freeholder" there shall be substituted "person who owns the freehold of that property", and

(b) in paragraph (b), for "freeholder" there shall be substituted "person who owns the freehold of that property".

3.—(1) Section 9 (the reversioner and other relevant landlords) shall be amended as follows.

(2) In subsection (1), after "any premises" there shall be inserted "the freehold of the whole of which is owned by the same person".

(3) In subsection (2)—

(a) after "such claim" there shall be inserted "as is mentioned in subsection (1)", and

(b) in paragraph (b), after "premises," there shall be inserted "every person who owns any freehold interest which it is proposed to acquire by virtue of section 1(2)(a),".

(4) After that subsection there shall be inserted—

"(2A) In the case of any claim to exercise the right to collective enfranchisement in relation to any premises the freehold of the whole of which is not owned by the same person—

(a) the reversioner in respect of the premises shall for the purposes of this Chapter be the person identified as such by Part IA of Schedule 1 to this Act, and

(b) every person who owns a freehold interest in the premises, every person who owns any freehold interest which it is proposed to acquire by virtue of section 1(2)(a), and every person who owns any leasehold interest which it is proposed to acquire under or by virtue of section 2(1)(a) or (b), shall be a relevant landlord for those purposes.".

(5) In subsection (3), after "subsection (2)" there shall be inserted "or (2A)".

4.—(1) Section 10 (premises with a resident landlord) shall be amended as follows.

(2) In subsection (1)(b)—

(a) for "the freeholder, or an adult member of the freeholder's" there shall be substituted "a relevant person, or an adult member of a relevant person's", and

(b) in sub-paragraph (i), after "premises" there shall be inserted "which is a qualifying flat".

(3) In subsection (2)—

(a) in paragraph (a)—

(i) for "freeholder" there shall be substituted "relevant person", and

(ii) after "Chapter", where it first occurs, there shall be inserted ", or, as the case may be, the amendments of this Chapter made by the Housing Act 1996,", and

(b) in paragraph (b)—

(i) for "freeholder, or an adult member of the freeholder's" there shall be substituted "relevant person, or an adult member of that person's", and

(ii) in sub-paragraph (i), after "premises" there shall be inserted "which is a qualifying flat".

(4) In subsection (4)—

(a) for "freehold interest" there shall be substituted "interest of a relevant person", and

(b) for "the freeholder" there shall be substituted "a relevant person".

(5) After that subsection there shall be inserted—

"(4A) For the purposes of this section a person is a relevant person, in relation to any premises, if he owns the freehold of the whole or any part of the premises.".

(6) In subsection (6) there shall be inserted at the end—

""qualifying flat", in relation to a relevant person, or an adult member of a relevant person's family, means a flat the freehold of the whole of which is owned by the relevant person.".

5.—(1) Section 11 (right of qualifying tenant to obtain information about superior interests etc.) shall be amended as follows.

(2) In subsection (1)—

(a) for "his immediate landlord", in both places, there shall be substituted "any immediate landlord of his", and

(b) for "the person who owns the freehold of" there shall be substituted "every person who owns a freehold interest in".

(3) In subsection (2)(b), for "the tenant's immediate landlord" there shall be substituted "any immediate landlord of the tenant".

(4) In subsection (3), for "the person who owns the freehold of" there shall be substituted "any person who owns a freehold interest in".

(5) In subsection (4), for paragraph (a) there shall be substituted—

"(a) to any person who owns a freehold interest in the relevant premises,

(aa) to any person who owns a freehold interest in any such property as is mentioned in subsection (3)(c),".

(6) In subsection (8)(b)(i), after "premises" there shall be inserted "or in any such property as is mentioned in subsection (3)(c)".

(7) In subsection (9), in the definition of "the relevant premises"—

(a) in paragraph (a), after "owns", where it second occurs, there shall be inserted ", or the persons who own the freehold interests in the flat own,", and

(b) in paragraph (b), after "owns" there shall be inserted ", or those persons own,".

6.—(1) Section 13 (notice by qualifying tenants of claim to exercise right to collective enfranchisement) shall be amended as follows.

(2) In subsection (2), in paragraph (a)—

(a) after "must" there shall be inserted—

"(i) in a case to which section 9(2) applies,",

and

(b) after "premises;" there shall be inserted "and

(ii) in a case to which section 9(2A) applies, be given to the person specified in the notice as the recipient;".

(3) After that subsection there shall be inserted—

"(2A) In a case to which section 9(2A) applies, the initial notice must specify—

(a) a person who owns a freehold interest in the premises, or

(b) if every person falling within paragraph (a) is a person who cannot be found or whose identity cannot be ascertained, a relevant landlord,

as the recipient of the notice.".

(4) In subsection (3)(d)(i), there shall be inserted at the end "or, if the freehold of the whole of the specified premises is not owned by the same person, each of the freehold interests in those premises".

7.—(1) Section 19 (effect of notice under section 13 on subsequent transactions by freeholder etc) shall be amended as follows.

(2) In subsection (1)(a)—

(a) for "the person who owns the freehold of the specified premises" there shall be substituted "any person who owns the freehold of the whole or any part of the specified premises or the freehold of any property specified in the notice under section 13(3)(a)(ii)", and

(b) in sub-paragraph (i), for the words from "any property" to the end there shall be substituted "that property".

(3) In subsection (2), for paragraph (a) there shall be substituted—

"(a) any person who owns the freehold of the whole or any part of the specified premises or the freehold of any property specified in the notice under section 13(3)(a)(ii) disposes of his interest in those premises or that property,".

(4) In subsection (4), for paragraph (a) there shall be substituted—

"(a) by any person who owns the freehold of the whole or any part of the specified premises or the freehold of any property specified in the notice under section 13(3)(a)(ii),".

8.—(1) Section 21 (reversioner's counter-notice) shall be amended as follows.

(2) In subsection (3)(d), for "the person who owns the freehold of the specified premises, or any other" there shall be substituted "any".

(3) In subsection (4), for "the person who owns the freehold of the specified premises or of any other" there shall be substituted "any".

9.—(1) Section 26 (application to court where relevant landlords cannot be found) shall be amended as follows.

(2) In subsection (1)(b), after "section 9(2)" there shall be inserted "or (2A)".

(3) In subsection (3), after "If" there shall be inserted ", in a case to which section 9(2) applies,".

(4) After that subsection there shall be inserted—

"(3A) Where in a case to which section 9(2A) applies—

(a) not less than two-thirds of the qualifying tenants of flats contained in any premises to which this Chapter applies desire to make a claim to exercise the right to collective enfranchisement in relation to those premises, and

(b) paragraph (b) of subsection (1) does not apply, but

(c) a copy of a notice of that claim cannot be given in accordance with Part II of Schedule 3 to any person to whom it would otherwise be required to be so given because he cannot be found or his identity cannot be ascertained,

the court may, on the application of the qualifying tenants in question, make an order dispensing with the need to give a copy of such a notice to that person.".

(5) In subsection (4), for "or (2)" there shall be substituted ", (2) or (3A)".

(6) In subsection (7), after "(2)" there shall be inserted "or (3A)".

10. In section 30 (effect on acquisition of institution of compulsory acquisition procedures), at the end of subsection (2)(a) there shall be inserted "or, where the freehold of the whole of the premises is not owned by the same person, any person who owns the freehold of part of them".

11.—(1) Section 34 (conveyance to nominee purchaser) shall be amended as follows.

(2) In subsection (1)—

(a) after "specified premises" there shall be inserted ", of a part of those premises", and

(b) after "those premises" there shall be inserted ", that part of those premises".

(3) In subsection (2), after "premises" there shall be inserted ", the part of the specified premises".

12.—(1) Section 36 (nominee purchaser required to grant leases back to former freeholder) shall be amended as follows.

(2) In subsection (1)—

(a) for "the freehold of" there shall be substituted "a freehold interest in", and

(b) for "freehold", where it second occurs, there shall be substituted "interest".

(3) In subsection (2), for "of the specified premises" there shall be substituted "interest concerned".

13. In section 38 (interpretation of Chapter I), in subsection (3), after "section 9(2)(b)" there shall be inserted "or (2A)(b)".

14. In Schedule 1 (conduct of proceedings by reversioner on behalf of other landlords), in Part I (identification of reversioner in case of premises with relevant landlords), in paragraph 1, after "2 to 4," there shall be inserted "in a case to which section 9(2) applies,".

15. In that Schedule, after Part I there shall be inserted—

"Part IA

The reversioner: premises with multiple freeholders

Initial reversioner

5A. Subject to paragraphs 5B to 5D, in a case to which section 9(2A) applies, the reversioner in respect of any premises is the person specified in the initial notice in accordance with section 13(2A) as the recipient.

Change of reversioner

5B. The court may, on the application of all the relevant landlords of any premises, appoint to be the reversioner in respect of those premises (in place of the person designated by paragraph 5A) such person as may have been determined by agreement between them.

5C. If it appears to the court, on the application of a relevant landlord of any premises—

(a) that the respective interests of the relevant landlords of those premises, the absence or incapacity of the person referred to in paragraph 5A or other special circumstances require that some person other than the person there referred to should act as the reversioner in respect of the premises, or

(b) that the person referred to in that paragraph is unwilling to act as the reversioner,

the court may appoint to be the reversioner in respect of those premises (in place of the person designated by paragraph 5A) such person as it thinks fit.

5D. The court may also, on the application of any of the relevant landlords or of the nominee purchaser, remove the reversioner in respect of any premises and appoint another person in his place, if it appears to the court proper to do so by reason of any delay or default, actual or apprehended, on the part of the reversioner.

5E. A person appointed by the court under any of paragraphs 5B to 5D—

(a) must be a relevant landlord; but

(b) may be so appointed on such terms and conditions as the court thinks fit.".

16. In Schedule 2 (special categories of landlords), in paragraph 1(1), in the definition of "Chapter I landlord", for "the reversioner or any other" there shall be substituted "a".

17.—(1) Part II of Schedule 3 (which makes provision for the giving of copies of the notice under section 13 to relevant landlords) shall be amended as follows.

(2) In paragraph 11, after "section 9(2)" there shall be inserted "or (2A)".

(3) In paragraph 12, in sub-paragraph (1), there shall be inserted at the beginning "In a case to which section 9(2) applies,".

(4) After that paragraph there shall be inserted—

"12A.—(1) In a case to which section 9(2A) applies, the qualifying tenants by whom the initial notice is given shall, in addition to giving the initial notice to the person specified in it as the recipient, give a copy of the notice to every other person known or believed by them to be a relevant landlord of the specified premises.

(2) The initial notice shall state whether copies are being given in accordance with sub-paragraph (1) to anyone other than the person specified in it as the recipient and, if so, to whom.".

(5) In paragraph 13(3)(a), after "12(2)" there shall be inserted "or, as the case may be, 12A(2)".

(6) In paragraph 14(2)(b)—

(a) after "12" there shall be inserted ", 12A", and

(b) for "either" there shall be substituted "any".

18.—(1) Schedule 6 (purchase price payable by nominee purchaser) shall be amended as follows.

(2) In paragraph 1(1) (interpretation)—

(a) the definition of "the freeholder" shall be omitted, and

(b) for the definition of "the valuation date" there shall be substituted—

""the valuation date" means—

(a) the date when it is determined, either by agreement or by a leasehold valuation tribunal under this Chapter, what freehold interest in the specified premises is to be acquired by the nominee purchaser, or

(b) if there are different determinations relating to different freehold interests in the specified premises, the date when determinations have been made in relation to all the freehold interests in the premises.".

(3) In paragraph 2 (price payable for the freehold of the specified premises), in sub-paragraph (1)—

(a) after "this paragraph," there shall be inserted "where the freehold of the whole of the specified premises is owned by the same person", and

(b) for "the specified" there shall be substituted "those".

(4) In paragraph 3(1A), after paragraph (b) there shall be inserted—

"(ba) an owner of an interest which the nominee purchaser is to acquire in pursuance of section 1(2)(a), or".

(5) After paragraph 5 there shall be inserted—

"Price payable for freehold of part of specified premises

5A.—(1) Where different persons own the freehold of different parts of the specified premises—

(a) a separate price shall be payable by the nominee purchaser for the freehold of each of those parts, and

(b) sub-paragraph (2) shall apply to determine the price so payable.

(2) Subject to sub-paragraph (3), the price payable by the nominee purchaser for the freehold of part of the specified premises shall be the aggregate of—

(a) the value of the freeholder's interest in the part as determined in accordance with paragraph 3, modified as mentioned in paragraph 5B, and

(b) the freeholder's share of the marriage value as determined in accordance with paragraph 4, modified as mentioned in paragraph 5C, and

(c) any amount of compensation payable to the freeholder under paragraph 5.

(3) Where the amount arrived at in accordance with sub-paragraph (2) is a negative amount, the price payable by the nominee purchaser for the freehold of the part shall be nil.

5B.—(1) In its application in accordance with paragraph 5A(2)(a), paragraph 3 shall have effect with the following modifications.

(2) In sub-paragraph (1)(a)(ii), there shall be inserted at the end "so far as relating to the part of the premises in which the freeholder's interest subsists".

(3) In sub-paragraph (1A), after paragraph (a) there shall be inserted—

"(aa) an owner of a freehold interest in the specified premises, or".

(4) In sub-paragraph (4)—

(a) the words "the whole of" shall be omitted, and

(b) for "2(1)(a)" there shall be substituted "5A(2)(a)".

5C.—(1) In its application in accordance with paragraph 5A(2)(b), paragraph 4 shall have effect with the following modifications.

(2) In sub-paragraph (2)—

(a) after "the specified premises" there shall be inserted "so far as relating to the part of the premises in which the freeholder's interest subsists",

(b) after "participating tenants", where it first occurs, there shall be inserted "in whose flats the freeholder's interest subsists", and

(c) in paragraph (a), for "the", where it second occurs, there shall be substituted "those".

(3) In sub-paragraph (3)—

(a) after "the specified premises" there shall be inserted "so far as relating to the part of the premises in which the freeholder's interest subsists", and

(b) in paragraph (a), for "2(1)(a)" there shall be substituted "5A(2)(a)".

(4) In sub-paragraph (4)(a), after "3(1)", where it first occurs, there shall be inserted "as applied by paragraph 5A(2)(a)".".

(6) For paragraph 8 there shall be substituted—

"8.—(1) Where the owner of the intermediate leasehold interest will suffer any loss or damage to which this paragraph applies, there shall be payable to him such amount as is reasonable to compensate him for that loss or damage.

(2) This paragraph applies to—

(a) any diminution in value of any interest of the owner of the intermediate leasehold interest in other property resulting from the acquisition of his interest in the specified premises; and

(b) any other loss or damage which results therefrom to the extent that it is referable to his ownership of any interest in other property.

(3) Without prejudice to the generality of paragraph (b) of sub-paragraph (2), the kinds of loss falling within that paragraph include loss of development value in relation to the specified premises to the extent that it is referable as mentioned in that paragraph.

(4) In sub-paragraph (3) "development value", in relation to the specified premises, means any increase in the value of the interest in the premises of the owner of the intermediate leasehold interest which is attributable to the possibility of demolishing, reconstructing or carrying out substantial works of construction on, the whole or a substantial part of the premises.".

(7) In paragraph 9 (owners of intermediate interests entitled to part of marriage value), in sub-paragraph (1), after "where" there shall be inserted "paragraph 2 applies and".

(8) After that paragraph there shall be inserted—

"9A.—(1) This paragraph applies where paragraph 5A applies and—

(a) the price payable for the freehold of a part of the specified premises includes an amount in respect of the freeholder's share of the marriage value, and

(b) the nominee purchaser is to acquire any intermediate leasehold interests which subsist in that part.

(2) The amount payable to the freeholder of the part in respect of his share of the marriage value shall be divided between the freeholder and the owners of the intermediate leasehold interests which subsist in that part in proportion to the value of their respective interests in the part (as determined for the purposes of paragraph 5A(2)(a) or paragraph 6(1)(b)(i), as the case may be).

(3) Where an intermediate leasehold interest subsists not only in the part of the specified premises in which the freeholder's interest subsists ("the relevant part") but also in another part of those premises—

(a) the value of the intermediate leasehold interest as determined for the purposes of paragraph 6(1)(b)(i) shall be apportioned between the relevant part and the other part of the specified premises in which it subsists, and

(b) sub-paragraph (2) shall have effect as if the reference to the value of the intermediate leasehold interest in the relevant part as determined for the purposes of paragraph 6(1)(b)(i) were to the value of that interest as determined on an apportionment in accordance with paragraph (a).

(4) Where the owner of an intermediate leasehold interest is entitled in accordance with sub-paragraph (2) to any part of the amount payable to the freeholder in respect of the freeholder's share of the marriage value, the amount to which he is so entitled shall be payable to him by the freeholder.".

(9) For paragraph 13 there shall be substituted—

"13.—(1) Where the owner of any such freehold or leasehold interest as is mentioned in paragraph 10(1) or (2) ("relevant interest") will suffer any loss or damage to which this paragraph applies, there shall be payable to him such amount as is reasonable to compensate him for that loss or damage.

(2) This paragraph applies to—

    (a) any diminution in value of any interest in other property belonging to the owner of a relevant interest, being diminution resulting from the acquisition of the property in which the relevant interest subsists; and

    (b) any other loss or damage which results therefrom to the extent that it is referable to his ownership of any interest in other property.

    (3) Without prejudice to the generality of paragraph (b) of sub-paragraph (2), the kinds of loss falling within that paragraph include loss of development value in relation to the property in which the relevant interest subsists to the extent that it is referable to his ownership of any interest in other property.

    (4) In sub-paragraph (3) "development value", in relation to the property in which the relevant interest subsists, means any increase in the value of the relevant interest which is attributable to the possibility of demolishing, reconstructing or carrying out substantial works of construction on, the whole or a substantial part of the property.".

    (10) In paragraph 14 (valuation of freehold and intermediate leasehold interests), in sub-paragraph (1)—

    (a) in paragraph (a), for "the", where it second occurs, there shall be substituted "a" and for "in accordance with paragraph 3" there shall be substituted "for the relevant purposes",

    (b) in paragraph (b), for "in accordance with paragraph 7" there shall be substituted "for the relevant purposes", and

    (c) for "the relevant" there shall be substituted "those".

    (11) In that paragraph, after sub-paragraph (3) there shall be inserted—

    "(3A) Where sub-paragraph (2) applies—

    (a) for the purposes of paragraph 5A(2)(a), and

    (b) in relation to an intermediate leasehold interest in relation to which there is more than one immediately superior interest,

any reduction in value made under that sub-paragraph shall be apportioned between the immediately superior interests.".

    (12) In that paragraph, in sub-paragraph (5)(a)—

    (a) for "the", where it first occurs, there shall be substituted "a", and

    (b) after "2(1)(a)" there shall be inserted "or, as the case may be, 5A(2)(a)".

    (13) In paragraph 15 (calculation of marriage value), there shall be inserted at the end—

    "(4) References in this paragraph to paragraph 4(2), (3) or (4) extend to that provision as it applies in accordance with paragraph 5A(2)(b).".

    (14) In paragraph 16 (apportionment of marriage value), in sub-paragraph (2), for "the", where it first occurs, there shall be substituted "a".

    (15) In paragraph 17 (adjustment of compensation), in sub-paragraph (4)(a), after "2(1)(c)" there shall be inserted ", 5A(2)(c)".

    (16) In that paragraph, there shall be inserted at the end—

    "(6) Where any reduction in value under sub-paragraph (2) of paragraph 14 is apportioned in accordance with sub-paragraph (3A) of that paragraph, any amount of compensation payable by virtue of this paragraph shall be similarly apportioned.".

    19. In Schedule 7 (conveyance to nominee purchaser on enfranchisement), in paragraph 1—

(a) for sub-paragraphs (a) and (b) there shall be substituted—

"(a) "the relevant premises" means, in relation to the conveyance of any interest, the premises in which the interest subsists;

(b) "the freeholder" means, in relation to the conveyance of a freehold interest, the person whose interest is to be conveyed;",

and

(b) for sub-paragraph (d) there shall be substituted—

"(d) "the appropriate time" means, in relation to the conveyance of a freehold interest, the time when the interest is to be conveyed to the nominee purchaser.".

20.—(1) Schedule 9 (grant of leases back to former freeholder) shall be amended as follows.

(2) In paragraph 1—

(a) for the definition of "the appropriate time" there shall be substituted—

""the appropriate time", in relation to a flat or other unit contained in the specified premises, means the time when the freehold of the flat or other unit is acquired by the nominee purchaser;", and

(b) for the definition of "the freeholder" there shall be substituted—

""the freeholder", in relation to a flat or other unit contained in the specified premises, means the person who owns the freehold of the flat or other unit immediately before the appropriate time;".

(3) In paragraph 2, in sub-paragraph (1), for "contained in the specified premises" there shall be substituted "falling within sub-paragraph (1A)", and after that sub-paragraph there shall be inserted—

"(1A) A flat falls within this sub-paragraph if—

(a) the freehold of the whole of it is owned by the same person, and

(b) it is contained in the specified premises.".

(4) In paragraph 3, in sub-paragraph (1), for "contained in the specified premises" there shall be substituted "falling within sub-paragraph (1A)", and after that sub-paragraph there shall be inserted—

"(1A) A flat falls within this sub-paragraph if—

(a) the freehold of the whole of it is owned by the same person, and

(b) it is contained in the specified premises.".

(5) In paragraph 5, in sub-paragraph (1), for "contained in the specified premises" there shall be substituted "falling within sub-paragraph (1A)", and after that sub-paragraph there shall be inserted—

"(1A) A unit falls within this sub-paragraph if—

(a) the freehold of the whole of it is owned by the same person, and

(b) it is contained in the specified premises.".

(6) In paragraph 6, for sub-paragraphs (1) and (2) there shall be substituted—

"(1) Sub-paragraph (2) applies where, immediately before the freehold of a flat or other unit contained in the specified premises is acquired by the nominee purchaser—

(a) those premises are premises with a resident landlord by virtue of the occupation of the flat or other unit by the freeholder of it, and

(b) the freeholder of the flat or other unit is a qualifying tenant of it.

(2) If the freeholder of the flat or other unit ("the relevant unit") by notice requires the nominee purchaser to do so, the nominee purchaser

shall grant to the freeholder a lease of the relevant unit in accordance with section 36 and paragraph 7 below; and, on the grant of such a lease to the freeholder, he shall be deemed to have surrendered any lease of the relevant unit held by him immediately before the appropriate time.".

(7) In that paragraph, in sub-paragraph (3), for "(1)(c)" there shall be substituted "(1)(b)".

SCHEDULE 11

COMPENSATION FOR POSTPONEMENT OF TERMINATION IN CONNECTION WITH INEFFECTIVE CLAIMS

Claims under Part I of the Leasehold Reform Act 1967

Section 116.

1.—(1) After section 27 of the Leasehold Reform Act 1967 there shall be inserted—   1967 c. 88.

"Compensation for postponement of termination in connection with ineffective claims.

27A.—(1) This section applies where, on or after 15th January 1999—

(a) a tenant of any property makes a claim to acquire the freehold or an extended lease of it, and

(b) the claim is not made at least two years before the term date of the tenancy in respect of which the claim is made ("the existing tenancy").

(2) The tenant shall be liable to pay compensation if the claim is not effective and—

(a) the making of the claim caused a notice served under paragraph 4(1) of Schedule 10 to the Local Government and Housing Act 1989 to cease to have effect and the date on which the claim ceases to have effect is later than four months before the termination date specified in the notice,   1989 c. 42.

(b) the making of the claim prevented the service of an effective notice under paragraph 4(1) of Schedule 10 to the Local Government and Housing Act 1989 (but did not cause a notice served under that provision to cease to have effect) and the date on which the claim ceases to have effect is a date later than six months before the term date of the tenancy, or

(c) the existing tenancy is continued under paragraph 3(1) of Schedule 3 to this Act by virtue of the claim.

(3) Compensation under subsection (2) above shall become payable at the end of the appropriate period and be the right of the person who is the tenant's immediate landlord at that time.

(4) The amount which the tenant is liable to pay under subsection (2) above shall be equal to the difference between—

(a) the rent for the appropriate period under the existing tenancy, and

(b) the rent which might reasonably be expected to be payable for that period were the property to which the existing tenancy relates let for a term equivalent to that period on the open market by a willing landlord on the following assumptions—

(i) that no premium is payable in connection with the letting,

(ii) that the letting confers no security of tenure, and

(iii) that, except as otherwise provided by this paragraph, the letting is on the same terms as the existing tenancy.

(5) For the purposes of subsection (2) above, a claim to acquire the freehold or an extended lease is not effective if it ceases to have effect for any reason other than—

(a) the acquisition in pursuance of the claim of the interest to which it relates, or

(b) the lapsing of the claim under any provision of this Act excluding the tenant's liability for costs.

(6) For the purposes of subsections (3) and (4) above, the appropriate period is—

(a) in a case falling within paragraph (a) of subsection (2) above, the period—

(i) beginning with the termination date specified in the notice mentioned in that paragraph, and

1989 c. 42.

(ii) ending with the earliest date of termination which could have been specified in a notice under paragraph 4(1) of Schedule 10 to the Local Government and Housing Act 1989 served immediately after the date on which the claim ceases to have effect, or, if the existing tenancy is terminated before then, with the date of its termination;

(b) in a case falling within paragraph (b) of subsection (2) above, the period—

(i) beginning with the later of six months from the date on which the claim is made and the term date of the existing tenancy, and

(ii) ending six months after the date on which the claim ceases to have effect, or, if the existing tenancy is terminated before then, with the date of its termination; and

(c) in a case falling within paragraph (c) of subsection (2) above, the period for which the existing tenancy is continued under paragraph 3(1) of Schedule 3 to this Act.

(7) For the purposes of this section—

(a) references to a claim to acquire the freehold or an extended lease shall be taken as references to a notice of a person's desire to acquire it under Part I of this Act and as including a claim made by a tenant not entitled to acquire it, and

(b) references to the date on which a claim ceases to have effect shall, in relation to a notice which is not a valid notice, be taken as references to the date on which the notice is set aside by the court or withdrawn or would, if valid, cease to have effect, that date being taken, where the notice is set aside, or would (if valid) cease to have effect, in consequence of a court order, to be the date when the order becomes final.

Modification of
section 27A
where change in
immediate
reversion.

27B.—(1) Where a tenant's liability to pay compensation under section 27A above relates to a period during which there has been a change in the interest immediately expectant on the determination of his tenancy, that section shall have effect with the following modifications.

(2) For subsections (3) and (4) there shall be substituted—

"(3) Compensation under subsection (2) above shall become payable at the end of the appropriate period and there shall be a separate right to compensation in respect of each of the interests which, during that period, have been immediately expectant on the determination of the existing tenancy.

(4) Compensation under subsection (2) above shall—

(a) in the case of the interest which is immediately expectant on the determination of the existing tenancy at the end of the appropriate period, be the right of the person in whom that interest is vested at that time, and

(b) in the case of an interest which ceases during the appropriate period to be immediately expectant on the determination of the existing tenancy, be the right of the person in whom the interest was vested immediately before it ceased to be so expectant.

(4A) The amount which the tenant is liable to pay under subsection (2) above in respect of any interest shall be equal to the difference between—

(a) the rent under the existing tenancy for the part of the appropriate period during which the interest was immediately expectant on the determination of that tenancy, and

(b) the rent which might reasonably be expected to be payable for that part of that period were the property to which the existing tenancy relates let for a term equivalent to that part of that period on the open market by a willing landlord on the following assumptions—

(i) that no premium is payable in connection with the letting,

(ii) that the letting confers no security of tenure, and

(iii) that, except as otherwise provided by this paragraph, the letting is on the same terms as the existing tenancy."

(3) In subsection (6), for "(3) and (4)" there shall be substituted "(3) to (4A)"."

(2) In section 21(1) of that Act (matters to be determined by leasehold valuation tribunal), after paragraph (c) there shall be inserted—

"(ca) the amount of any compensation payable under section 27A;".

Claims under Chapter I of Part I of the Leasehold Reform, Housing and Urban Development Act 1993

2.—(1) After section 37 of the Leasehold Reform, Housing and Urban Development Act 1993 there shall be inserted—

1993 c. 28.

"Landlord's right to compensation in relation to ineffective claims

Compensation for postponement of termination in connection with ineffective claims.

37A.—(1) This section applies where a claim to exercise the right to collective enfranchisement in respect of any premises is made on or after 15th January 1999 by tenants of flats contained in the premises and the claim is not effective.

(2) A person who is a participating tenant immediately before the claim ceases to have effect shall be liable to pay compensation if—

   (a) the claim was not made at least two years before the term date of the lease by virtue of which he is a qualifying tenant ("the existing lease"), and

   (b) any of the conditions mentioned in subsection (3) is met.

(3) The conditions referred to above are—

   (a) that the making of the claim caused a notice served under paragraph 4(1) of Schedule 10 to the Local Government and Housing Act 1989 in respect of the existing lease to cease to have effect and the date on which the claim ceases to have effect is later than four months before the termination date specified in the notice,

   (b) that the making of the claim prevented the service of an effective notice under paragraph 4(1) of Schedule 10 to the Local Government and Housing Act 1989 in respect of the existing lease (but did not cause a notice served under that provision in respect of that lease to cease to have effect) and the date on which the claim ceases to have effect is a date later than six months before the term date of the existing lease, and

   (c) that the existing lease has been continued under paragraph 6(1) of Schedule 3 by virtue of the claim.

(4) Compensation under subsection (2) shall become payable at the end of the appropriate period and be the right of the person who is the tenant's immediate landlord at that time.

(5) The amount which a tenant is liable to pay under subsection (2) shall be equal to the difference between—

   (a) the rent for the appropriate period under the existing lease, and

   (b) the rent which might reasonably be expected to be payable for that period were the property to which the existing lease relates let for a term equivalent to that period on the open market by a willing landlord on the following assumptions—

      (i) that no premium is payable in connection with the letting,

      (ii) that the letting confers no security of tenure, and

      (iii) that, except as otherwise provided by this paragraph, the letting is on the same terms as the existing lease.

(6) For the purposes of subsections (4) and (5), the appropriate period is—

   (a) in a case falling within paragraph (a) of subsection (3), the period—

(i) beginning with the termination date specified in the notice mentioned in that paragraph, and

(ii) ending with the earliest date of termination which could have been specified in a notice under paragraph 4(1) of Schedule 10 to the Local Government and Housing Act 1989 in respect of the existing lease served immediately after the date on which the claim ceases to have effect, or, if the existing lease is terminated before then, with the date of its termination;

1989 c. 42.

(b) in a case falling within paragraph (b) of subsection (3), the period—

(i) beginning with the later of six months from the date on which the claim is made and the term date of the existing lease, and

(ii) ending six months after the date on which the claim ceases to have effect, or, if the existing lease is terminated before then, with the date of its termination; and

(c) in a case falling within paragraph (c) of subsection (3), the period for which the existing lease is continued under paragraph 6(1) of Schedule 3.

(7) In the case of a person who becomes a participating tenant by virtue of an election under section 14(3), the references in subsections (3)(a) and (b) and (6)(b)(i) to the making of the claim shall be construed as references to the making of the election.

(8) For the purposes of this section—

(a) references to a claim to exercise the right to collective enfranchisement shall be taken as references to a notice given, or purporting to be given (whether by persons who are qualifying tenants or not), under section 13,

(b) references to the date on which a claim ceases to have effect shall, in the case of a claim made by a notice which is not a valid notice under section 13, be taken as references to the date on which the notice is set aside by the court or is withdrawn or would, if valid, cease to have effect or be deemed to have been withdrawn, that date being taken, where the notice is set aside, or would, if valid, cease to have effect, in consequence of a court order, to be the date when the order becomes final, and

(c) a claim to exercise the right to collective enfranchisement is not effective if it ceases to have effect for any reason other than—

(i) the application of section 23(4), 30(4) or 31(4),

(ii) the entry into a binding contract for the acquisition of the freehold and other interests falling to be acquired in pursuance of the claim, or

(iii) the making of an order under section 24(4)(a) or (b) or 25(6)(a) or (b) which provides for the vesting of those interests.

Modification of
section 37A
where change in
immediate
reversion.

37B.—(1) Where a tenant's liability to pay compensation under section 37A relates to a period during which there has been a change in the interest immediately expectant on the determination of his lease, that section shall have effect with the following modifications.

(2) For subsections (4) and (5) there shall be substituted—

"(4) Compensation under subsection (2) shall become payable at the end of the appropriate period and there shall be a separate right to compensation in respect of each of the interests which, during that period, have been immediately expectant on the determination of the existing lease.

(5) Compensation under subsection (2) above shall—

(a) in the case of the interest which is immediately expectant on the determination of the existing lease at the end of the appropriate period, be the right of the person in whom that interest is vested at that time, and

(b) in the case of an interest which ceases during the appropriate period to be immediately expectant on the determination of the existing lease, be the right of the person in whom the interest was vested immediately before it ceased to be so expectant.

(5A) The amount which the tenant is liable to pay under subsection (2) above in respect of any interest shall be equal to the difference between—

(a) the rent under the existing lease for the part of the appropriate period during which the interest was immediately expectant on the determination of that lease, and

(b) the rent which might reasonably be expected to be payable for that part of that period were the property to which the existing lease relates let for a term equivalent to that part of that period on the open market by a willing landlord on the following assumptions—

(i) that no premium is payable in connection with the letting,

(ii) that the letting confers no security of tenure, and

(iii) that, except as otherwise provided by this paragraph, the letting is on the same terms as the existing lease."

(3) In subsection (6), for "(4) and (5)" there shall be substituted "(4) to (5A)"."

(2) In section 91(2) of that Act (matters to be determined by leasehold valuation tribunal), after paragraph (c) there shall be inserted—

"(ca) the amount of any compensation payable under section 37A;".

Claims under Chapter II of Part I of the Leasehold Reform, Housing and Urban Development Act 1993

1993 c. 28.

3.—(1) After section 61 of the Leasehold Reform, Housing and Urban Development Act 1993 there shall be inserted—

"Landlord's right to compensation in relation to ineffective claims

Compensation for postponement of termination in connection with ineffective claims.

61A.—(1) This section applies where, on or after 15th January 1999—

(a) a tenant of a flat makes a claim to acquire a new lease of the flat, and

(b) the claim is not made at least two years before the term date of the lease in respect of which the claim is made ("the existing lease").

(2) The tenant shall be liable to pay compensation if the claim is not effective and—

(a) the making of the claim caused a notice served under paragraph 4(1) of Schedule 10 to the Local Government and Housing Act 1989 to cease to have effect and the date on which the claim ceases to have effect is later than four months before the termination date specified in the notice,

1989 c. 42.

(b) the making of the claim prevented the service of an effective notice under paragraph 4(1) of Schedule 10 to the Local Government and Housing Act 1989 (but did not cause a notice served under that provision to cease to have effect) and the date on which the claim ceases to have effect is a date later than six months before the term date of the existing lease, or

(c) the existing lease is continued under paragraph 5(1) of Schedule 12 by virtue of the claim.

(3) Compensation under subsection (2) shall become payable at the end of the appropriate period and be the right of the person who is the tenant's immediate landlord at that time.

(4) The amount which the tenant is liable to pay under subsection (2) shall be equal to the difference between—

(a) the rent for the appropriate period under the existing lease, and

(b) the rent which might reasonably be expected to be payable for that period were the property to which the existing lease relates let for a term equivalent to that period on the open market by a willing landlord on the following assumptions—

(i) that no premium is payable in connection with the letting,

(ii) that the letting confers no security of tenure, and

(iii) that, except as otherwise provided by this paragraph, the letting is on the same terms as the existing lease.

(5) For the purposes of subsections (3) and (4), the appropriate period is—

(a) in a case falling within paragraph (a) of subsection (2), the period—

(i) beginning with the termination date specified in the notice mentioned in that paragraph, and

(ii) ending with the earliest date of termination which could have been specified in a notice under paragraph 4(1) of Schedule 10 to the Local Government and Housing Act 1989 served

immediately after the date on which the claim
ceases to have effect, or, if the existing lease is
terminated before then, with the date on which it is
terminated;

(b) in a case falling within paragraph (b) of subsection (2),
the period—

(i) beginning with the later of six months from
the date on which the claim is made and the term
date of the existing lease, and

(ii) ending six months after the date on which the
claim ceases to have effect, or, if the existing lease is
terminated before then, with the date of its
termination; and

(c) in a case falling within paragraph (c) of subsection (2),
the period for which the existing lease is continued
under paragraph 5(1) of Schedule 12.

(6) For the purposes of subsection (2), a claim to a new lease
is not effective if it ceases to have effect for any reason other
than—

(a) the application of section 47(1) or 55(2), or

(b) the acquisition of the new lease in pursuance of the
claim.

(7) For the purposes of this section—

(a) references to a claim to acquire a new lease shall be
taken as references to a notice given, or purporting to
be given (whether by a qualifying tenant or not),
under section 42, and

(b) references to the date on which a claim ceases to have
effect shall, in the case of a claim made by a notice
which is not a valid notice under section 42, be taken
as references to the date on which the notice is set
aside by the court or is withdrawn or would, if valid,
cease to have effect or be deemed to have been
withdrawn, that date being taken, where the notice is
set aside, or would, if valid, cease to have effect, in
consequence of a court order, to be the date when the
order becomes final.

Modification of
section 61A
where change in
immediate
reversion.

61B.—(1) Where a tenant's liability to pay compensation
under section 61A relates to a period during which there has
been a change in the interest immediately expectant on the
determination of his lease, that section shall have effect with the
following modifications.

(2) For subsections (3) and (4) there shall be substituted—

"(3) Compensation under subsection (2) shall become
payable at the end of the appropriate period and there shall be
a separate right to compensation in respect of each of the
interests which, during that period, have been immediately
expectant on the determination of the existing lease.

(4) Compensation under subsection (2) above shall—

(a) in the case of the interest which is immediately
expectant on the determination of the existing lease at
the end of the appropriate period, be the right of the
person in whom that interest is vested at that time,
and

(b) in the case of an interest which ceases during the appropriate period to be immediately expectant on the determination of the existing lease, be the right of the person in whom the interest was vested immediately before it ceased to be so expectant.

(4A) The amount which the tenant is liable to pay under subsection (2) above in respect of any interest shall be equal to the difference between—

(a) the rent under the existing lease for the part of the appropriate period during which the interest was immediately expectant on the determination of that lease, and

(b) the rent which might reasonably be expected to be payable for that part of that period were the property to which the existing lease relates let for a term equivalent to that part of that period on the open market by a willing landlord on the following assumptions—

(i) that no premium is payable in connection with the letting,

(ii) that the letting confers no security of tenure, and

(iii) that, except as otherwise provided by this paragraph, the letting is on the same terms as the existing lease."

(3) In subsection (5), for "(3) and (4)" there shall be substituted "(3) to (4A)"."

(2) In section 91(2) of that Act (matters to be determined by leasehold valuation tribunal), after paragraph (c) there shall be inserted—

"(cb) the amount of any compensation payable under section 61A;".

SCHEDULE 12

Section 121.

ADMINISTRATION OF HOUSING BENEFIT, &c

Administration of housing benefit

1.—(1) Section 134 of the Social Security Administration Act 1992 (arrangements for housing benefit) is amended as follows.

1992 c. 5.

(2) For subsection (1) (administering authority and form of benefit) substitute—

"(1) Housing benefit provided by virtue of a scheme under section 123 of the Social Security Contributions and Benefits Act 1992 (in this Part referred to as "the housing benefit scheme") shall be funded and administered by the appropriate housing authority or local authority.

1992 c. 4.

(1A) Housing benefit in respect of payments which the occupier of a dwelling is liable to make to a housing authority shall take the form of a rent rebate or, in prescribed cases, a rent allowance funded and administered by that authority.

The cases that may be so prescribed do not include any where the payment is in respect of property within the authority's Housing Revenue Account.

(1B) In any other case housing benefit shall take the form of a rent allowance funded and administered by the local authority for the area in which the dwelling is situated or by such other local authority as is specified by an order made by the Secretary of State.".

(3) In subsection (2)(b) omit the words "or rates".

(4) Omit subsections (3), (4), (6) and (7).

(5) For subsection (5) (agreements with other authorities for carrying out of functions) substitute—

"(5) Authorities may—

(a) agree that one shall discharge functions relating to housing benefit on another's behalf; or

(b) discharge any such functions jointly or arrange for their discharge by a joint committee.

(5A) Nothing in this section shall be read as excluding the general provisions of the Local Government Act 1972 or the Local Government (Scotland) Act 1973 from applying in relation to the housing benefit functions of a local authority.".

(6) In subsection (9) for the words from "the rebates or allowances" to the end substitute "the housing benefit which will be paid by the authority in any year will not exceed the permitted total or any subsidiary limit specified by order of the Secretary of State.".

(7) In subsection (11) for the words from "the rebates or allowances" to the end substitute "the housing benefit paid by them during the year exceeds the permitted total or any subsidiary limit specified by order of the Secretary of State.".

(8) For subsection (12) substitute—

"(12) The Secretary of State—

(a) shall by order specify the permitted total of housing benefit payable by any authority in any year; and

(b) may by order specify one or more subsidiary limits on the amount of housing benefit payable by any authority in any year in respect of any matter or matters specified in the order.

The power to specify the permitted total or a subsidiary limit may be exercised by fixing an amount or by providing rules for its calculation.".

Administration of council tax benefit

2. In section 138 of the Social Security Administration Act 1992 (council tax benefit: nature of benefit), at the end of subsection (1) insert—

"References in any enactment or instrument (whenever passed or made) to payment, in relation to council tax benefit, include any of those ways of giving the benefit.".

3.—(1) Section 139 of the Social Security Administration Act 1992 (arrangements for council tax benefit) is amended as follows.

(2) For subsections (4) and (5) (agreements with other authorities for carrying out of functions) substitute—

"(4) Nothing in this section shall be read as excluding the general provisions of the Local Government Act 1972 or the Local Government (Scotland) Act 1973 from applying in relation to the council tax benefit functions of a local authority.".

(3) In subsection (7) for the words from "the benefits which will be allowed" to the end substitute "the amount of benefit which will be paid by them in any year will not exceed the permitted total or any subsidiary limit specified by order of the Secretary of State.".

(4) In subsection (9) for the words from "the benefits allowed by it" to the end substitute "the amount of benefit paid by them in any year exceeds the permitted total or any subsidiary limit specified by order of the Secretary of State.".

(5) For subsection (10) substitute—

"(10) The Secretary of State—

(a) shall by order specify the permitted total of council tax benefit payable by any authority in any year; and

(b) may by order specify one or more subsidiary limits on the amount of council tax benefit payable by any authority in any year in respect of any matter or matters specified in the order.

The power to specify the permitted total or a subsidiary limit may be exercised by fixing an amount or by providing rules for its calculation.".

Subsidy

4. After section 140 of the Social Security Administration Act 1992 insert—   1992 c. 5.

"Subsidy

Subsidy.   140A.—(1) For each year the Secretary of State shall pay a subsidy to each authority administering housing benefit or council tax benefit.

(2) He shall pay—

(a) rent rebate subsidy to each housing authority;

(b) rent allowance subsidy to each local authority; and

(c) council tax benefit subsidy to each billing authority or levying authority.

(3) In the following provisions of this Part "subsidy", without more, refers to subsidy of any of those descriptions.

Calculation of amount of subsidy.   140B.—(1) The amount of subsidy to be paid to an authority shall be calculated in the manner specified by order made by the Secretary of State.

(2) Subject as follows, the amount of subsidy shall be calculated by reference to the amount of relevant benefit paid by the authority during the year, with any additions specified in the order but subject to any deductions so specified.

In the case of a housing authority in England and Wales, any Housing Revenue Account rebates paid by them shall be excluded from the total.

(3) The order may provide that the amount of subsidy in respect of any matter shall be a fixed sum or shall be nil.

(4) The Secretary of State may deduct from the amount which would otherwise be payable by way of subsidy such amount as he considers it unreasonable to pay by way of subsidy.

(5) The Secretary of State may pay to an authority as part of the subsidy an additional amount in respect of the costs of administering the relevant benefit.

Any such additional amount shall be a fixed sum specified by, or shall be calculated in the manner specified by, an order made by the Secretary of State.

(6) In this section "relevant benefit" means housing benefit or council tax benefit, as the case may be.

(7) Nothing in this section shall be taken to imply that any such addition or deduction as is mentioned in subsection (2) or (4) above may not be determined by reference to—

(a) the amount of relevant benefit paid by the authority during a previous year; or

(b) the amount of subsidy paid to the authority in respect of a previous year, under this section.

(8) The amount of subsidy payable to an authority shall be calculated to the nearest pound, disregarding an odd amount of 50 pence or less and treating an odd amount exceeding 50 pence as a whole pound.

Payment of subsidy.

140C.—(1) Subsidy shall be paid by the Secretary of State in such instalments, at such times, in such manner and subject to such conditions as to claims, records, certificates, audit or otherwise as may be provided by order of the Secretary of State.

(2) The order may provide that if an authority has not, within such period as may be specified in the order, complied with the conditions so specified as to claims, records, certificate, audit or otherwise, the Secretary of State may estimate the amount of subsidy payable to the authority and employ for that purpose such criteria as he considers relevant.

(3) Where subsidy has been paid to an authority and it appears to the Secretary of State—

(a) that subsidy has been overpaid; or

(b) that there has been a breach of any condition specified in an order under this section,

he may recover from the authority the whole or such part of the payment as he may determine.

Without prejudice to other methods of recovery, a sum recoverable under this subsection may be recovered by withholding or reducing subsidy.

(4) An order made by the Secretary of State under this section may be made before, during or after the end of the year or years to which it relates.

Rent rebate subsidy: accounting provisions.

140D.—(1) Rent rebate subsidy is payable—

(a) in the case of a local authority in England and Wales, for the credit of a revenue account of theirs other than their Housing Revenue Account or Housing Repairs Account;

(b) in the case of a local authority in Scotland, for the credit of their rent rebate account;

(c) in the case of a development corporation in England and Wales or the Development Board for Rural Wales, for the credit of their housing account; and

(d) in the case of a new town corporation in Scotland or Scottish Homes, for the credit of the account to which rent rebates granted by them, or it, are debited.

(2) Every local housing authority in England and Wales shall for each year carry to the credit of their Housing Revenue Account from some other revenue account of theirs which is not a Housing Repairs Account an amount equal to the aggregate of—

(a) so much of each Housing Revenue Account rebate paid by them during the year as was paid—

(i) in the exercise of a discretion conferred by the housing benefit scheme; or

(ii) in pursuance of any modification of that scheme under section 134(8)(b) above; and

(b) unless the authority otherwise determine, so much of each such rebate as was paid in pursuance of such modifications of that scheme as are mentioned in section 134(8)(a) above.

Supplementary provisions

Financing of joint arrangements.

140E.—(1) Where two or more authorities make arrangements for the discharge of any of their functions relating to housing benefit or council tax benefit—

(a) by one authority on behalf of itself and one or more other authorities; or

(b) by a joint committee,

the Secretary of State may make such payments as he thinks fit to the authority or committee in respect of their expenses in carrying out those functions.

(2) The provisions of sections 140B and 140C (subsidy: calculation and supplementary provisions) apply in relation to a payment under this section as in relation to a payment of subsidy.

(3) The Secretary of State may (without prejudice to the generality of his powers in relation to the amount of subsidy) take into account the fact that an amount has been paid under this section in respect of expenses which would otherwise have been met in whole or in part by the participating authorities.

No requirement for annual orders.

140F.—(1) Any power under this Part to make provision by order for or in relation to a year does not require the making of a new order each year.

(2) Any order made under the power may be revoked or varied at any time, whether before, during or after the year to which it relates.

Interpretation: Part VIII.

140G. In this Part, unless the context otherwise requires—

"Housing Repairs Account" means an account kept under section 77 of the Local Government and Housing Act 1989;

1989 c. 42.

"Housing Revenue Account" means the account kept under section 74 of the Local Government and Housing Act 1989, and—

(a) references to property within that account have the same meaning as in Part VI of that Act, and

(b) "Housing Revenue Account rebate" means a rebate debited to that account in accordance with that Part;

"rent rebate subsidy" and "rent allowance subsidy" shall
be construed in accordance with section 134 above;

"year" means a financial year within the meaning of the
Local Government Finance Act 1992.".

Transitional provision

5.—(1) The Secretary of State may by order make such transitional provision,
and such consequential provision and savings, as appear to him appropriate in
connection with the coming into force of the provisions of this Schedule.

(2) Without prejudice to the generality of that power, the order may provide
for the recovery by the withholding or reduction of subsidy payable under the
provisions inserted by paragraph 4 above of any amount which would have been
recoverable under the provisions of Part VIII of the Social Security
Administration Act 1992 repealed by this Act.

(3) Section 189(3) to (7) of the Social Security Administration Act 1992
(general provisions as to regulations and orders) apply in relation to the power
conferred by sub-paragraph (1) as they apply in relation to a power conferred by
that Act to make an order.

(4) A statutory instrument containing an order under this paragraph shall be
subject to annulment in pursuance of a resolution of either House of Parliament.

SCHEDULE 13

HOUSING BENEFIT AND RELATED MATTERS: CONSEQUENTIAL AMENDMENTS

Rent Act 1977 (c.42)

1. In section 63(7) of the Rent Act 1977 (expenditure on rent officers to be met
by Secretary of State), in paragraph (a), for "or an order under section 121 of the
Housing Act 1988" substitute "or an order under section 122 of the Housing
Act 1996".

Housing Act 1985 (c.68)

2. In section 425(2)(b) of the Housing Act 1985 (housing subsidy: local
contribution differential), for "section 135" substitute "section 140A".

Social Security Administration Act 1992 (c.5)

3.—(1) The Social Security Administration Act 1992 is amended as follows.

(2) In section 5(3) (regulations about benefit: information required by a rent
officer), for "section 121 of the Housing Act 1988" substitute "section 122 of the
Housing Act 1996".

(3) In section 116(4) (legal proceedings for offences: definition of "appropriate
authority")—

(a) omit paragraph (a);

(b) in paragraph (b), for "that subsection" substitute "section 134
below"; and

(c) in paragraph (c), for "that subsection" substitute "that section".

(4) In section 176 (consultation with representative organisations), in
subsection (1)(b) for "section 134(12), 135, 139 or 140 above" substitute "any
provision of Part VIII above".

(5) In section 189(8) (requirement for consent of the Treasury), for "135, 140"
substitute "140B, 140C".

(6) In section 191 (interpretation: general)—

(a) at the appropriate place insert—

""council tax benefit scheme" shall be construed in accordance with section 139(1) above;";

(b) in the definition of "rate rebate", "rent rebate" and "rent allowance", omit the reference to rate rebate;

(c) omit the definitions of "rates" and "rating authority".

Leasehold Reform, Housing and Urban Development Act 1993 (c.28)

4. In section 135(8) of the Leasehold Reform, Housing and Urban Development Act 1993 (programmes for disposals of dwelling-houses by local authorities), for "section 135(1) of the Social Security Administration Act 1992 (housing benefit finance)" substitute "section 140A of the Social Security Administration Act 1992 (subsidy)".

SCHEDULE 14

INTRODUCTORY TENANCIES: CONSEQUENTIAL AMENDMENTS

Housing Act 1985 (c.68)

1. In section 88(1) of the Housing Act 1985 (cases where the secure tenant is a successor) after paragraph (e) insert "or

(f) the tenancy was previously an introductory tenancy and he was a successor to the introductory tenancy.".

2. In section 104(2) of the Housing Act 1985 (provision of information about secure tenancies) for the words "on the grant of the tenancy" substitute "when the secure tenancy arises".

3. After section 115 of the Housing Act 1985 insert—

"Meaning of "introductory tenancy".   115A. In this Part "introductory tenancy" has the same meaning as in Chapter I of Part V of the Housing Act 1996.".

4. In section 117 of the Housing Act 1985 (index of defined expressions: Part IV) insert at the appropriate place—

"introductory tenancy   section 115A".

5. In Schedule 1 to the Housing Act 1985 (tenancies which are not secure tenancies) after paragraph 1 insert—

"Introductory tenancies

1A. A tenancy is not a secure tenancy if it is an introductory tenancy or a tenancy which has ceased to be an introductory tenancy—

(a) by virtue of section 133(3) of the Housing Act 1996 (disposal on death to non-qualifying person), or

(b) by virtue of the tenant, or in the case of a joint tenancy every tenant, ceasing to occupy the dwelling-house as his only or principal home.".

Section 155(6).

SCHEDULE 15

ARREST FOR ANTI-SOCIAL BEHAVIOUR: POWERS OF HIGH COURT AND COUNTY
COURT TO REMAND

Introductory

1.—(1) The provisions of this Schedule apply where the court has power to remand a person under section 155(2) or (5) (arrest for breach of injunction, &c.).

(2) In this Schedule "the court" means the High Court or a county court and includes—

(a) in relation to the High Court, a judge of that court, and

(b) in relation to a county court, a judge or district judge of that court.

Remand in custody or on bail

2.—(1) The court may—

(a) remand him in custody, that is, commit him to custody to be brought before the court at the end of the period of remand or at such earlier time as the court may require, or

(b) remand him on bail, in accordance with the following provisions.

(2) The court may remand him on bail—

(a) by taking from him a recognizance, with or without sureties, conditioned as provided in paragraph 3, or

(b) by fixing the amount of the recognizances with a view to their being taken subsequently, and in the meantime committing him to custody as mentioned in sub-paragraph (1)(a).

(3) Where a person is brought before the court after remand, the court may further remand him.

3.—(1) Where a person is remanded on bail, the court may direct that his recognizance be conditioned for his appearance—

(a) before that court at the end of the period of remand, or

(b) at every time and place to which during the course of the proceedings the hearing may from time to time be adjourned.

(2) Where a recognizance is conditioned for a person's appearance as mentioned in sub-paragraph (1)(b), the fixing of any time for him next to appear shall be deemed to be a remand.

(3) Nothing in this paragraph affects the power of the court at any subsequent hearing to remand him afresh.

4.—(1) The court shall not remand a person for a period exceeding 8 clear days, except that—

(a) if the court remands him on bail, it may remand him for a longer period if he and the other party consent, and

(b) if the court adjourns a case under section 156(1) (remand for medical examination and report), the court may remand him for the period of the adjournment.

(2) Where the court has power to remand a person in custody it may, if the remand is for a period not exceeding 3 clear days, commit him to the custody of a constable.

Further remand

5.—(1) If the court is satisfied that a person who has been remanded is unable by reason of illness or accident to appear or be brought before the court at the expiration of the period for which he was remanded, the court may, in his absence, remand him for a further time.

This power may, in the case of a person who was remanded on bail, be exercised by enlarging his recognizance and those of any sureties for him to a later time.

(2) Where a person remanded on bail is bound to appear before the court at any time and the court has no power to remand him under sub-paragraph (1), the court may in his absence enlarge his recognizance and those of any sureties for him to a later time.

The enlargement of his recognizance shall be deemed to be a further remand.

(3) Paragraph 4(1) (limit of period of remand) does not apply to the exercise of the powers conferred by this paragraph.

Postponement of taking of recognizance

6. Where under paragraph 2(2)(b) the court fixes the amount in which the principal and his sureties, if any, are to be bound, the recognizance may afterwards be taken by such person as may be prescribed by rules of court, with the same consequences as if it had been entered into before the court.

SCHEDULE 16   Section 173.

ALLOCATION OF HOUSING ACCOMMODATION: CONSEQUENTIAL AMENDMENTS

Housing Act 1985 (c.68)

1. In section 106 of the Housing Act 1985 (information about allocation of secure tenancies) at the end insert—

"(6) The provisions of this section do not apply to a landlord authority which is a local housing authority so far as they impose requirements corresponding to those to which such an authority is subject under sections 166 and 168 of the Housing Act 1996 (provision of information about housing registers and allocation schemes).".

2.—(1) Schedule 1 to the Housing Act 1985 (tenancies which are not secure tenancies) is amended as follows.

(2) In paragraph 2 (premises occupied in connection with employment) at the beginning of sub-paragraph (1), (2) and (3) insert in each case "Subject to sub-paragraph (4B)".

(3) In sub-paragraph (4) of that paragraph—

(a) at the beginning insert "Subject to sub-paragraph (4A) and (4B)", and

(b) omit the words from "until" to the end.

(4) After sub-paragraph (4) of that paragraph insert—

"(4A) Except where the landlord is a local housing authority, a tenancy under sub-paragraph (4) shall become a secure tenancy when the periods during which the conditions mentioned in sub-paragraph (1), (2) or (3) are not satisfied with respect to the tenancy amount in aggregate to more than three years.

(4B) Where the landlord is a local housing authority, a tenancy under sub-paragraph (1), (2), (3) or (4) shall become a secure tenancy if the authority notify the tenant that the tenancy is to be regarded as a secure tenancy.".

(5) In paragraph 5 (temporary accommodation for persons taking up employment) in sub-paragraph (1)—

(a) for the words from the beginning to first "grant" substitute "Subject to sub-paragraphs (1A) and (1B), a tenancy is not a secure tenancy", and

(b) omit from "unless" to the end.

(6) After sub-paragraph (1) of that paragraph insert

"(1A) Except where the landlord is a local housing authority, a tenancy under sub-paragraph (1) shall become a secure tenancy on the expiry of one year from the grant or on earlier notification by the landlord to the tenant that the tenancy is to be regarded as a secure tenancy.

(1B) Where the landlord is a local housing authority, a tenancy under sub-paragraph (1) shall become a secure tenancy if at any time the authority notify the tenant that the tenancy is to be regarded as a secure tenancy.".

(7) In paragraph 10 (student lettings) in sub-paragraph (1)—

(a) for the words from the beginning to "sub-paragraph (3)" substitute "Subject to sub-paragraphs (2A) and (2B), a tenancy of a dwelling-house is not a secure tenancy", and

(b) omit from "unless" to the end.

(8) After sub-paragraph (2) of that paragraph insert—

"(2A) Except where the landlord is a local housing authority, a tenancy under sub-paragraph (1) shall become a secure tenancy on the expiry of the period specified in sub-paragraph (3) or on earlier notification by the landlord to the tenant that the tenancy is to be regarded as a secure tenancy.

(2B) Where the landlord is a local housing authority, a tenancy under sub-paragraph (1) shall become a secure tenancy if at any time the authority notify the tenant that the tenancy is to be regarded as a secure tenancy.".

(9) In sub-paragraph (3) of that paragraph for the words "sub-paragraph (1)" substitute "sub-paragraph (2A)".

Asylum and Immigration Act 1996 (c. 49)

3.—(1) Section 9 of the Asylum and Immigration Act 1996 (entitlement to housing accommodation and assistance) is amended as follows.

(2) In subsection (1) (entitlement to housing accommodation)—

(a) for "housing authority" substitute "local housing authority within the meaning of the Housing Act 1985", and

(b) for "the accommodation Part" substitute "Part II of that Act".

(3) After subsection (4) insert—

"(5) This section does not apply in relation to any allocation of housing accommodation to which Part VI of the Housing Act 1996 (allocation of housing accommodation) applies.

SCHEDULE 17

HOMELESSNESS: CONSEQUENTIAL AMENDMENTS

Local Authority Social Services Act 1970 (c.42)

1. In Schedule 1 to the Local Authority Social Services Act 1970 (enactments conferring functions assigned to Social Services Committee) for the entry relating to the Housing Act 1985 substitute—

"Housing Act 1996　　　　　　Co-operation in relation to homeless
Section 213(1)(b)　　　　　　persons and persons threatened
　　　　　　　　　　　　　　with homelessness.".

Greater London Council (General Powers) Act 1984 (c.xxvii)

2. In section 39 of the Greater London Council (General Powers) Act 1984 (occupants removed from buildings to have priority housing need) for "Part III of the Housing Act 1985 (housing the homeless)" substitute "Part VII of the Housing Act 1996 (homelessness)".

Housing Act 1985 (c.68)

3. In Schedule 1 to the Housing Act 1985 (tenancies which are not secure tenancies), for paragraph 4 (accommodation for homeless persons) substitute—

"Accommodation for homeless persons

4. A tenancy granted in pursuance of any function under Part VII of the Housing Act 1996 (homelessness) is not a secure tenancy unless the local housing authority concerned have notified the tenant that the tenancy is to be regarded as a secure tenancy.".

Housing (Scotland) Act 1987 (c.26)

4. In section 42 of the Housing (Scotland) Act 1987 (application of Part II to cases arising in England and Wales: request for co-operation)—

(a) in subsection (1) for "section 67(1) of the Housing Act 1985" substitute "section 198(1) of the Housing Act 1996"; and

(b) in subsections (2) and (3) for "section 72 of the Housing Act 1985" substitute "section 213 of the Housing Act 1996".

SCHEDULE 18

MISCELLANEOUS PROVISIONS

PART I

HOUSING MANAGEMENT

Repeal of Part IV of the Housing Act 1988

1. Part IV of the Housing Act 1988 (change of landlord: secure tenants) is hereby repealed.　　　　　　　　　1988 c. 50.

Payments to encourage local housing authority tenants to move to other accommodation

2.—(1) A local housing authority may make payments to or for the benefit of a tenant or licensee of a dwelling-house within its Housing Revenue Account with a view to assisting or encouraging that person to move to qualifying accommodation.

(2) In sub-paragraph (1) "qualifying accommodation" means a dwelling-house made available to the person concerned as tenant or licensee by any of the following—

    (a) the local housing authority making the grant or any other local housing authority; or

    (b) a registered social landlord.

1989 c. 42.

(3) The reference in sub-paragraph (1) to a dwelling-house being within the Housing Revenue Account of a local housing authority is to a dwelling-house to which section 74(1) of the Local Government and Housing Act 1989 for the time being applies.

(4) In this paragraph—

1985 c. 68.

"dwelling-house" has the meaning given by section 112 of the Housing Act 1985; and

"tenant" does not include a tenant under a long tenancy as defined in section 115 of that Act.

Consultation with respect to housing management

3.—(1) Part II of the Housing Act 1985 (provision of housing accommodation) is amended as follows.

(2) After section 27B insert—

"Consultation with respect to housing management

Consultation with respect to management.

27BA.—(1) The Secretary of State may make regulations for imposing requirements on a local housing authority to consult tenants, or to consider representations made to them by tenants, with respect to the exercise of their management functions (including proposals as to the exercise of those functions), in relation to any of the authority's houses or other land held for a related purpose.

(2) The regulations may include provision requiring a local housing authority to consult tenants, or consider representations made by tenants, with respect to—

    (a) the terms of a written specification to be prepared by the authority of functions proposed to be exercised by the authority or another person;

    (b) a proposal of the authority to exercise management functions themselves;

    (c) any person whom the authority propose to invite to submit a bid to exercise any of their management functions;

    (d) the standards of service for the time being achieved by the authority or (as the case may be) the person with whom they have entered into a management agreement;

    (e) a proposal to enforce the standards of service required by a management agreement.

(3) The requirements imposed on a local housing authority by the regulations may include provision with respect to—

    (a) the tenants to be consulted or whose representations are to be considered;

    (b) the means by which consultation is to be effected (including the arrangements to be made for tenants to consider the matters on which they have been consulted);

    (c) the arrangements to be made for tenants to make representations to the authority;

    (d) the action to be taken by the authority where representations are made.

(4) The regulations may include provision requiring a local housing authority to consult representatives of tenants, or to consider representations made to them by such representatives, as well as (or instead of) the tenants themselves; and accordingly, references in subsections (1) to (3) above to tenants include references to such representatives.

(5) The regulations may include provision for particular questions arising under them to be determined by a local housing authority on whom they impose requirements.

(6) Nothing in subsections (2) to (5) above shall be taken as prejudicing the generality of subsection (1).

(7) Regulations under this section—

    (a) may make different provision with respect to different cases or descriptions of case, including different provision for different areas,

    (b) may contain such incidental, supplementary or transitional provisions as appear to the Secretary of State to be necessary or expedient, and

    (c) shall be made by statutory instrument which shall be subject to annulment in pursuance of a resolution of either House of Parliament.

(8) Except as otherwise provided by the regulations, in the case of secure tenants, the provisions of the regulations shall apply in place of the provisions of section 105 (consultation on matters of housing management).

(9) Except as otherwise provided by the regulations, in the case of introductory tenants, the provisions of the regulations shall apply in place of the provisions of section 137 of the Housing Act 1996 (consultation on matters of housing management).

(10) References in this section to the management functions of a local housing authority in relation to houses or land shall be construed in the same way as references to any such functions in section 27.".

(3) In section 20(1) (application of housing management provisions) for "section 27B" substitute "section 27BA".

(4) In section 27 (management agreements), after subsection (5) insert—

"(5A) Nothing in section 6 of the Local Government Act 1988 (restrictions on authority carrying out functional work) shall apply in

1988 c. 9.

relation to any management functions which, in pursuance of a management agreement, are carried out by the manager as agent of the local housing authority.".

(5) In section 27AB (management agreements with tenant management organisations), in subsection (7)(b)(i), for the words from "section 27A" to the end substitute "regulations under section 27BA (consultation with respect to management)".

PART II

HOUSING FINANCE

Housing Revenue Account: directions as to certain matters

1989 c. 42.

4.—(1) In Part VI of the Local Government and Housing Act 1989 (housing finance), after section 78 (directions as to proper accounting practices) insert—

"Directions as to treatment of service charges, &c.

78A.—(1) The Secretary of State may give directions as to what items or amounts are to be regarded as referable to property within a local housing authority's Housing Revenue Account where one or more parts of a building have been disposed of but the common parts remain property within that account.

(2) Any such direction also has effect for the purposes of any Housing Repairs Account kept by the authority.

(3) Directions under this section may give the authority a discretion as to whether items or amounts are accounted for in the Housing Revenue Account or any Housing Repairs Account or in another revenue account.

(4) In this section "common parts" includes the structure and exterior of the building and common facilities provided, whether in the building or elsewhere, for persons who include the occupiers of one or more parts of the building.

Directions as to accounting for work subject to competitive tendering.

78B.—(1) This section applies where work is carried out by a local housing authority which has successfully bid for the work on a competitive basis.

(2) The Secretary of State may give directions—

(a) to secure that the amount debited to the Housing Revenue Account or any Housing Repairs Account of the authority in respect of the work reflects the amount of the authority's successful bid for the work rather than expenditure actually incurred;

(b) allowing an authority to credit to its Housing Revenue Account any surpluses reasonably attributable to work undertaken on or in connection with property within that account.

(3) Directions under subsection (2)(a) may make provision for determining the amount to be treated as the amount of the authority's successful bid.

References in this Part to expenditure shall be construed as references to the amount falling to be debited in accordance with the directions.

(4) Directions under subsection (2)(b) may make provision as to the ascertainment of the surpluses referred to and the circumstances in which a surplus is or is not to be taken to be attributable to property within an authority's Housing Revenue Account.".

(2) The above amendment has effect for the financial year beginning on 1st April 1997 and subsequent financial years.

Housing Revenue Account subsidy: final decision on amount

5.—(1) In Part VI of the Local Government and Housing Act 1989 (housing finance), after section 80 (calculation of Housing Revenue Account subsidy) insert— 1989 c. 42.

"Final decision on amount of Housing Revenue Account subsidy.

80A.—(1) The Secretary of State shall, as soon as he thinks fit after the end of the year, make a final decision as to the amount (if any) of Housing Revenue Account subsidy payable to a local housing authority for that year and notify the authority in writing of his decision.

(2) Once notified to the authority the decision is conclusive as to the amount (if any) payable by way of subsidy and shall not be questioned in any legal proceedings.

(3) Where the amount of Housing Revenue Account subsidy paid to an authority is less than the amount finally decided, the authority is entitled to be paid the balance.

(4) Where Housing Revenue Account subsidy has been paid to an authority in excess of the amount finally decided, the Secretary of State may recover the excess, with interest from such time and at such rates as he thinks fit.

Without prejudice to other methods of recovery, a sum recoverable under this subsection may be recovered by withholding or reducing subsidy.

(5) Nothing in this section affects any power of the Secretary of State to vary a determination as to the amount of subsidy before the final decision is made.".

(2) The above amendment applies in relation to the amount of subsidy payable—

(a) to authorities in England for the financial year beginning on 1st April 1996 and subsequent years; and

(b) to authorities in Wales for such financial years as the Secretary of State may specify by order made by statutory instrument.

Abolition of exchequer contributions for agricultural housing

6.—(1) No contribution shall be made by the Secretary of State by virtue of Part II of Schedule 15 to the Housing Act 1985 (exchequer contributions for agricultural housing) in respect of any year after the year ending on 31st March 1996. 1985 c. 68.

(2) Part II of Schedule 15 to that Act is amended as follows.

(3) For the heading substitute—

"Annual Grants for Agricultural Housing".

(4) For paragraph 1 substitute—

"Annual grants by local housing authorities

1.—(1) Annual grants shall, notwithstanding the abolition of exchequer contributions by paragraph 6(1) of Schedule 18 to the Housing Act 1996, continue to be payable by local housing authorities in respect of agricultural housing provided in pursuance of arrangements made under section 46 of the Housing (Financial Provisions) Act 1958. 1958 c. 42.

(2) Subject to the provisions of this Part of this Schedule, such annual grants are payable, in respect of any house as to which the Secretary of State originally undertook to make annual contributions under section 46 of the Housing (Financial Provisions) Act 1958, for the remainder of the 40 year period for which that undertaking was given.

(3) The amount paid by way of annual grant to the owner of a house shall not be less than the amount of the last annual contribution paid by the Secretary of State in respect of the house.".

(5) For paragraph 2(1) substitute—

"Conditions of payment of annual grant

2.—(1) It is a condition of the payment of a grant in respect of a house in any year that throughout the year the house—

(a) is reserved for members of the agricultural population, and

(b) if let, is let at a rent not exceeding the limit applicable in accordance with the following provisions of this paragraph,

and that in the opinion of the local housing authority all reasonable steps have been taken to secure the maintenance of the house in a proper state of repair during the year.".

(6) In paragraph 3(1), for "contribution" substitute "grant".

(7) For paragraph 4 substitute—

"4. A grant shall not be made or shall be reduced, as the local housing authority think fit, if (before the grant is paid) the local housing authority are of the opinion that during the whole or the greater part of the period to which the payment of the grant is referable the house has not been available as a dwelling fit for habitation, unless the authority is satisfied that that could not with reasonable diligence have been achieved.".

(8) In paragraph 5 omit the words "the Secretary of State or".

(9) After paragraph 5 insert—

"Commutation of future annual grant

6.—(1) A local authority may make an offer in writing to the person who is for the time being the owner of a house as respects which annual grant is payable under this Part of this Schedule to pay a lump sum in lieu of—

(a) the annual grant payable for the year in which the offer is accepted; and

(b) any further payments of annual grant that would (apart from this paragraph) be payable for the remainder of the period for which the original arrangements under section 46 of the Housing (Financial Provisions) Act 1958 were made.

(2) An owner may accept an offer made under this paragraph by notice in writing to the local housing authority.

(3) Subject to sub-paragraph (4) below, where such an offer is accepted the local housing authority shall pay to the owner a lump sum calculated in such manner as the authority may determine.

(4) A lump sum shall not be paid as respects a house unless the local housing authority are satisfied that the conditions in this Part of this Schedule have been observed throughout the year preceding the date on which the lump sum would otherwise be paid.

(5) On payment of a lump sum under this paragraph to the owner of a house—

(a) no further annual grants under this Part of this Schedule shall be payable in respect of the house; and

(b) the conditions described in this Part of this Schedule shall cease to apply to the house.".

(10) Nothing in this paragraph affects the operation of Part II of Schedule 15 to the Housing Act 1985 in respect of any year ending before 1st April 1996.

1985 c. 68.

PART III

ORDERS IN RELATION TO PROPERTY IN FAMILY AND MATRIMONIAL PROCEEDINGS, &c.

Housing Act 1980 (c.51)

7. In section 54(2) of the Housing Act 1980 (prohibition on assignment of protected shorthold tenancy or protected tenancy of dwelling-house), for "except in pursuance of an order under section 24 of the Matrimonial Causes Act 1973" substitute—

"except in pursuance of an order under—

(a) section 24 of the Matrimonial Causes Act 1973 (property adjustment orders in connection with matrimonial proceedings),

(b) section 17(1) of the Matrimonial and Family Proceedings Act 1984 (property adjustment orders after overseas divorce, &c.), or

(c) paragraph 1 of Schedule 1 to the Children Act 1989 (orders for financial relief against parents).".

Housing Act 1985 (c.68)

8.—(1) Section 39 of the Housing Act 1985 (exempted disposals) is amended as follows.

(2) In subsection (1), for paragraph (c) substitute—

"(c) it is a disposal of the whole of the house in pursuance of any such order as is mentioned in subsection (3);".

(3) After subsection (2) add—

"(3) The orders referred to in subsection (1)(c) are orders under—

(a) section 24 or 24A of the Matrimonial Causes Act 1973 (property adjustment orders or orders for the sale of property in connection with matrimonial proceedings),

(b) section 2 of the Inheritance (Provision for Family and Dependants) Act 1975 (orders as to financial provision to be made from estate),

(c) section 17 of the Matrimonial and Family Proceedings Act 1984 (property adjustment orders or orders for the sale of property after overseas divorce, &c.), or

(d) paragraph 1 of Schedule 1 to the Children Act 1989 (orders for financial relief against parents).".

9. In section 88(2) of the Housing Act 1985 (cases where secure tenant is a successor) after "proceedings)" insert "or section 17(1) of the Matrimonial and Family Proceedings Act 1984 (property adjustment orders after overseas divorce, &c.)".

10. In section 89 of the Housing Act 1985 (succession to periodic tenancy), for subsection (3) substitute—

"(3) Where there is no person qualified to succeed the tenant, the tenancy ceases to be a secure tenancy—

(a) when it is vested or otherwise disposed of in the course of the administration of the tenant's estate, unless the vesting or other disposal is in pursuance of an order made under—

(i) section 24 of the Matrimonial Causes Act 1973 (property adjustment orders made in connection with matrimonial proceedings),

(ii) section 17(1) of the Matrimonial and Family Proceedings Act 1984 (property adjustment orders after overseas divorce, &c.), or

(iii) paragraph 1 of Schedule 1 to the Children Act 1989 (orders for financial relief against parents); or

(b) when it is known that when the tenancy is so vested or disposed of it will not be in pursuance of such an order.".

11. In section 90(3) of the Housing Act 1985 (devolution of secure tenancy), for paragraph (a) and the word "or" at the end of the paragraph substitute—

"(a) the vesting or other disposal is in pursuance of an order made under—

(i) section 24 of the Matrimonial Causes Act 1973 (property adjustment orders in connection with matrimonial proceedings),

(ii) section 17(1) of the Matrimonial and Family Proceedings Act 1984 (property adjustment orders after overseas divorce, &c.), or

(iii) paragraph 1 of Schedule 1 to the Children Act 1989 (orders for financial relief against parents), or".

12. In section 91(3) of the Housing Act 1985 (cases where assignment of secure tenancy permitted), for paragraph (b) substitute—

"(b) an assignment in pursuance of an order made under—

(i) section 24 of the Matrimonial Causes Act 1973 (property adjustment orders in connection with matrimonial proceedings),

(ii) section 17(1) of the Matrimonial and Family Proceedings Act 1984 (property adjustment orders after overseas divorce, &c.), or

(iii) paragraph 1 of Schedule 1 to the Children Act 1989 (orders for financial relief against parents);".

13. In section 99B(2) of the Housing Act 1985 (persons qualifying for compensation for improvements) for paragraph (e) substitute—

"(e) a person to whom the tenancy was assigned by the improving tenant in pursuance of an order made under—

(i) section 24 of the Matrimonial Causes Act 1973 (property adjustment orders in connection with matrimonial proceedings),

(ii) section 17(1) of the Matrimonial and Family Proceedings Act 1984 (property adjustment orders after overseas divorce, &c.), or

(iii) paragraph 1 of Schedule 1 to the Children Act 1989 (orders for financial relief against parents);".

14. In section 101(3) of the Housing Act 1985 (rent not increased on account of tenant's improvements: qualifying persons) for paragraph (c) substitute—

"(c) a person to whom the tenancy was assigned by the tenant in pursuance of an order made under—

(i) section 24 of the Matrimonial Causes Act 1973 (property adjustment orders in connection with matrimonial proceedings),

(ii) section 17(1) of the Matrimonial and Family Proceedings Act 1984 (property adjustment orders after overseas divorce, &c.), or

(iii) paragraph 1 of Schedule 1 to the Children Act 1989 (orders for financial relief against parents);".

15.—(1) Section 160 of the Housing Act 1985 (exempted disposals in relation to right to buy) is amended as follows.

(2) In subsection (1), for paragraph (c) substitute—

"(c) it is a disposal of the whole of the dwelling-house in pursuance of any such order as is mentioned in subsection (3);".

(3) After subsection (2) add—

"(3) The orders referred to in subsection (1)(c) are orders under—

(a) section 24 or 24A of the Matrimonial Causes Act 1973 (property adjustment orders or orders for the sale of property in connection with matrimonial proceedings),

(b) section 2 of the Inheritance (Provision for Family and Dependants) Act 1975 (orders as to financial provision to be made from estate),

(c) section 17 of the Matrimonial and Family Proceedings Act 1984 (property adjustment orders or orders for the sale of property after overseas divorce, &c.), or

(d) paragraph 1 of Schedule 1 to the Children Act 1989 (orders for financial relief against parents).".

16. In section 171B(4)(b) of the Housing Act 1985 (extent of preserved right to buy: qualifying successors of tenant), after sub-paragraph (ii) insert—

"or

(iii) a property adjustment order under section 17(1) of the Matrimonial and Family Proceedings Act 1984 (property adjustment orders after overseas divorce, &c.), or

(iv) an order under paragraph 1 of Schedule 1 to the Children Act 1989 (orders for financial relief against parents),".

17. In paragraph 1(2) of Schedule 6A to the Housing Act 1985 (obligation to redeem landlord's share: excluded disposals), for paragraph (c) substitute—

"(c) it is a disposal in pursuance of an order under—

(i) section 24 or 24A of the Matrimonial Causes Act 1973 (property adjustment orders or orders for the sale of property in connection with matrimonial proceedings),

(ii) section 2 of the Inheritance (Provision for Family and Dependants) Act 1975 (orders as to financial provision to be made from estate),

(iii) section 17 of the Matrimonial and Family Proceedings Act 1984 (property adjustment orders or orders for the sale of property after overseas divorce, &c.), or

(iv) paragraph 1 of Schedule 1 to the Children Act 1989 (orders for financial relief against parents),".

Landlord and Tenant Act 1987 (c.31)

18. In section 4(2) of the Landlord and Tenant Act 1987 (right of first refusal: excluded disposals), for paragraph (c) substitute—

(c) a disposal in pursuance of an order made under—

(i) section 24 of the Matrimonial Causes Act 1973 (property adjustment orders in connection with matrimonial proceedings),

(ii) section 24A of the Matrimonial Causes Act 1973 (orders for the sale of property in connection with matrimonial proceedings) where the order includes provision requiring the property concerned to be offered for sale to a person or class of persons specified in the order,

(iii) section 2 of the Inheritance (Provision for Family and Dependants) Act 1975 (orders as to financial provision to be made from estate),

(iv) section 17(1) of the Matrimonial and Family Proceedings Act 1984 (property adjustment orders after overseas divorce, &c.),

(v) section 17(2) of the Matrimonial and Family Proceedings Act 1984 (orders for the sale of property after overseas divorce, &c.) where the order includes provision requiring the property concerned to be offered for sale to a person or class of persons specified in the order, or

(vi) paragraph 1 of Schedule 1 to the Children Act 1989 (orders for financial relief against parents);".

Housing Act 1988 (c.50)

19.—(1) Paragraph 4 of Schedule 11 to the Housing Act 1988 (repayment of discount on disposal: exempted disposals) is amended as follows.

(2) In sub-paragraph (1), for paragraph (c) substitute—

"(c) it is a disposal of the whole of the house in pursuance of any such order as is mentioned in sub-paragraph (4) below;".

(3) After sub-paragraph (3) add—

"(4) The orders referred to in sub-paragraph (1)(c) above are orders under—

(a) section 24 or 24A of the Matrimonial Causes Act 1973 (property adjustment orders or orders for the sale of property in connection with matrimonial proceedings),

(b) section 2 of the Inheritance (Provision for Family and Dependants) Act 1975 (orders as to financial provision to be made from estate),

(c) section 17 of the Matrimonial and Family Proceedings Act 1984 (property adjustment orders or orders for the sale of property after overseas divorce, &c.), or

(d) paragraph 1 of Schedule 1 to the Children Act 1989 (orders for financial relief against parents).".

PART IV

OTHER HOUSING PROVISIONS

Abolition of consent requirements for exercise of certain housing powers

1985 c. 68.   20. Section 16 of the Housing Act 1985 (consent requirements for exercise of certain housing powers) shall cease to have effect.

Amendments of section 133 of the Housing Act 1988

21.—(1) Section 133 of the Housing Act 1988 (consent required for certain subsequent disposals) is amended as follows.　　　1988 c. 50.

(2) After subsection (1) insert—

"(1A) This section does not apply if the original disposal was made before the date on which this section comes into force.".

The amendment made by this sub-paragraph shall be deemed always to have had effect.

(3) After subsection (2) insert—

"(2A) Consent required for the purposes of this section may be given either generally to all persons who may require such consent or to any particular person or description of person who may require such consent.".

(4) After subsection (5) insert—

"(5A) A person seeking any consent required by virtue of this section is not required to consult a tenant of the land or house proposed to be disposed of if—

(a) consent is sought for the disposal of the land or house to that tenant or to persons including that tenant; or

(b) consent is sought subject to the condition that the land or house is vacant at the time of the disposal;

and, accordingly, subsection (5) does not apply in either case.".

Abolition of requirements for Treasury consent

22.—(1) Any requirement in the following enactments for the consent or approval of the Treasury shall cease to have effect—

(a) in the Rent Act 1977—　　　1977 c. 42.

　　section 63(2) (schemes for appointment of rent officers), and

　　Schedule 10 (rent assessment committees);

(b) Schedule 26 to the Local Government, Planning and Land Act 1980 (urban development corporations);　　　1980 c. 65.

(c) in the Housing Act 1985—　　　1985 c. 68.

　　section 156(4) (liability to repay discount: approved lending institutions), and

　　section 429A (financial assistance for persons concerned with housing management);

(d) in the Housing Associations Act 1985—　　　1985 c. 69.

　　section 85(2) (meaning of "recognised body"), and

　　paragraphs 5 and 6 of Schedule 6 (remuneration, allowances and pensions);

(e) Schedule 7 to the Housing Act 1988 (constitution of housing action trusts);

(f) Schedule 17 to the Leasehold Reform, Housing and Urban Development Act 1993 (constitution of the Urban Regeneration Agency).　　　1993 c. 28.

(2) In Schedule 10 to the Rent Act 1977 (rent assessment committees), in paragraph 9(c), for "the Minister for the Civil Service" substitute "the Secretary of State".

(3) The amendments in this paragraph do not extend to Scotland.

Sch. 18

1985 c. 68.

Disposal of dwelling-houses subject to secure tenancies: consultation requirements

23. In section 106A of the Housing Act 1985 (consultation before disposal to private sector landlord) at the end insert—

"(3) That Schedule, and this section, do not apply in relation to any disposal of an interest in land by a local authority if—

(a) the interest has been acquired by the authority (whether compulsorily or otherwise) following the making of an order for compulsory purchase under any enactment, other than section 290 (acquisition of land for clearance),

(b) the order provides that the interest is being acquired for the purpose of disposal to a registered social landlord, and

(c) such a disposal is made within one year of the acquisition.

(4) In this section "registered social landlord" has the same meaning as in Part I of the Housing Act 1996.".

Powers of local housing authorities to acquire land for housing purposes

24.—(1) In section 17(2) of the Housing Act 1985 (acquisition of land for housing purposes) at end insert "or facilities which serve a beneficial purpose in connection with the requirements of persons for whom housing accommodation is provided".

1989 c. 42.

(2) In section 74(3)(b) of the Local Government and Housing Act 1989 (land excluded from Housing Revenue Account) at end insert "or facilities which serve a beneficial purpose in connection with the requirements of persons for whom housing accommodation is provided".

Housing action trusts

1988 c. 50.

25.—(1) In section 63 of the Housing Act 1988 (objects etc of housing action trusts)—

(a) in subsection (1)(d) after "conditions" insert "of those living"; and

(b) after subsection (2) insert—

"(2A) For the avoidance of doubt it is hereby declared that it is immaterial for the purposes of this section whether action taken by a housing action trust for achieving its objects or exercising the powers conferred on it by subsection (2) above also—

(a) benefits persons who do not live in the designated area; or

(b) improves the social conditions or general environment of an area outside the designated area.".

(2) In section 64 of that Act (proposals for area of housing action trust) in subsections (1) and (5) after "in" insert "relation to".

Preserved right to buy

26.—(1) In section 171B of the Housing Act 1985 (qualifying persons in relation to preserved right to buy)—

(a) in subsection (4)(a), at the end insert "or in whom that assured tenancy vested under section 17 of the Housing Act 1988 (statutory succession to assured tenancy)"; and

(b) in subsection (5)(b), for "subsection (4)(a) or (b)" substitute "subsection (4)".

(2) The amendment made by sub-paragraph (1)(a) does not apply in relation to qualifying disposals (within the meaning of Part V of the Housing Act 1985) made before, or made under a contract entered into before, the day on which this paragraph comes into force.

1985 c. 68.

Local authority assistance in connection with mortgages

27.—(1) Section 442 of the Housing Act 1985 (agreements by local authority to indemnify mortgagees) is amended as follows.

(2) In subsection (1)—

   (a) for the words from the beginning to "house" (in the second place it appears) substitute "A local authority may enter into an agreement with a person or body making an advance on the security of a house (or a building to be converted into a house)";

   (b) for "society or body" (in both places) substitute "mortgagee".

(3) After subsection (1) insert—

   "(1A) The local authority may only enter into the agreement if the advance is for one or more of the purposes specified in subsection (1) of section 435; and subsections (2) to (4) of that section apply in relation to power to enter into such an agreement as they apply to the power to make an advance under that section.".

(4) In subsection (2) for "building society or recognised body" substitute "mortgagee";

(5) Subsections (4) and (5) shall cease to have effect.

28. In section 443 of the Housing Act 1985 (local authority contributions to mortgage costs)—

   (a) in subsection (1), for "a building society or recognised body" substitute "any person or body"; and

   (b) subsections (2) and (3) shall cease to have effect.

29.—(1) For section 444 of the Housing Act 1985 (meaning of "recognised body" and "relevant advance") substitute—

"Relevant advances for the purposes of section 443.   444. The expression "relevant advance" in section 443 (contributions to mortgage costs) means an advance made to a person whose interest in the house (or building to be converted into a house) on the security of which the advance is made is, or was, acquired by virtue of a conveyance of the freehold, or a grant or assignment of a long lease, by a housing authority.".

(2) Any reference in an agreement made under section 442 of the Housing Act 1985 before the date on which this paragraph comes into force which defines the expression "recognised body" by reference to section 444 of that Act shall (notwithstanding the amendment made by sub-paragraph (1) of this paragraph) continue to have the same meaning as it had immediately before that date.

30. In paragraph 21(d) of Schedule 13 to the Local Government (Wales) Act 1994 (Residuary Body a local authority for purposes of section 442 of Housing Act 1985)—

1994 c. 19.

   (a) omit the words from "(so" to "subsection (1)(b))", and

   (b) after "local authority" insert "agreement to indemnify mortgagee and".

Section 227.

SCHEDULE 19

REPEALS

PART I

SOCIAL RENTED SECTOR

Chapter	Short title	Extent of repeal
1985 c. 69.	Housing Associations Act 1985.	Sections 3 to 8. Section 9(1) and (4). Section 11. Sections 13 to 33. Section 36A. Section 67. Section 69(1)(e) and (g). Schedules 2 and 3.
1988 c. 9.	Local Government Act 1988.	Section 24(5)(a) and (c).
1988 c. 50.	Housing Act 1988.	Sections 48 and 49. Section 55(1)(a). Section 58. Section 79(6) to (10). In section 92(2), the words from "but" to the end. In Schedule 6, paragraphs 3 to 6 and 9 to 23.
1989 c. 42.	Local Government and Housing Act 1989.	Section 182.
1993 c. 10.	Charities Act 1993.	In Schedule 6, paragraph 21(3).
1993 c. 28.	Leasehold Reform, Housing and Urban Development Act 1993.	Section 134.

PART II

HOUSES IN MULTIPLE OCCUPATION

Chapter	Short title	Extent of repeal
1985 c. 68.	Housing Act 1985.	In section 365(5), the words "and (e)". In section 368(3), the words from "and if" to the end. Part XII. Section 619(1).
1989 c. 42.	Local Government and Housing Act 1989.	In Schedule 9— (a) paragraphs 45 to 47 and 53(2), (b) in paragraph 53(3) the words from "after" to "(2A)" and" and the words "of that subsection",

Chapter	Short title	Extent of repeal
		(c) paragraphs 55(2), 63, 66 and 68(2). In Schedule 11, paragraphs 75 and 76.

Part III

Tenants' rights

Chapter	Short title	Extent of repeal
1985 c. 70.	Landlord and Tenant Act 1985.	In section 19(3), the words "within the meaning of Part I of the Arbitration Act 1996". Section 19(4).
1987 c. 31.	Landlord and Tenant Act 1987.	In section 4(2)(aa), the words ""consisting of the creation of an estate or interest". In section 20(1), the definition of "the new landlord". In section 20(2), the words "or counter-offer" in each place where they occur. Section 24(2)(a)(ii). Section 31(5). In section 60(1), the definition of "rent assessment committee".
1996 c. 23.	Arbitration Act 1996.	In Schedule 3, paragraph 43.

Part IV

Assured tenancies

Chapter	Short title	Extent of repeal
1985 c. 68.	Housing Act 1985.	In section 553(2)(b), the words "or under section 20(1)(c) of that Act (notice served in respect of assured shorthold tenancies)".
1988 c. 50.	Housing Act 1988.	Section 20(7). In section 22, in subsection (1), the words from "in respect of" to "above" and, in subsection (2), the word "or" after paragraph (a). In Schedule 17, paragraph 60(c).

Part V

Leasehold reform

Chapter	Short title	Extent of repeal
1993 c. 28.	Leasehold Reform, Housing and Urban Development Act 1993.	In section 1, in subsection (3), the words "the freehold of it is owned by the person who owns the freehold of the relevant premises and" and, in subsection (7), the definition of "the freeholder". In section 3(1)(a), the words "and the freehold of the whole of the building or of that part of the building is owned by the same person". In section 10(6), the definition of "the freeholder". In section 11(4)(i), the words "as is mentioned in subsection (3)(c)". In section 13, in subsection (3)(a)(iii), the words "of the person who owns the freehold of the specified premises" and "by him" and subsections (4), (6) and (7). In section 39, in subsection (3), the word "and" at the end of paragraph (b), and subsection (6). In Schedule 6, in paragraph 1(1), the definition of "the freeholder".

Part VI

Housing benefit and related matters

Chapter	Short title	Extent of repeal
1988 c. 50.	Housing Act 1988.	Section 121.
1988 c. 43.	Housing (Scotland) Act 1988.	Section 70.
1992 c. 4.	Social Security Contributions and Benefits Act 1992.	Section 130(5).

SCH. 19

Chapter	Short title	Extent of repeal

1992 c. 5.	Social Security Administration Act 1992.	Section 116(4)(a).
		In section 134—
		  (a) in subsection (2)(b), the words "or rates";
		  (b) subsections (3), (4), (6) and (7).
		Sections 135 to 137.
		Section 140.
		In section 191—
		  (a) in the definition of "rate rebate", "rent rebate" and "rent allowance", the reference to rate rebate;
		  (b) the definitions of "rates" and "rating authority".

1992 c. 6.	Social Security (Consequential Provisions) Act 1992.	In Schedule 2, paragraph 104.
1992 c. 14.	Local Government Finance Act 1992.	In Schedule 9, paragraph 21.
1994 c. 39.	Local Government etc. (Scotland) Act 1994.	In Schedule 13, in paragraph 175, in sub-paragraph (3) the words "138(1), 139(2), (5) and (6) and 140(1), (2), (4) and (7)" and sub-paragraph (4).

PART VII

ALLOCATION OF HOUSING ACCOMODATION

Chapter	Short title	Extent of repeal
1985 c. 68.	Housing Act 1985.	Section 22. In Schedule 1, in paragraph 2(4) the words from "until" to the end and in paragraphs 5(1) and 10(1) the words from "unless" to the end.
1996 c. 49.	Asylum and Immigration Act 1996.	In section 9(4), the definitions of "the accommodation Part", "housing authority" and "licence to occupy" and, in the definition of "tenancy" the words ", in relation to England and Wales,".

PART VIII

HOMELESSNESS

Chapter	Short title	Extent of repeal
1985 c. 68.	Housing Act 1985.	Part III.
1985 c. 71.	Housing (Consequential Provisions) Act 1985.	In Schedule 2, paragraphs 19 and 60(3).
1986 c. 63.	Housing and Planning Act 1986.	Section 14.
1987 c. 26.	Housing (Scotland) Act 1987.	In Schedule 23, paragraph 30(1).
1988 c. 50.	Housing Act 1988.	Section 1(6) and (7). Section 70.
1993 c. 23.	Asylum and Immigration Appeals Act 1993.	Sections 4 and 5. Schedule 1.
1994 c. 39.	Local Government etc. (Scotland) Act 1994.	In Schedule 13, paragraph 142(2).
1996 c. 49.	Asylum and Immigration Act 1996.	In section 9, subsection (2), in subsection (3)(a) the words "or assistance" and in subsection (4) the definition of "the homelessness Part".

PART IX

CHANGE OF LANDLORD: SECURE TENANTS

Chapter	Short title	Extent of repeal
1985 c. 68.	Housing Act 1985.	In section 32(1) and 43(1), the words from "and Part IV" to "tenants)".
1985 c. 69.	Housing Associations Act 1985.	In section 9(1), the word ", 105(6)".
1988 c. 50.	Housing Act 1988.	In section 79(2)(a), the words "either" and "or under section 94 below". Sections 93 to 114. In Schedule 2, in Ground 6, the paragraph beginning "For the purposes of this ground, every acquisition under Part IV". Schedule 12. In Schedule 17, paragraphs 38 and 39.
1989 c. 42.	Local Government and Housing Act 1989.	Section 174. In Schedule 11, paragraphs 107 and 109.

Chapter	Short title	Extent of repeal
S.I. 1990/778.	Local Authorities (Capital Finance) (Consequential Amendments) Order 1990.	In the Schedule, paragraph 2.
1993 c. 28.	Leasehold Reform, Housing and Urban Development Act 1993.	Section 124(4) to (6). In Schedule 10, paragraph 1(2)(d).
1995 c. 8.	Agricultural Tenancies Act 1995.	In the Schedule, paragraph 33.
1995 c. 38.	Civil Evidence Act 1995.	In Schedule 1, paragraph 14.

PART X

CONSULTATION WITH RESPECT TO HOUSING MANAGEMENT

Chapter	Short title	Extent of repeal
1985 c. 68.	Housing Act 1985.	Sections 27A and 27AA.
1993 c. 28.	Leasehold Reform, Housing and Urban Development Act 1993.	Sections 130 and 131.

PART XI

ABOLITION OF EXCHEQUER CONTRIBUTIONS FOR AGRICULTURAL HOUSING

Chapter	Short title	Extent of repeal
1985 c. 68.	Housing Act 1985.	In section 432, the entry for Part II of Schedule 15. In Schedule 15, Part II.

PART XII

ABOLITION OF CERTAIN CONSENT REQUIREMENTS

Chapter	Short title	Extent of repeal
1985 c. 68.	Housing Act 1985.	Section 16.

Part XIII

Removal of Treasury consent requirements

Chapter	Short title	Extent of repeal
1977 c. 42.	Rent Act 1977.	In section 63(2)(a), the words "with the consent of the Treasury". In Schedule 10, in paragraphs 7, 7A and 8, the words "with the consent of the Minister for the Civil Service".
1980 c. 65.	Local Government, Planning and Land Act 1980.	In Schedule 26, in paragraphs 8, 9 and 10, the words "with the consent of the Minister for the Civil Service" and, in paragraph 12(5), the words "given with the consent of the Minister for the Civil Service".
1985 c. 68.	Housing Act 1985.	In section 156(4), the words "with the consent of the Treasury". In section 429A, in subsections (1) and (3), the words "with the consent of the Treasury" and "with the like consent" and, in subsection (5), the words "with the consent of the Treasury".
1985 c. 69.	Housing Associations Act 1985.	In section 85(2), the words "with the consent of the Treasury". In Schedule 6, in paragraphs 5(1) and 6(1), the words "with the consent of the Treasury".
1988 c. 50.	Housing Act 1988.	In Schedule 7, in paragraph 8, the words "with the approval of the Treasury", in paragraph 9, the words "with the approval of the Treasury" and "with that approval", in paragraphs 10 and 12(2), the words "with the approval of the Treasury" and, in paragraph 12(5), the words "given with the consent of the Treasury".

Chapter	Short title	Extent of repeal
1993 c. 28.	Leasehold Reform Housing and Urban Development Act 1993.	In Schedule 17, paragraphs 2(4) and 3(8) and, in paragraph 5(5), the words "with the approval of the Treasury".

PART XIV

LOCAL AUTHORITY ASSISTANCE IN CONNECTION WITH MORTGAGES

Chapter	Short title	Extent of repeal
1974 c. 39.	Consumer Credit Act 1974.	In section 16(1)(ff), "444(1)".
1985 c. 68.	Housing Act 1985.	Section 442(4) and (5). Section 443(2) and (3). In section 459, the entry for "recognised body".
1986 c. 53.	Building Societies Act 1986.	In Schedule 18, paragraph 18(2).
1994 c. 19.	Local Government (Wales) Act 1994.	In Schedule 13, in paragraph 21(d) the words from "(so" to "subsection (1)(b))".

Printed in the UK by The Stationery Office Limited under the authority and superintendence of Peter Macdonald, Controller of Her Majesty's Stationery Office and Queen's Printer of Acts of Parliament.

1st Impression August 1996
3rd Impression March 1997

Dd 5066402 3/97 51.00 56219